ANN SERANNE'S
Good Food
With a Blender

ANN SERANNE'S
Good Food
With a Blender

by Ann Seranne

William Morrow & Company, Inc.   New York

Library of Congress Cataloging in Publication Data

Smith, Margaret Ruth (date)
  Ann Seranne's good food with a blender.

  1. Blenders (Cookery) I. Title. II. Title: Good
food with a blender.
TX840.B5S54   641.5′89   74-6254
ISBN 0-688-00297-8

Contents

8   *Contents*

Introduction

ELECTRIC blenders have come a long way in the past few years—perhaps too far! The beautiful simplicity of this compact, efficient appliance has been disguised by the addition of multiple speeds, each supposedly designed for a specific blending technique, when in essence most of these actions can be accomplished on three of the various speeds. Complication has by no means destroyed efficiency, but it has served to confuse the consumer.

When the electric blender was marketed in America more than thirty-five years ago, it was one of the first wholly original pieces of kitchen equipment invented in centuries. It had a simple switch. When the switch was flicked up, the powerful blending action began; when the switch was flicked down, the action stopped. It was used gratefully to take the drudgery out of tiresome kitchen chores such as puréeing, grating, chopping, crumbing, and homogenizing.

Later, two-speed models were a step in the right direction, for these enabled the homemaker to begin a blending action on low speed and switch to high. It avoided the sudden surge in the container of thin liquids, such as soup, which often resulted in more soup on the ceiling than in the saucepan.

One more speed in the middle range is, in my estimation, advantageous, giving you LOW, MEDIUM, and HIGH. Additional speeds are superfluous and unnecessary, for a few seconds' longer blending on a lower speed will give the same result as less blending on a higher speed. And when one is dealing with seconds, no cook is going to quarrel with the loss of a couple of them.

But blender manufacturers began to compete with one another for point-of-sale "improvements," or gimmicks, and one model was merchandized with 32 different buttons, or speeds. It gave the salesman something to talk about, but it gave most homemakers a headache!

Today blenders are available with 7, 8, 14, or 20 different buttons, with automatic timers, red lights that flash on and off, and other special features, none of which improve the efficiency or flexibility of the electric blender.

My advice to you, if you do not have a blender and have decided to buy one, is to look at all the different models. Every manufacturer has what is known as "the top of the line," and therefore the most expensive. It has a certain snob appeal, and probably lots of buttons, but it does no more or less than a less expensive model. So, don't buy the most expensive or the cheapest. Select one in the middle price range and you will have invested in a great precision appliance that will save you many hours of food preparation in the kitchen.

Once you have selected your blender, take a few minutes to read the literature enclosed with it, then set it up on a clean, dry surface in the most convenient spot in your kitchen. Plug it into the handiest electric outlet and LEAVE IT THERE, always ready to use. You will find that it will come in handy several times each day.

HOW TO USE YOUR BLENDER

There's nothing to it, for an electric blender is an essentially simple appliance. If it is a multiple-speed blender, using it is a little like learning to play a scale on the piano, switching from one key or button to another. It will actually talk to you, if you listen!

Turn your blender on LOW speed, then push each button successively from lowest to highest and you will hear the increase in revolutions per minute (R.P.M.'s) as the blades pick up speed.

The range of most blenders is from 3,000 R.P.M.'s on LOW to 22,000 R.P.M.'s on HIGHEST speed. The middle range or MEDIUM speeds are anywhere from 8,000 to 10,000 R.P.M.'s, and you will find yourself using these three speeds in almost all your blending.

It's a good idea to get into the habit of beginning most blender actions by pressing LOW speed first. As soon as the blades are in full action, switch to MEDIUM or HIGH, depending on how thick the mixture is in the container. If you have a mixture in the container which is too thick to be blended on one of the middle-speed buttons, the sound of the whirling blades will tell you so. They will slow down, labor to churn the mixture, and may even cease to spin. To correct this, switch to a higher or the highest speed. If the motor still labors, turn off your blender and stir the mixture with a slim rubber spatula to introduce some air, or add a few drops of liquid. If you allow the motor to run when the blades have stopped spinning, you will burn it out, and it won't be anybody's fault but yours.

Once you have mastered the few basic techniques of using your blender, you will find that you will use it not only for simple kitchen chores, cutting your preparation time of many dishes to seconds, but for the preparation of whole dishes, even meals, in your blender without recourse to range or refrigerator. You can turn out salads, sauces, desserts, dips, spreads, soups, beverages, and a host of other dishes literally in seconds.

So good luck with "blender cooking." There is not much a blender cannot do, and what it does do, it does to perfection.

Happy Blending!

ANN SERANNE

Five Blender Tips

1. What your blender will not do

Your electric blender cannot beat egg whites to the maximum volume needed for meringues or frostings. It cannot mash potatoes or knead a stiff cooky or bread dough. It cannot grind raw meats for sausages or hamburgers or extract juice from fruit or vegetables. From there on, the sky's the limit!

2. Which speed to use

In general, use LOW speeds, or the first couple of buttons, for whipping cream, making mayonnaise, Hollandaise, and other egg sauces.

Use MEDIUM speeds, or the center of the scale buttons, for chopping, crumbing, and shredding.

Use HIGH speeds, or the last couple of buttons, for grating hard cheeses and nuts, for puréeing cooked fruits and soft vegetables, and for making frozen daiquiris and fruit sherbets.

3. Stop the motor to add ingredients

Most of the recipes in this book are written in numbered steps, and many of the steps involve the addition of ingredients to the blender container. STOP THE MOTOR BEFORE EACH ADDITION, except when the recipe specifies that you should add an ingredient "with the blades spinning" or "with the motor on."

4. Never overwork your motor with too heavy a load

A. If mixture stops blending, turn off motor and stir. Or, remove cover and use a rubber bottle scraper or spatula to pull mixture from sides of container to center. Do not dip too deeply or you will hit the spinning blades.

B. A slim bottle scraper is also an invaluable aid in removing chopped mixtures and thick purées from the container. Hold container firmly in left hand and invert over serving dish or bowl. Rotate blades while scraping food away from sides of container.

5. Cleaning your blender container is a cinch without disassembling

If it is not convenient to wash your blender container directly after use, fill it with water to keep the food from drying on sides and around the blades. When ready to wash:

A. Fill container ½ full of hot water. Add a few drops detergent or soap flakes. Cover.

B. Press LOW button. As soon as blades reach full speed, press HIGH button. Blend for 30 seconds.

C. Rinse container and return to blender base to air dry.

Twenty-Nine Basic Techniques

* Recipes in this book use an asterisk when the following basic techniques are required. If you have forgotten how to do them, refer to this section.

1. CRUMB BREAD in 3 seconds for croquettes and stuffings.

Tear 1 slice bread into container. Cover and blend on HIGH speed until bread is crumbed. Repeat as needed. For buttered crumbs, simply butter slices before tearing into container.

2 slices bread = 1 cup crumbs

2. CRUMB CRACKERS, ZWIEBACK, AND OTHER DRY BISCUITS in 3 seconds for crumb crusts and tortes.

Break 8 crackers into container. Cover and blend on HIGH speed until crackers are crumbed. Repeat as needed.

8 graham cracker squares = ½ cup cracker crumbs
6 Zwieback = ½ cup Zwieback crumbs
1 cup potato chips = ½ cup potato chip crumbs
12 thin pretzels = ½ cup pretzel crumbs
¾ cup cornflakes = ½ cup cornflake crumbs

3. CRUMB BREAD AND CHEESE FOR AU GRATIN TOPPINGS in 3 seconds.

Tear 1 slice bread into container. Add ¼ cup diced Swiss, Gruyère, or Cheddar cheese. Cover and blend on HIGH speed until bread is crumbed. Repeat as needed.

4. GRATE HARD CHEESES FOR SPAGHETTI in 6 seconds.

Empty ½ to 1 cup diced Parmesan or Romano cheese into container. Cover and blend on HIGH speed until cheese is coarsely or finely grated to taste. Repeat as needed.

1 cup diced hard cheese = ⅞ cup grated cheese

5. GRATE NUTS OR CHOCOLATE in 6 seconds for cakes and cookies.

Empty 1 cup nut meats (4 ounces) or 6 ounces chocolate bits into container. Cover and blend on HIGH speed until nuts or chocolate is grated.

1 cup walnut meats (4 oz.) = 1 cup grated nuts
1 package chocolate bits (6 oz.) = 1 cup grated chocolate
2 squares chocolate, diced (2 oz.) = scant ½ cup grated chocolate

6. GRATE COCONUT in 10 seconds for curries, desserts, and pie and cake toppings.

Empty ½ to 1 cup diced fresh coconut into container. Cover and blend on HIGH speed until coconut is grated. If a few large chunks remain, turn off motor, toss coconut with a rubber spatula, and blend again briefly.

7. SHRED SEMISOLID CHEESES in 5 seconds for sauces.

In grating semisolid cheeses with a high oil content, a few chunks of fresh bread added to the container absorb the oil and keep the cheese free-flowing into the blades. It will not change the flavor of any recipes in which you are using grated cheese.

Be sure the container is completely dry. Tear 3 small cubes fresh bread into container. Add ½ cup diced Swiss, Cheddar, or Gruyère cheese. Cover and blend on HIGH speed until cheese is shredded.

½ cup diced cheese plus 3 small cubes bread = ½ cup shredded cheese

8. SHRED COOKED HAM, CHICKEN, MEAT in 5 seconds for loaves, croquettes, or casseroles.

As in the grinding of semisolid cheese, a few cubes of bread added to the container with the meat will keep it free-flowing.

Tear 3 small cubes bread into container. Add ½ cup diced meat. Cover and blend on HIGH speed until meat is shredded. Repeat as needed.

½ cup diced cooked meat plus 3 small cubes bread = ¾ cup shredded meat

9. SHRED CARROTS, RADISHES, APPLES, PARSLEY for salads.

Cover container and press HIGH speed. If cover has an inner removable cap, take it out. Otherwise tilt cover back far enough to allow you to drop a whole carrot, a few radishes, or a whole stalk of celery, and so on, directly into the revolving blades. Turn off motor and empty shredded vegetable into a bowl. Repeat as needed.

1 medium carrot = ½ cup shredded carrot
1 medium apple, peeled and cored = ½ cup shredded apple
1 medium onion, peeled and halved = ½ cup shredded onion
1 large stalk celery = ½ cup shredded celery
½ cup stemmed parsley = ½ cup shredded parsley
6 radishes = ½ cup shredded radish

10. GRIND COFFEE BEANS in 15 seconds.

Empty ½ to 1 cup coffee beans into container. Cover and blend on HIGH speed for 15 seconds for percolator coffee-maker; 60 seconds for vacuum or drip coffee-maker.

11. PULVERIZE LUMP OR GRANULATED SUGAR in 30 to 60 seconds.

Empty 1 cup sugar lumps (24 large) into container. Cover and blend on HIGH speed until sugar is pulverized.

24 large lumps = 1 cup fine granulated sugar
1 cup granulated sugar = 1¼ cups pulverized sugar

12. WATER-CHOP CABBAGE AND OTHER CRISP RAW VEGETABLES in 2 seconds for cole slaw, soups, casseroles.

Fill container three-quarters full of coarsely cut cabbage. Add a few pieces of sliced carrot and green pepper, if desired. Add cold water to barely cover vegetables. Cover container and rest hand lightly on the cover. Press HIGH speed. WATCH CAREFULLY. As the last piece of vegetable is pulled from top of container down into the blades, press OFF. This takes only 2 to 3 seconds. Pour chopped vegetables into a sieve to drain.

13. CHOP AND REFRESH STICKY FRUIT SUCH AS RAISINS, DATES, CANDIED FRUIT in 5 seconds for cakes and cookies.

Measure 1 cup fruit into container. Add water to cover fruit. Cover and blend on HIGH speed for 5 seconds. Drain before using.

14. MIX AND REFRESH FROZEN JUICES OR CANNED OR FROZEN SOUPS in 15 seconds.

Empty partially defrosted juice or soup or canned soup into container. Add desired amount of water. Cover and press LOW speed. As soon as blades reach full speed, press HIGH and blend for 15 seconds.

15. RECONSTITUTE AND AERATE DRY MILK SOLIDS in 10 seconds.

Measure dry milk solids and water into container. Cover. Blend on LOW speed until blended.

16. CHILL BEVERAGES in 15 seconds.

Fill container half full of liquid. Add 3 or 4 ice cubes. Cover and blend on MEDIUM speed until ice is melted.

17. RESTORE CURDLED CUSTARDS in 5 seconds.

Empty hot, curdled custard into container. Cover and blend on LOW speed for just 5 seconds. Empty into serving dish and chill until set.

18. SMOOTH LUMPY GRAVIES AND SAUCES in 5 seconds.

Empty sauce or gravy into container. Cover and blend on LOW speed for 5 seconds.

19. BLEND CAKE MIXES in 60 seconds.

Follow package directions. Put liquid, eggs, and half the cake mix into container. Blend on LOW speed for 15 seconds. Empty in remaining mix, cover and blend on MEDIUM speed for 45 seconds, stopping to stir down around sides of container, if necessary.

20. BLEND INSTANT PUDDINGS in 10 seconds.

Follow package directions. Empty liquid into container. Add dry mix. Cover and blend on LOW speed for 10 seconds.

21. BLEND PANCAKE AND POPOVER BATTERS

Follow package directions or your own recipe. Put eggs and liquid into container first. Add dry ingredients. Cover and blend on MEDIUM speed until all dry ingredients are moistened, stopping to stir down around sides of container, if necessary. Do not overblend. If blades stop revolving, switch to HIGH speed.

22. BLEND FLOUR AND WATER in 10 seconds to thicken sauces and gravies.

For each cup sauce or gravy to be thickened, measure 4 tablespoons water and 2 tablespoons flour into container. Cover and blend on MEDIUM speed for 10 seconds.

23. BLEND INSTANT MASHED POTATOES

Follow directions on package for 4 servings. Pour hot liquid and seasonings into container. Cover and press LOW speed. As soon as blades reach full speed, remove cover and pour in potatoes. Blend until well mixed.

24. MAKE SHERBETS AND FROZEN DAIQUIRIS

Measure liquids into container, filling container no more than ¼ full, but enough to cover the blades generously. Cover and turn blender on HIGH speed. Remove cover or inner cap of cover. Add 3 or 4 ice cubes, one at a time. Continue to add ice cubes until liquid freezes, stirring mixture down occasionally with a rubber spatula.

25. MAKE COCONUT MILK AND CREAM in 30 seconds for desserts and beverages.

Empty into container 1 cup diced fresh coconut. Add 2 cups boiling water. Cover and blend on HIGH speed for 30 seconds. Empty coconut and liquid into a strainer set into a small bowl and press coconut with back of a wooden spoon to extract all the coconut milk. If this milk is allowed to stand, the coconut cream will rise to the surface and may be spooned off, giving you about ½ cup coconut cream and 1 cup coconut milk.

26. MAKE SOUR-CREAM TOPPING FOR BAKED POTATOES in 15 seconds.

Empty 1 cup commercial sour cream into container. Add 2 tablespoons coarsely cut chives or green onion tops. Cover and blend on LOW speed until chives or onion tops are finely chopped.

27. MAKE LOW-CALORIE SOUR CREAM in 30 seconds from cottage cheese.

Empty ½ cup water, milk, buttermilk, or yogurt into container. Add 8 ounces cream-style cottage cheese, a pinch of salt, and 1 tablespoon lemon juice. Cover and blend on HIGH speed until smooth and creamy.

28. WHIP CREAM THICKLY

Pour 1 cup cold whipping cream into container. Add 1 tablespoon confectioners' sugar. Cover and press LOW speed. Remove cover and watch closely, for you don't want to churn the cream to butter. (If you get into trouble, see page 77.) As soon as the cream begins to set around the blades, turn off motor. Stir with a rubber spatula and blend again for a few seconds, repeating the stirring and blending as often as needed to make the cream the consistency desired.

29. MAKE CHOCOLATE SAUCE in 20 seconds for ice cream.

Empty 6 ounces semisweet chocolate pieces into container. Add ⅓ cup boiling water, hot strong coffee, or fruit juice. Cover and blend on MEDIUM speed for 20 seconds. Serve warm or cold.

A MINI-COURSE
IN BLENDER COOKING

A Mini-Course
in Blender Cooking

LEARN TO USE your blender by making these eighteen basic blender recipes. In the past twenty years, many new techniques in blender "cooking" have been developed, giving wider scope to the blender. I can immodestly take credit for developing and perfecting such favorite shortcut recipes as Hollandaise sauce, chocolate butter-cream frosting, instant-set gelatin desserts, and others, for I have been a dedicated disciple of the electric blender since the very first model was marketed and spent fifteen years as food consultant for one of the leading blender manufacturers. Next to a stove and refrigerator, I honestly consider the electric blender the most essential electric appliance for every home kitchen.

Begin right now to learn how to use your blender. Try one of the recipes in this section for a soup, salad dressing, sauce, or dessert for dinner tonight. Or perhaps you'd like to begin by making some very fresh, homemade peanut butter, better than any you can buy, for sandwiches for the children. If you happen to have some left-over cooked vegetables in your refrigerator, you might make a blended hot soup to serve with the sandwiches for supper.

HOW TO MAKE FRESH
PEANUT BUTTER in 1 minute

1. Be sure blender container is completely dry.

2. Empty 1 cup shelled roasted peanuts (6-ounce can) into container. Cover, and blend on HIGH speed for 5 seconds. That's all it takes to give you ground peanuts for cookies, cakes, or dessert toppings. Leave them in the container.

3. Add 1 tablespoon peanut or vegetable oil. Cover and blend on HIGH speed.

4. LISTEN TO YOUR BLENDER TALK TO YOU! After about 10 seconds, the motor will begin to reach a high pitch. This means it has done all the work at the moment that it will do on HIGH speed. Turn the motor to LOW and let the blades churn the ground nuts into peanut butter. This will take about 60 seconds. If necessary, stop the motor occasionally and stir the mixture down with a thin rubber spatula.

5. Use the rubber spatula or a bottle scraper to remove the peanut butter from the container.

1 cup peanuts = ¾ cup (6 ounces) fresh peanut butter

HOW TO MAKE CREAM OF VEGETABLE SOUP in 30 seconds

Serves 4.   Here's a marvelous cream soup that can be made from practically any vegetable—freshly cooked, canned, or leftover from dinner the previous day. It has infinite variations, but the basic recipe demonstrates the technique of making a purée, the basis of all creamed soups. The vegetable may be carrots, spinach, broccoli, cauliflower, peas, string beans, squash, beets, lima beans, or any combination.

To make a purée, always begin with ENOUGH LIQUID TO COVER THE BLADES, or about ½ cup. The liquid may be chicken or beef stock, milk, tomato juice, vegetable juice, fruit juice, wine, or even water.

1	thin slice onion	½	teaspoon salt or celery salt
1½	cups chicken, beef, or vegetable broth		Dash of pepper
½	cup cooked potatoes, mashed or diced	1	cup milk or cream or ½ cup of each
1	cup cooked vegetable	1	tablespoon butter

1. Put the onion slice and ½ cup broth into container. Cover and blend on HIGH speed for 10 seconds to liquefy the onion so that it will cook quickly.

2. Add potatoes, cover, and blend on HIGH speed for 10 seconds.

3. Add remaining broth, the vegetable, salt, and pepper. Cover, rest hand lightly on cover, and blend on HIGH speed for 5 seconds.

4. With blades spinning, remove cover or inner cap and gradually pour in the milk or cream.

5. Pour soup into a saucepan, add butter, and bring to a simmer over moderate heat, stirring constantly. Or heat over simmering water to serving temperature, stirring occasionally.

VARIATIONS:

Along with the cooked vegetable, add ¼ cup parsley clusters; or 1 stalk celery with leaves, coarsely chopped; or ½ teaspoon dried tarragon, sweet basil, thyme, or oregano.

BASIC BISQUES

Follow Cream of Vegetable Soup recipe, substituting ⅔ cup cooked dried seafood, meat, or poultry in place of the cooked vegetables.

CURRIED FISH BISQUE

Follow Cream of Vegetable Soup recipe, using ⅔ cup cooked haddock or cod fish, flaked to remove any bones, in place of the cooked vegetables. Add ½ to 1 teaspoon curry powder along with the pepper.

HOW TO MAKE A THICK BANANA FROSTED in 10 seconds

Makes 1 large drink

YOUR BLENDER PURÉES soft fresh or cooked fruits and blends them with a liquid to make a great variety of fruit-flavored beverages that actually cannot be made in any other way.

1   cup milk
1   large scoop vanilla ice cream
1   banana, peeled

1. Put milk and ice cream into container. Cover and blend on HIGH speed for 5 seconds.

2. With blades spinning, remove cover or inner cap, and slice in banana.

3. Do not overblend. As soon as mixture is smooth and still thick, pour into large glass and enjoy.

VARIATIONS:

1. Add malted milk in quantity desired.

2. Use any of the following fruits in place of the banana: ½ cup sliced raw or canned peaches or apricots; ½ cup pitted, stewed prunes; 1 cup diced cantaloupe or honeydew melon; 2 slices fresh or canned pineapple; or half a 10-ounce package frozen strawberries, cubed.

CREAMY BLUE CHEESE DIP

Makes 1 pint

8 ounces sour cream
6 ounces blue cheese
1 clove garlic
5–6 parsley clusters
1 tablespoon coarsely cut chives or green onion
Few drops of Tabasco

Put all ingredients into container. Cover and blend on HIGH speed for 30 seconds or until smooth.

IF VORTEX CEASES TO FORM in a heavy mixture such as a dip, remove blender cover, and carefully break the surface with a rubber spatula, pulling mixture from sides of container into center. This will introduce air, and the vortex will be recreated. An alternate method is to add a few drops of liquid. Be careful not to dip the spatula too deeply; it must not touch the blades.

HOW TO MAKE A BLENDER CREAM SAUCE in 6 seconds

Makes 2 cups

YOUR BLENDER EMULSIFIES liquid, fat, and flour . . . and that means that it breaks butter down into such fine particles that they stay in suspension in the flour-liquid mixture for a very long time without separating. Because of this unique emulsifying action, your blender can turn out tricky cream sauces that can never lump or become greasy. Reason enough for investing in a blender!

The following method for making a velvety cream sauce in seconds has become one of the most popular blender techniques of the century, for it has gotten many a novice cook over this early culinary hump, and it gets the experienced cook off to a running start in the preparation of many dishes. It also demonstrates one of the fundamental rules of blender cooking, which is NEVER TO FILL YOUR CONTAINER MORE THAN HALF FULL WITH A HOT LIQUID, SAUCE, OR SOUP. You could be burned quite badly.

4	tablespoons flour
4	tablespoons soft butter
½	teaspoon salt
¼	teaspoon black pepper, mustard, or cayenne pepper
2	cups hot milk or part broth and part cream

1. Put flour, butter, salt, pepper, and ½ cup of the hot liquid into container. Cover and begin blending on HIGH speed.

2. With blades spinning, remove inner cap or cover, and gradually pour in remaining hot milk mixture.

THIN CREAM SAUCE: Use only 2 tablespoons each of butter and flour.

THICK CREAM SAUCE: Use 6 tablespoons each of butter and flour.

Now THAT you've made your sauce, you'll want to use it. Pour it into a saucepan, cook over low heat for 3 minutes, and use for creamed fish or chicken. Or pour it over 1 quart meat, fish, vegetables, rice, or pasta in a casserole, mix well, and bake according to recipe instructions. Here's a specific use for tonight's dinner:

SCALLOPED CAULIFLOWER AU GRATIN

Serves 6

1	large head cauliflower
2	cups blender cream sauce, uncooked
1	thin slice onion
½	teaspoon dried thyme
1	slice buttered bread

1. Preheat oven to 350° F. Butter a 2-quart casserole.

2. Wash and trim the cauliflower and separate it into flowerettes. Cook in boiling salted water for 5 to 6 minutes, or until just fork tender. Drain, and empty into casserole.

3. Pour half the cream sauce from container over the cauliflower.

4. Add the onion slice and thyme to remaining sauce in container. Cover and blend on HIGH speed for 10 seconds. Pour into casserole and mix well.

5. Make buttered crumbs: Clean and thoroughly dry container. Tear in the buttered bread, cover, and blend on HIGH speed for 5 seconds. Sprinkle on top of casserole.

6. Bake in preheated oven for 20 to 25 minutes.

VARIATIONS:

Use cabbage or broccoli in place of cauliflower. Small cooked onions are also divine; for these, you don't need to add the onion slice to the cream sauce, but do double the quantity of thyme.

IF YOU WILL MAKE the next two dishes in your blender for supper some evening—macaroni and cheese and cole slaw with mayonnaise dressing—you'll be convinced once and for all that you could never again exist without a blender.

A GOOD DISH OF MACARONI AND CHEESE

Serves 4

8	ounces elbow macaroni	½	teaspoon salt
1½	slices bread	¼	teaspoon coarse black pepper
2	cups diced Cheddar cheese	2	cups hot milk or part milk and
2	tablespoons soft butter		part cream
2	tablespoons flour		

1. Cook the macaroni according to package directions until barely tender. Drain, rinse, and empty into a 2-quart baking dish.

2. While the macaroni is cooking, crumb 1 slice of bread: Tear the slice into container, cover, and blend on HIGH speed for 5 seconds. Empty crumbs out onto piece of waxed paper.

3. Now shred part of the cheese: Tear remaining ½ slice bread into container. Add ½ cup of the diced cheese, cover, and blend on HIGH speed

until cheese is shredded. Empty out onto waxed paper and mix with the crumbs.

4. For the cheese sauce, put butter, flour, salt, pepper, and 1 cup of the hot milk into container. Cover and blend on HIGH speed for 20 seconds. With blades revolving, remove cover or inner cap, and pour in remaining hot milk. Add the remaining cheese, a handful at a time, and continue to blend for 20 seconds longer.

5. Pour cheese sauce over the macaroni and mix well. Sprinkle the crumbs and cheese over the top, and set aside until ready to bake.

6. To bake, preheat oven to 350° F. Bake the macaroni and cheese for 25 to 30 minutes.

SERVE THE MACARONI and cheese with cole slaw salad. The cole slaw will demonstrate another basic blender technique that you will use frequently in recipes throughout this book, which is the LIQUID METHOD FOR CHOPPING VEGETABLES. This method is used when you want to chop more than just a carrot, a stalk of celery, or a small quantity of onion or parsley. With this method you can fill the container to the top with crisp vegetables for gazpacho, relishes, and pickles. Sometimes you will use the water or other liquid in the recipes; other times you will drain off the liquid, as in this recipe for cole slaw. Yes, some of the water-soluble nutrients are lost, but think of how much time is saved.

HOW TO MAKE COLE SLAW

Serves 4

½   head medium cabbage, coarsely cut
1   small onion, quartered
1   small carrot, coarsely cut
½   green pepper, cut into strips

1. Fill container loosely to the top with half the vegetables. Add enough water to barely cover the vegetables, or about 2 cups.

2. Cover container and blend on HIGH speed for JUST 2 to 3 seconds. WATCH CAREFULLY, and the second that the last piece of vegetable from the top of the container takes a nose-dive down into the spinning blades, turn

motor OFF. It's a good idea to have your finger on the OFF button, ready to push. Empty vegetables into a sieve to drain thoroughly.

3. Repeat with remaining vegetables, then empty all drained vegetables into a salad bowl, and chill.

HOMEMADE MAYONNAISE

Mayonnaise is the basis of the dressing you're going to use on the cole slaw you just made. If you've never made homemade mayonnaise, you don't know what you've missed. You can make it with all vegetable oils, a combination of them, or with all or part pure olive oil. Any way you make it, it is far superior to the commercial varieties and much less expensive.

Another great thing about it is that you can vary the flavor by using lemon juice in place of vinegar. And you can season it with garlic or herbs to your heart's content.

Making mayonnaise is a typical example of how quickly your blender can homogenize a mixture of oil and egg. In other recipes for homemade mayonnaise, the oil must be beaten into the egg mixture with the utmost care, just drop by drop, or the oil, being of less density than the egg, will separate and float on top of the egg.

By using an electric blender, however, you can blend the ingredients together so thoroughly that they cannot separate or curdle IF YOU WILL FOLLOW THESE DIRECTIONS EXACTLY.

HOW TO MAKE PERFECT
BLENDER MAYONNAISE in 15 seconds

Makes 1⅓ cups

1	egg
2	tablespoons vinegar or lemon juice
½	teaspoon dry mustard
¼	teaspoon salt
1	cup salad oil

1. Break the egg into the container. Add vinegar or lemon juice, mustard, salt, and ¼ cup of the oil.

2. Cover and blend on LOW speed.

3. IMMEDIATELY remove inner cap or cover, and pour in remaining oil in quite a fast stream (do not add it drop by drop). All the oil must be added by the end of 15 seconds blending time.

4. A few drops of oil may remain on the surface of the mayonnaise. Without turning blender off, switch to HIGH, and blend for just 3 seconds more.

NOTE: Should the mixture fail to thicken, pour three-quarters of it into a measuring cup. Add another egg to the mixture left in the container, and start again at step 2, adding the mixture in the measuring cup in the same manner that you originally added the oil.

CREAMY MAYONNAISE SALAD DRESSING

Make this when you are ready to serve the cole slaw.

½   cup blender mayonnaise
3   tablespoons light cream
1   teaspoon prepared mustard
¼   cup wine vinegar
6   tablespoons salad oil

1. Put all ingredients into container, cover, and blend on HIGH speed for 5 seconds.

2. Pour the dressing over the cole slaw, toss lightly, and correct seasoning with salt and pepper.

HOW TO MAKE
POTATO PANCAKES in 30 seconds

Serves 4.   This method illustrates the liquid method of shredding vegetables without afterward draining away the liquid. In this case, eggs supply the necessary liquid.

2   eggs
¼   cup flour or 2 tablespoons matzo meal

1   thin slice onion
1   teaspoon salt
    Dash of white pepper
3   cups diced raw potatoes (2 large Idahos)

1. Put all ingredients, except potatoes, into container. Cover and blend on HIGH speed for 20 seconds.

2. With blades spinning, remove cover and add potatoes. As soon as the last piece of potato is added, turn the blender OFF.

3. Pour batter onto a hot greased griddle and cook until nicely browned on both sides.

TURKEY OR CHICKEN HASH

Serves 4.   A quick and economical luncheon dish. Serve it with hot corn muffins (page 278) and a green salad with a favorite salad dressing (see Index).

2	tablespoons butter	1/4	cup cream or milk
2	cups diced cooked turkey or	1	egg
	chicken meat	1/2	teaspoon dry mustard
1	slice bread	1/4	teaspoon dried thyme
1/2	medium onion, thickly sliced	1/4	teaspoon salt
1/2	green pepper, cut in strips		
1/2	cup chicken broth		

1. Preheat oven to 350° F. Butter a shallow casserole or pie plate, using half the butter.

2. Put 1/2 cup turkey or chicken meat and a few pieces of the bread into container. Cover and blend on HIGH speed until meat is shredded. Empty into mixing bowl and repeat until all turkey or chicken and the bread slice have been shredded.

3. Put all remaining ingredients except butter into container. Cover and blend on HIGH speed for 6 seconds. Pour over the shredded meat and mix well.

4. Spread the hash in the prepared casserole or pie plate, dot with remaining butter, and bake in the preheated oven for 20 to 25 minutes. Garnish with parsley and serve hot.

HOW TO MAKE A FABULOUS
CHOCOLATE TORTE in 10 minutes

Serves 8.   Your blender is not only an aid in the preparation of family favorites, but can enable you to become a real epicurean cook—the easy way. Try this chocolate mousse torte for dessert tonight, and you'll be convinced that the sky's the limit! It's very rich, so cut the pieces small.

1	tablespoon soft butter	⅔	cup sugar
4	graham cracker squares	1	tablespoon vanilla extract
8	eggs	1	cup heavy cream
8	ounces semisweet chocolate pieces	1	tablespoon confectioners' sugar
⅓	cup strong coffee, very hot		

1.   Spread the soft butter around sides and on the bottom of a 9-inch pie plate.

2.   MAKE BLENDER CRUMBS. Break graham crackers into container. Cover and blend on HIGH speed for 3 seconds, or until crackers are crumbed. Sprinkle crumbs on bottom and sides of the pie plate.

3.   Preheat oven to 350° F.

4.   Separate eggs, dropping whites into a large mixing bowl and yolks into a cup.

5.   Empty chocolate pieces into container and add hot coffee. Cover and blend on HIGH speed for 10 seconds, or until chocolate mixture is smooth. With blades spinning, remove inner cap or cover, and add egg yolks, sugar, and vanilla. Continue to blend on HIGH speed until smooth.

6.   Beat egg whites with a rotary or electric beater until stiff and glossy. (Do not beat so long that the whites become dry.) Empty the chocolate mixture over the egg whites, scraping out every last bit with a slim rubber spatula, and fold with a large metal spoon until egg whites are gently incorporated into the chocolate mixture. This is now chocolate mousse.

7.   Pour just enough chocolate mousse into the prepared pie plate to come level with the edge. Bake in the preheated oven for 25 minutes. Remove from oven and let cool for 1 hour. The mousse will sink in the middle as it cools, forming a pie or torte shell.

8.   Meanwhile, chill remaining chocolate mousse in refrigerator. When the shell has cooled, fill it with the chilled, uncooked mousse, and return the torte to the refrigerator for a couple of hours.

9.   BLENDER-WHIP THE CREAM: Empty heavy cream into clean container.

Cover and blend on HIGH speed until the cream begins to set around the blades. Add the confectioners' sugar, stir with rubber spatula, and blend again for a few seconds. Stop and stir, and repeat as often as needed until the cream is very thick.

10. Spread the cream over the top of the torte. Or make this a culinary masterpiece by using a pastry bag fitted with a small star tube: make a criss-cross lattice pattern over the top, then pipe a fluted edge all around the edge of the torte shell. Keep cold, but remove from refrigerator about 30 minutes before serving.

HOW TO MAKE A MOLDED CHICKEN MOUSSE in 2 minutes

Serves 4

2	tablespoons lemon juice	2	cups diced white meat of
1	envelope plain gelatin		chicken
1	thin slice onion	1	teaspoon dried tarragon
½	cup boiling water	1	cup heavy cream
½	cup mayonnaise (page 27)		

1. Put lemon juice and gelatin into container. Add onion slice and boiling water. Cover and blend on HIGH speed for 40 to 60 seconds. This comparatively long blending time is necessary to liquefy the gelatin completely so that it will set the mousse. If in doubt, overblend rather than underblend.

2. Add mayonnaise, chicken, and tarragon. Cover, and start blending on HIGH speed. With blades spinning, remove cover or inner cap, and gradually pour in the cream. Blend for 30 seconds longer, until mixture is smooth.

3. Pour into a 4-cup mold, and chill until firm.

4. To unmold: Loosen mousse around edges of mold with a silver knife. Lower mold carefully into water that is just hot to the hand, being careful not to let any water run into the mold. Count 3 seconds, then invert the mousse on a cold serving plate.

SALMON MOUSSE VARIATION

Use a 1-pound can of salmon, drained, in place of the chicken. Substitute dill weed for the tarragon.

Blend-and-Set Fruit Desserts

THE technique of making gelatin desserts that actually set as they are blending is one of my claims to culinary fame. Like many new food discoveries, it happened quite by accident, but once the phenomenon had taken place, it took many weeks of testing to perfect the technique and make it foolproof. I called this "cooking with ice." Originally, crushed ice was used in the recipes, but, since few homemakers have an ice crusher and smashing ice to fine bits in a towel is tedious work, I decided to work out the technique with ice cubes when I began thinking about this new blender book. If you make the Fruit Snow which follows just once, you will realize the infinite variations that are possible of this recipe and of others in the dessert chapter. While I have here used heavy cream right out of the refrigerator—simply because I have an inordinate fondness for creamy rich desserts—you can use light cream or cold milk, or ice-cold water, for that matter, made by melting a few ice cubes in a cup of water. For really low-calorie desserts, you may use a sugar substitute equivalent to the amount of sugar specified in the recipe. For additional nourishment, you may add whole eggs or leftover yolks or whites.

HOW TO MAKE
A FRUIT SNOW in 2 minutes

Serves 6

1	cup hot, but not boiling, water
2	envelopes plain gelatin
½	cup sugar
One	6-ounce can concentrated lime, orange, or lemon juice, or fruitade, partially defrosted.
One	8-ounce container cold cream or milk
6–8	ice cubes

1. Put the hot water and gelatin into the container. Cover and blend on HIGH speed for 40 to 60 seconds.

2. With blades spinning, remove cover or inner cap, and add sugar. Continue to blend for 3 seconds longer to dissolve sugar thoroughly.

3. Add the concentrated juice, cover, and start blending on HIGH speed.

With blades spinning, remove cover and pour in the cold milk or cream. Then with blades still spinning, drop in ice cubes, one at a time, until the mixture begins to thicken. Be sure each ice cube is thoroughly incorporated before adding the next.

4. Pour the setting dessert into crumb crust, or 4-cup mold, or individual serving dishes. Serve immediately or refrigerate until serving time.

NOTE: Ice can vary in temperature from 32° F. to below zero, depending on how cold your refrigerator or freezer is kept. Thus, in warm weather it may be necessary to let the dessert stand in the refrigerator for 3 to 5 minutes before it is sufficiently set to serve.

HOW TO MAKE A
FRUIT SHERBET in 1 minute

Serves 2 or 3

3 ounces (½ can) frozen concentrated fruit juice, partially defrosted
2 tablespoons sugar or the equivalent of sugar substitute
2 cups cracked ice cubes

1. Put all ingredients into container, cover, and start blending on HIGH speed. As mixture freezes around the blades it will stop churning. Remove cover, and with a rubber spatula, carefully break surface, pulling the frost from sides of container into the center.

2. When fruit juice and ice are the consistency of fine snow, turn off blender, and spoon the sherbert into serving dishes.

FROZEN DAIQUIRIS are made in the same way

Serves 2. Put into container 3 ounces light rum, 1½ tablespoons lime juice, 1 tablespoon sugar or the equivalent of sugar substitute, and 2 cups cracked ice. Follow directions for fruit sherbets.

BABY'S DINNER is ready in seconds

You can feed your baby the same foods that you eat, in moderation. I don't think I'd start him off on a lamb curry or chili con carne, but most any roasted meat and cooked vegetable can be turned into a dinner for him. Extra or special nutrients that your baby needs or that are prescribed by your doctor—such as dry milk or a special formula, raw or cooked egg yolks, or vitamins—may be blended in.

6   tablespoons hot tomato juice, broth, or formula
¼   cup diced, cooked vegetables
½   cup diced, cooked meat, poultry or fish

Put all ingredients into blender container. Cover and blend on HIGH speed for 20 seconds, or until smooth.

FOR COARSELY CHOPPED DINNER

Reduce amount of liquid to 4 tablespoons, and blend for about 6 seconds only.

FOR FRUIT PURÉES

Measure 2 tablespoons orange, pineapple, apple, cranberry, or prune juice into container. Add ½ cup fresh or canned diced apricots, peaches, or pitted prunes, 1 sliced banana or ½ cup diced apple. Cover and blend on HIGH speed for 10 seconds, or until fruit is puréed.

FOR PURÉED VEGETABLES

Measure ¼ cup hot vegetable cooking water, tomato juice, or milk and 1 teaspoon soft butter into container. Add ¾ cup diced cooked carrots, cauliflower, asparagus, sweet potato, or green beans, or drained spinach, cooked lima beans or peas, or cooked shredded cabbage. Cover and blend on HIGH speed for 1 minute, or until smooth.

TIME-SAVING TIP

Blend enough vegetables, dinners, or fruit purées to fill an ice cube tray. Fill tray, replace metal divider, and freeze. When purée is solid, remove the metal divider, empty the frozen cubes into a plastic bag, and store in the freezer section of your refrigerator. To thaw, heat over simmering water.

SOUPS

Soups

IF YOU BOUGHT an electric blender for no other reason than to make soups, it would pay for itself in just a few months, for one of the basic functions of the blender is to reduce cooked vegetables or soft fruits to a smooth purée. It eliminates the time-consuming, messy, and dull chore of pressing vegetables through a sieve or food mill.

With some liquid added to this purée, and spices, herbs, or flavor vegetables like onion or celery, hundreds of differently flavored soups may be made in seconds from freshly cooked vegetables or from leftovers that might otherwise find themselves in the garbage disposal.

Not one speck of food need be thrown away. Leftover potato, rice, or macaroni may be used to thicken a cream soup in place of flour. Leftover gravies from roasts or stews, even spoonfuls of leftover casseroles or baked dishes may be added to the purée. The liquid may be milk, broth, tomato, or vegetable juice, and a small amount of cream may be added at the end of the blending for a richer soup. All you do is simply blend, heat, and serve. Or chill for a cold soup in summertime.

When beef or chicken stock are specified in a recipe, they may be the broth from boiled beef or poached chicken, they may be canned, or they may be made by dissolving a bouillon cube in 1 cup hot water. And, because alternate liquids have been suggested in many of the recipes, always correct the seasoning of the soup with salt before serving.

In this chapter are some wonderfully good soups, quickly made in your blender. They are just a beginning. You take it from there, but with this word of caution: When making hot soups, never fill your blender container more than half full of a hot, thin liquid. Be certain to cover the container and rest your hand lightly on the cover before turning the blender on. Boiling-hot soup can cause a nasty burn! Once the blades have reached full speed and the surge of liquid in the container has subsided, you may then raise the cover or remove the inner cap, and with the motor on, add more of the ingredients to fill the entire container.

If a blender is new to you, I recommend that you first make the Cream of Vegetable Soup (page 21) to familiarize yourself with the technique of soup making before progressing to the recipes that follow. Serve the soup with a square of hot cornbread or a muffin for a nutritious and flavorful lunch—prepared literally in seconds.

Creamy Hot Soups

CREAM OF ALMOND SOUP

Makes 3 1/4 cups

1 tablespoon butter
1 tablespoon finely diced onion
One 10 1/2-ounce can condensed
    chicken soup with rice
1/8 teaspoon dry mustard
1/2 cup slivered almonds, toasted

1 cup milk
1/8 teaspoon mace
1/2 cup light cream
Extra toasted almond slivers
    for garnish

1. Melt butter over moderate heat. Add onion and cook for about 2 minutes. Empty into container.

2. Add remaining ingredients in order listed. Cover and blend on MEDIUM speed for 30 seconds.

3. Pour blended mixture into saucepan. Heat thoroughly, but do not boil, stirring frequently. Correct seasoning, if necessary.

4. Serve with a garnish of slivered, toasted almonds.

CREAM OF ASPARAGUS OR ZUCCHINI SOUP

Serves 6

1 pound fresh asparagus or zuc-
    chini, washed
1 small onion, quartered
1 cup chicken broth
1 teaspoon salt

1/4 teaspoon pepper
1/2 teaspoon sweet basil
1 1/2 cups milk
1/2 cup cream

1. Discard coarse white ends from asparagus stalks, or trim and slice zucchini thickly.

2. Combine in saucepan the prepared vegetable, onion, chicken broth, salt, pepper, and sweet basil. Bring to a boil and simmer 20 minutes.

3. Empty vegetable and liquid into container. Cover, then turn motor on HIGH speed.

4. With motor running, remove lid and gradually add ½ cup milk. Blend until smooth.

5. Return blended purée to saucepan and stir in remaining milk and the cream. Heat to serving temperature, stirring occasionally.

SPINACH CHEESE SOUP

Serves 4

1 cup cooked spinach	½ cup shredded Cheddar cheese
3 cups milk	Dash of cayenne pepper
1 tablespoon soft butter	Salt to taste
1 tablespoon flour	

1. Into container, put the spinach, 1 cup of the milk, the butter, and flour. Cover and blend on HIGH speed for 15 seconds.

2. Empty into a saucepan and add remaining milk, cheese, and cayenne pepper. Heat to boiling, stirring constantly.

3. Correct seasoning with salt and serve immediately—or keep hot over simmering water until ready to serve.

CRÈME OLGA
(Scallions and Raw Mushroom Soup)

Serves 6

3 bunches green onions (about 15)	½ teaspoon white pepper
¾ pound fresh mushrooms	4 cups chicken broth or part milk and part broth
¼ pound butter (1 stick)	2 tablespoons flour
1 teaspoon salt	1½ cups light cream

1. Wash and trim green onions, using both the white and green parts. Cut coarsely. Wash and dry mushrooms. Slice one-third of them, and set aside. Quarter remaining mushrooms.

2. In a saucepan, melt the butter, add scallions, salt, and pepper, and cook over low heat for 10 minutes. Add 2 cups of the stock or milk, bring to a boil, and simmer for 10 minutes.

3. Empty contents of saucepan into container. Add the flour and the quartered mushrooms. Cover and blend on HIGH speed for 30 seconds.

4. Return mixture to saucepan and stir in remaining stock or milk and the cream. Heat to simmering and cook for 3 minutes, stirring frequently.

5. Add the reserved sliced mushrooms and serve hot.

CREAM OF FRESH MUSHROOM SOUP

Serves 4

½	pound fresh mushrooms, washed and sliced	2	tablespoons flour
½	small onion, diced	¾	teaspoon salt
4	tablespoons butter (½ stick)	⅛	teaspoon white pepper
1	cup chicken broth or milk	1	cup milk
		½	cup cream

1. Sauté mushrooms and onion in half the butter for 5 to 6 minutes, or until mushrooms are tender.

2. Empty vegetables into container and add 1 cup chicken broth or milk, the flour, salt, pepper, and remaining butter. Cover and blend on HIGH speed for 10 seconds, or until mushrooms are finely chopped.

3. Empty into a saucepan and stir in the milk and cream. Heat to serving temperature and serve hot.

CURRIED LIMA BEAN SOUP

Serves 6

One	10-ounce package baby lima beans	⅛	teaspoon white pepper
2	tablespoons butter	¼	teaspoon marjoram
⅓	cup sliced green onions	4	parsley clusters
1	teaspoon curry powder	One	13¾-ounce can chicken broth
½	cup water	½	cup light cream
½	teaspoon salt		Chopped chives or parsley for garnish

1. In a saucepan, combine lima beans, butter, green onions, curry

powder, and water. Bring to a boil, partially cover, and simmer for 15 minutes, or until beans are tender.

2.   Empty contents of saucepan into container. Add salt, pepper, marjoram, and parsley. Cover and blend on HIGH speed for 20 seconds. Without turning off motor, remove cover, and add broth and cream.

3.   Chill soup, and serve cold with a sprinkling of chopped chives or parsley.

POTAGE DU CURÉ
(Cream of Tomato and Leek Soup)

Serves 8

One   2-pound, 2-ounce can tomatoes
  6   leeks, white part only, washed
        and coarsely cut
  3   carrots, coarsely cut
  ½   bunch parsley

½   teaspoon coarsely ground
      black pepper
1   pint heavy cream
Salt to taste

1.   Empty tomatoes with juice into a large saucepan. Add leeks, carrots, parsley, and pepper. Bring to a boil and simmer for 45 minutes, or until vegetables are very soft.

2.   Blend 2 cups at a time on HIGH speed until smooth and empty into top of a double saucepan. Continue until all soup is blended.

3.   Stir in cream, add salt to taste, and cook over simmering water until very hot.

POTAGE CHOU-FLEUR AU FROMAGE
(Cauliflower Soup with Cheese)

Serves 6

One   10-ounce package frozen
        cauliflower
  1   tablespoon butter
  ½   teaspoon salt
  1   cup boiling water
  ⅛   teaspoon pepper

½ medium onion, coarsely
    chopped
½ teaspoon curry powder
One 10-ounce can frozen potato
    soup, partially defrosted
½ cup cream
½ cup grated Parmesan cheese

1. Into a small saucepan, put the cauliflower, butter, salt, water, pepper, onion, and curry powder. Cover and simmer for 8 to 10 minutes.

2. Empty cauliflower and liquid into container. Add potato soup and cream. Cover and press button for LOW speed. When blades have reached full speed, switch to HIGH, and blend for 20 seconds.

3. Heat. Keep hot over simmering water until ready to serve, stirring occasionally.

4. Serve hot and pass the grated cheese on the side.

LENTIL SOUP

Serves 6 to 8

1 cup lentils
1 large onion, quartered
½ cup diced, cooked ham
1 stalk celery with leaves,
    coarsely cut
1 carrot, coarsely cut

¼ cup parsley clusters
¼ teaspoon Tabasco sauce
3 teaspoons salt
¼ teaspoon pepper
2 teaspoons paprika
1 cup sour cream

1. Put lentils in container, cover and blend on HIGH speed for 20 seconds, or until lentils are ground. Empty into a large saucepan.

2. Now place in container onion, ham, celery, carrot, parsley, Tabasco, salt, pepper, and paprika. Cover ingredients with cold water to within 1 inch from top of container. Cover and blend on HIGH speed for 5 seconds, or until vegetables are finely chopped. Empty into saucepan with lentils. Stir to mix.

3. Add 1 quart water, and bring to a boil. Simmer, covered, for 40 minutes, stirring occasionally.

4. Into blender, put 1 cup hot soup and 1 cup sour cream. Cover and blend on HIGH speed for 5 seconds, or until smooth. Stir into rest of soup and heat to serving temperature, stirring occasionally.

CHICKEN SOUP AVGOLEMONO

Serves 4

3   tablespoons raw rice
3   cups seasoned chicken broth
2   egg yolks
    Juice of 1 lemon
    Thin yellow rind of ½ lemon
1   cup heavy cream

1. In a saucepan, simmer rice and chicken broth for 30 minutes. Remove from heat and empty into container. Cover and begin blending on LOW speed. Add 2 egg yolks, lemon juice, and rind. Cover and switch to HIGH speed. Blend for 10 seconds, then remove cover, and with motor on, pour in the cream.

2. Reheat in a saucepan to serving temperature, stirring constantly and taking care not to let the soup boil. Or cool, and serve well chilled.

Bisques

NEPTUNE BISQUE

Serves 6

1   cup freshly shucked clams
1½   cups milk
1   cup diced raw potato
      (1 medium)
1   stalk celery, coarsely cut
1   small onion, quartered
¼   teaspoon thyme
⅛   teaspoon pepper
6–8 parsley clusters
1   tablespoon chopped chives
½   teaspoon salt
½   cup cream

1. Into container, put clams, ½ cup of the milk, potato, celery, onion, thyme, pepper, parsley, chives, and salt. Cover and blend on HIGH speed for 20 seconds.

2. With motor on, remove lid and gradually pour in remaining milk.

3. Empty mixture into a saucepan, bring to a boil, and cook over low heat for 10 minutes, stirring frequently.

4. Stir in the cream and keep hot over simmering water until ready to serve.

SALMON BISQUE

Serves 6 to 8

1½ cups milk
One 10-ounce can frozen potato soup, thawed
1 cup chicken broth
2 teaspoons onion juice
One 1-pound can salmon with liquid
1 cup light cream
Fresh dill for garnish

1. In a saucepan, heat milk, potato soup, chicken broth, and onion juice. Bring just to a simmer, then remove from heat, and stir in salmon with liquid.

2. Blend 2 cups at a time. Cover, begin on LOW speed, then switch to HIGH.

3. Stir in cream and chill until very cold. Garnish with fresh dill.

CLAM BISQUE

Serves 4

One 10½-ounce can condensed celery soup
1 cup cream, or half milk and half cream
One 7½-ounce can minced clams
½ teaspoon tarragon
½ cup clam juice
2 tablespoons sherry
Tabasco sauce to taste

1. Put all ingredients into the container. Cover and blend on MEDIUM speed for 20 seconds, or until smooth.

2. Heat over simmering water, and serve.

LOBSTER BISQUE

Serves 4

1½ cups milk
 2   tablespoons soft butter
One 5-ounce can lobster meat,
       drained, or 1 cup cooked
       lobster
     Dash of Tabasco sauce

¼   cup parsley clusters
½   teaspoon salt
    Dash of pepper
1   tablespoon dry sherry
1   cup cream

1. Pour milk into container. Add butter, lobster meat, Tabasco, parsley, salt, pepper, and sherry. Cover and blend on HIGH speed for 30 seconds, or until smooth.

2. Empty into a saucepan and stir in cream. Heat to serving temperature, stirring occasionally.

EASY OYSTER BISQUE

Serves 4

2   tablespoons butter
4   green onions, coarsely cut
1   cup dry white wine
One 7-ounce can frozen oysters,
       defrosted

½   cup milk
⅛   teaspoon Tabasco sauce
1   egg yolk
1   cup cream
1   tablespoon sherry

1. Melt the butter in a small saucepan. Add green onions, and sauté for 2 to 3 minutes. Add white wine, and simmer for 5 minutes.

2. Empty oysters and oyster liquor into container. Add milk. Cover and blend on HIGH speed for 10 seconds.

3. With motor on, remove cover, and add the green onions and liquid from saucepan and the Tabasco. Blend for 10 seconds longer.

4. Empty mixture into saucepan and heat to serving temperature.

5. Just before serving, blend the egg yolk, cream, and sherry with a little of the hot soup. Stir egg mixture into remaining soup, and heat to serving temperature (do not boil). Serve hot.

Clear Vegetable Soups

VEGETABLE BORSCHT WITH BOILED POTATO

Serves 6

2 cups coarsely cut cabbage
5 medium beets, peeled and
    quartered   water-chopped in blender*
1 medium onion, quartered
1 carrot, coarsely cut
2 teaspoons sugar
1 tablespoon tomato catsup
2 tablespoons vinegar or
    lemon juice
2 teaspoons salt
¼ teaspoon pepper
2 cups water
Two 10½-ounce cans beef
    consommé
6 small, peeled, boiled potatoes

1. Fill container loosely with cut vegetables, add cold water, and water-chop. Drain vegetables and empty into a large saucepan. Repeat until all vegetables are coarsely chopped.

2. Add all other ingredients to saucepan, except potatoes. Bring to a boil and simmer 20 minutes.

3. Serve hot with a potato in each serving.

BROCCOLI SOUP

Serves 6

One 10-ounce package frozen broccoli spears
1 small onion, quartered
1 cup water
½ teaspoon salt
    Dash of pepper
Two 10½-ounce cans beef consommé

1. Into a saucepan, put the broccoli, onion, water, salt, and pepper. Cover and simmer for 20 minutes.

2. Empty vegetables and liquid into container. Cover and blend on HIGH speed for 10 seconds.

3. Leave motor on. Remove lid and gradually pour in the beef consommé.

4. Heat to serving temperature.

NOTE: This is good served with crisp croutons.

EGG-DROP SOUP

Serves 6

1   egg
2   green onions, coarsely cut
6–8 parsley clusters
2   tablespoons soy sauce
1   quart hot chicken broth

1. Put the egg, onions, parsley, and soy sauce into container. Cover and blend on HIGH speed for 5 seconds, or until greens are minced.

2. Bring hot chicken broth to a rapid boil. Slowly stir the egg mixture into the hot soup so that it separates into egg threads.

3. Serve hot.

FRENCH ONION SOUP

Serves 4

½   cup diced Parmesan cheese   1½   cups water
3   large onions, coarsely cut   1   teaspoon salt
Two 10½-ounce cans beef   ½   teaspoon pepper
       consommé   4   slices toasted French bread

1. Empty cheese into container. Cover and blend on HIGH speed for 15 seconds. Empty grated cheese onto waxed paper and set aside.

2. Into container, put onions and beef consommé. Cover and blend on HIGH speed for about 3 seconds, or until onions are coarsely chopped.

3. Empty chopped onions into saucepan, add water, salt, and pepper. Bring to a boil and simmer for 15 minutes.

4. Pour soup into 4 individual casserole dishes. Top each serving with a slice of toast and sprinkle heavily with grated cheese.

5. Broil 4 to 5 inches from source of heat for 5 minutes, or until top is golden and crusty.

LOW-CALORIE VEGETABLE SOUP

Serves 4

1½	cups water	1	cup coarsely cut celery
2	beef bouillon cubes	1½	cups tomato or vegetable juice
½	cup coarsely diced onion		Salt and pepper to taste
1	cup coarsely sliced carrot	1	tablespoon chopped parsley

1. Pour 1 cup of the water into container. Add bouillon cubes and vegetables. Cover and blend on HIGH speed for 2 seconds, or until vegetables are coarsely chopped.

2. Empty mixture into a saucepan, add remaining water and tomato juice, and bring to a boil. Simmer for 10 minutes.

3. Season to taste with salt and pepper and serve with a sprinkle of chopped parsley.

POTAGE VERT

Serves 4

3	tablespoons butter	½	bunch watercress
¼	cup sliced green onions	1	cup spinach leaves
2	cups diced raw potatoes	2	cups shredded lettuce
1	teaspoon salt		Chopped chives or parsley for
2	cups chicken broth		garnish

1. In a saucepan, melt butter and in it cook onions over moderate heat for 5 minutes. Add potatoes, salt, and chicken broth. Bring to a boil, cover, and simmer 10 minutes.

2. Meanwhile, discard coarse stems from watercress. Wash the watercress and spinach.

3. Add watercress, spinach, and lettuce to mixture in saucepan, and simmer for 5 minutes longer, or until potatoes are tender.

4. Pour off about 1 cup of the broth and set aside. Empty remaining vegetables and broth into container. Cover, and blend on HIGH speed for 30 seconds, or until smooth.

5. Return purée and reserved broth to saucepan, and reheat.

6. Serve with a sprinkling of chopped chives or parsley in each cup.

Serve-Hot-or-Cold Soups

MINTED CUCUMBER SOUP

Serves 6

1 large cucumber (or 2 medium-size)	3 tablespoons flour
4 large green onions, coarsely cut	1 cup chicken broth
½ cup water	3 sprigs fresh mint
½ teaspoon salt	½ cup cream or milk
¼ teaspoon pepper	Mint and sour cream for garnish

1. Wash cucumber, trim ends, and peel half. Cut both peeled and unpeeled cucumber in chunks, and put into a saucepan with the green onions, water, salt, and pepper. Cover, and simmer for 10 minutes, or until vegetables are tender.

2. Empty vegetables and juice into container, and add the flour, chicken broth, and mint. Cover, and blend on HIGH speed. With motor on, remove cover, and gradually pour in the cream or milk.

3. Empty soup into a saucepan, and bring to a boil, stirring frequently. Serve hot, or chill and serve cold. Garnish with chopped fresh mint and a dab of sour cream.

CREAM OF POTATO SOUP

Serves 2

1 small onion, coarsely cut
2 tablespoons butter
2 medium potatoes, freshly cooked and quartered
One 10½-ounce can condensed cream of chicken soup

Few clusters of parsley
½ cup cream of milk
¼ cup sour cream
Chopped chives for garnish

1. In a small skillet, sauté the onion in the butter for 6 minutes, or until tender but not browned.

2. Empty onion and butter into container. Add potatoes, soup, parsley, and cream or milk. Cover and blend on HIGH speed for 15 seconds, or until smooth.

3. Empty into a bowl, or saucepan, and stir in sour cream.

4. Serve hot or cold with a sprinkling of chives on each serving.

BORSCHT WITH SOUR CREAM

Serves 4

1 cup cooked or canned, sliced or diced beets
1 cup beet liquor
1½ cups beef broth

2 tablespoons lemon juice
Dash of pepper
1 egg
½ cup sour cream

1. Put beets and beet liquor into container. Cover and blend on HIGH speed for about 30 seconds.

2. With motor on, remove cover and add beef broth, lemon juice, pepper, egg, and half the sour cream.

3. Serve hot or chilled with a spoonful of the remaining sour cream on top of each serving. Correct seasoning with salt if necessary before serving.

NOTE: When serving hot, add a hot boiled potato to each serving, if desired.

Definitely Cold Soups

FRESH TOMATO SOUP

Serves 4

2 large beefsteak tomatoes, cut in sections
½ large Bermuda onion, coarsely cut
1 clove garlic
1 cup water
1 teaspoon salt
Freshly ground black pepper

½ teaspoon dried dill weed or several sprays fresh dill
2 tablespoons flour
½ cup light cream
Chopped chives, fresh dill, or peeled, seeded, chopped tomato for garnish

1. In a saucepan, combine tomatoes, onion, garlic, half the water, salt, pepper, and dill. Bring to a boil, partially cover, and simmer 30 minutes.

2. Combine remaining water and flour. Stir into soup and cook 3 minutes, stirring constantly.

3. Empty half the contents of saucepan into blender container. Cover and blend on HIGH speed 20 seconds. Strain through a sieve into a bowl. Repeat with remaining cooked mixture.

4. Cool over ice. Correct seasoning and stir in cream. Keep cold until ready to serve. Serve with a garnish of chopped chives, fresh dill, or tomato.

CHICKEN AVOCADO SOUP

Serves 4

2½ cups chicken broth
1 ripe avocado, peeled, pitted, and sliced
1 teaspoon salt
Dash of white pepper

2 tablespoons sherry
¼ cup cream, whipped
A few chopped pistachio nuts for garnish

1. Pour the chicken broth into container and add avocado, salt, pepper, and sherry. Cover and press LOW button. As soon as blades reach full speed, press MEDIUM or HIGH button and blend for 30 seconds, or until smooth.

2. Pour purée into a bowl and chill thoroughly.

3. Serve each portion topped with a dab of whipped cream and a sprinkling of pistachio nuts.

BUTTERMILK SOUP

Serves 4

3 cups buttermilk
5 green onions, trimmed, washed, and coarsely cut
½ cucumber, peeled and seeded
½ cup parsley clusters
½ cup fresh dill or 2 teaspoons dried dill weed
½ teaspoon pepper

1. Into container, put 2 cups of the buttermilk, the green onion, cucumber, parsley, dill, and pepper. Cover and press LOW button. As soon as blades reach full speed, switch to HIGH. Blend for 30 seconds.

2. With motor on, remove cover and pour in remaining buttermilk. Chill and serve cold.

NOTE: ½ pound cooked shrimp, peeled and deveined, may be added along with the onion and cucumber.

JELLIED HERB MADRILÈNE

Serves 6

Two 10½-ounce cans beef consommé with gelatin added
1 lemon, peeled, seeded, and coarsely cut
1 envelope plain gelatin
½ teaspoon sweet basil or tarragon
½ cup sherry
1½ cups tomato juice
Salt to taste
6 thin lemon slices for garnish

1. Put 1 can of the consommé, the lemon, gelatin, and herb into container. Cover and blend on HIGH speed for 30 seconds.

2. Empty into a saucepan and add sherry. Bring slowly to a simmer, stirring constantly, and remove from heat.

3. Stir in remaining consommé, tomato juice, and salt to taste. Chill until set.

4. Serve in bouillon cups with a slice of lemon on each serving.

NOTE: If desired, top each serving with a spoonful of red caviar and a dab of sour cream.

CHILLED CANTALOUPE SOUP

Serves 3

1   cup orange juice
1   tablespoon lemon juice
2   cups diced cantaloupe
⅛   teaspoon salt

Put ingredients into container in order listed. Cover and blend on HIGH speed for 15 seconds. Serve very cold.

DILLED VICHYSSOISE

Serves 6

2   cups peeled, diced, raw pota-   ½   teaspoon salt
    toes (2 medium)   ⅛   teaspoon white pepper
2   leeks, white part only, coarsely   ½   teaspoon dill weed
    cut   1   cup milk
1   small onion, coarsely cut   1   cup cream
1   cup chicken broth   Chopped chives for garnish

1. Put potatoes into container. Add leeks, onion, chicken broth, salt, pepper, and dill weed. Cover and blend on HIGH speed 20 seconds. With motor on, remove lid, and gradually pour in the milk.

2. Empty mixture into a saucepan and cook over very low heat for 10 minutes, stirring frequently.

3. Return soup to container, filling container only one-quarter full. Cover and press HIGH button. As soon as blades reach full speed, remove cover, and gradually pour in remaining soup.

4. Pour soup into a bowl, stir in cream, and chill thoroughly. Serve garnished with chopped chives.

GAZPACHO

Serves 6

1 clove garlic, halved	2 large ripe tomatoes, peeled and cut in sections
1 egg	
1/8 teaspoon cayenne pepper	1/2 green pepper, seeded and cut in strips
1/2 teaspoon salt	
3 tablespoons cider or wine vinegar	1 medium cucumber, peeled and coarsely cut
1/4 cup olive oil	1/2 cup beef consommé
1/2 small onion, peeled and quartered	

1. Into container, put the garlic, egg, cayenne pepper, salt, vinegar, and olive oil. Cover and blend on LOW speed for 5 seconds.

2. Add remaining ingredients, cover, and blend on HIGH speed for 30 seconds. Chill and serve very cold.

NOTE: Often crisp garlic croutons are passed with this soup.

Instant Cold Soups

A GREAT VARIETY of smooth, icy cold vegetable soups have become popular during the past ten years for quick luncheon dishes. Here are but a few. Use your own imagination to create your own flavors using the same technique as in these sample recipes.

CURRIED CHICKEN (Senegalese)

Serves 4

Into container, put a 10½-ounce can cream of chicken soup, 1 teaspoon curry powder, and ½ cup milk. Cover and blend on HIGH speed 15 seconds. Remove cover and, with blades spinning, empty in 1 cup ice cubes. Pour in ½ cup milk or, preferably, cream, and blend for 10 seconds longer. Garnish with chopped chives or chopped cucumber.

MOCK VICHYSSOISE

Serves 3

Into container, put a 10½-ounce can frozen condensed cream of potato soup, partially defrosted, 1 thin slice onion, a dash of pepper, and ½ cup sour cream. Cover and blend on HIGH speed 15 seconds. Remove cover and, with blades spinning, empty in 1 cup ice cubes. Blend until ice cubes are melted. Garnish with chopped radishes or green onions.

TOMATO CUCUMBER SOUP

Serves 3

Empty a 10½-ounce can condensed tomato soup into container. Add ½ cucumber, peeled, seeded, and sliced, 2 green onions, coarsely cut, ½ teaspoon salt, and a dash of pepper. Cover and blend on HIGH speed 10 seconds. Remove cover and, with blades spinning, empty in 1 cup ice cubes. Pour in ½ cup heavy cream and blend until ice cubes are melted. Garnish with chopped fresh dill or parsley.

APPETIZERS,
DIPS & SPREADS

Appetizers, Dips & Spreads

ONE of the most popular uses for an electric blender is the making of dips and spreads to serve at cocktail time. Cheese, mayonnaise, sour cream, or a mixture of these, are usually the basis of such dips or spreads, and many flavor changes can be rung by the addition or substitution of one spice or herb for another. Most spreads may be converted into dips by increasing the amount of liquid, and conversely, a little less liquid in a dip can turn it into a spread for sandwiches or crackers.

Dips and spreads, which are so in keeping with our casual living today, are easy to make in seconds in a blender. Serve them in attractive bowls, surrounded by crackers or a colorful array of crisp vegetables.

On some occasions, you may prefer a more elaborate appetizer, so we'll begin this chapter with a few spectacular blended dishes, many of which can double as quick luncheon or supper dishes, and all of which can fill the need of a snack at almost any time of the day.

Appetizer Pies

CRAB AND CHEESE QUICHE
WITH SAVORY CRUMB CRUST

Serves 6 to 8 for an appetizer, 4 as a luncheon dish

1 cup corn flakes or other flaky cereal	3 egg yolks
4 tablespoons melted butter (½ stick)	½ cup cream
	3 tablespoons flour
½ teaspoon dill weed or tarragon	½ teaspoon salt
3 egg whites	⅛ teaspoon pepper
6 ounces canned or frozen king crab meat	1 tablespoon coarsely cut chives or green onion tops
1 cup cream-style cottage cheese (8 ounces)	1 tablespoon lemon juice

1. Make Savory Crumb Crust: Empty corn flakes into container. Cover and blend on HIGH speed until cereal is crumbed. Empty crumbs into a bowl and mix with the melted butter and dill weed or tarragon. Press onto bottom and around sides of an 8- or 9-inch pie plate.

2. In a clean bowl, beat egg whites until stiff, but not dry. Set aside. Preheat oven to 350°F.

3. Put cottage cheese, egg yolks, cream, flour, salt, pepper, chives, and lemon juice into container. Cover and blend on HIGH speed until smooth. Pick over crab meat to remove any cartilage, then add crab meat to mixture. Cover and blend on HIGH speed just until last piece of crab meat is pulled down into blades.

4. Pour over egg whites and fold together until lightly mixed. Turn into prepared pie plate and bake in preheated oven for 30 to 35 minutes. Serve hot.

VARIATION: Substitute a 7¾-ounce can of salmon for the crab meat.

ONION CHEESE PIE

Makes one 9-inch pie

* 1 cup blender-crumbed cheese crackers
2 tablespoons poppy seeds
½ cup melted butter (1 stick)
3 cups sliced sweet onion
2 tablespoons butter

1 cup cubed Cheddar cheese
1 cup hot milk or cream
3 egg yolks
½ teaspoon salt
¼ teaspoon thyme
⅛ teaspoon black pepper

1. Combine cheese-cracker crumbs, poppy seeds, and melted butter. Press onto bottom and sides of a buttered 9-inch pie plate. Bake in a preheated 350° F. oven for 10 minutes. Remove from oven and set aside.

2. Sauté onion in the 2 tablespoons butter in a skillet over low heat, stirring frequently, for 20 minutes, or until limp and golden.

3. Spread onions in bottom of baked cracker crust.

4. Put remaining ingredients into container. Cover and blend on HIGH speed for 20 seconds.

5. Pour blended mixture into cracker crust over onions.

6. Bake in preheated 350° F. oven for 25 to 30 minutes, or until custard is brown and set.

7. Serve hot.

CREAM CHEESE PIE

Serves 8 as an appetizer, 4 to 6 as a luncheon dish

* 16   melba toast rounds,
         blender-crumbed
   4   tablespoons melted butter
         (½ stick)
   2   tablespoons lemon juice
   2   envelopes plain gelatin
   ½   cup hot milk
 One   8-ounce package cream cheese,
         diced

   2   eggs
   1   pint sour cream
   8   large stuffed green olives
   3   green onions, coarsely cut
   ½   green pepper, coarsely cut
   ½   teaspoon salt
   ¼   teaspoon Tabasco sauce
         Pimiento strips and anchovies
           for garnish

1. Blender-crumb half the toast rounds, empty into mixing bowl, and repeat with remaining toast.

2. Mix crumbs with melted butter and press into bottom and around sides of a buttered 9-inch pie plate.

3. Put lemon juice into container. Add gelatin and hot milk. Cover and blend on HIGH speed for 40 to 60 seconds.

4. Add cream cheese, and sour cream, cover, and blend on HIGH speed until mixture is smooth, stopping to stir down if necessary.

5. Add olives, green onions, green pepper, salt, and Tabasco. Cover and blend on HIGH speed just until vegetables are finely chopped.

6. Pour into prepared pie plate and chill for several hours, or overnight.

7. Before serving garnish with pimiento and anchovies.

Pâtés

PÂTÉ CASANOVA

Makes a 1½-pound loaf

¾ pound soft butter (3 sticks)
1 small onion, sliced
1 pound chicken livers, cleaned and halved
1 bay leaf
½ teaspoon salt
¼ teaspoon pepper
2 tablespoons sherry or Marsala wine
2 tablespoons brandy

1. In a skillet, melt 1 stick of the butter, add onion, and sauté until lightly browned. Add chicken livers and bay leaf and cook for about 10 minutes, or until livers are lightly browned. Add salt, pepper, and sherry or Marsala, and simmer for 5 minutes.

2. Empty contents of skillet into container, cover, and start blending on HIGH speed. With blades spinning, remove cover or inner cap and gradually add remaining butter and the brandy. Blend for 1 minute longer, or until mixture is smooth.

3. Pack mixture into an 8 × 4 × 2-inch loaf pan lined with aluminum foil. Chill for 6 hours or overnight.

4. Turn out onto serving platter. Slice thinly and serve with pumpernickel bread.

CHICKEN LIVER AND MUSHROOM PÂTÉ

Makes about 2 cups

2 tablespoons butter
½ pound chicken livers, cleaned and quartered
One 3-ounce can mushroom bits and pieces, drained
2 tablespoons coarsely cut chives
½ cup mayonnaise
¼ cup parsley clusters
2 tablespoons dry sherry
⅛ teaspoon salt
Dash of pepper

1. In a skillet, melt butter and in it sauté the chicken livers over moderate heat, stirring frequently, until pink color disappears.

2. Empty livers and butter into container and add remaining ingredients. Cover and blend on HIGH speed until smooth, stopping to stir down if necessary. Chill before serving.

LIVER PÂTÉ BOULE DE NEIGE

Makes one 3-inch ball

½ pound liverwurst, peeled and
    diced
2 tablespoons brandy
2 tablespoons mayonnaise

¼ teaspoon curry powder
2 green onions, coarsely cut
4 ounces cream cheese, cubed
2 tablespoons cream

1. Put liverwurst, brandy, mayonnaise, curry powder, and green onions into container. Cover and blend on HIGH speed until smooth, stopping to stir down if necessary.

2. Scrape mixture out of container into a small bowl, using a slim rubber spatula, pack down firmly, and chill for 3 to 4 hours, or overnight.

3. Unmold onto serving platter.

4. Put cream cheese and cream into container. Cover and blend on HIGH speed until smooth. Frost the ball with the cream cheese mixture; keep cold until serving time.

PÂTÉ GOURMET

Makes about 4 cups. Rich and velvety smooth, this excellent pâté keeps well and freezes equally well. Serve with French bread or melba toast.

6 tablespoons salted butter
    (¾ stick)
½ cup chopped onion
1 pound chicken livers,
    cleaned and halved
¼ cup Cognac

2 to 4 tablespoons heavy cream
¼ pound sweet butter (1 stick)
1 teaspoon sherry
1½ teaspoons salt
¼ teaspoon curry powder

1. In large skillet, melt half the salted butter, and in it sauté the onion over moderate heat for about 8 minutes, or until soft and transparent but not brown. Transfer to blender container.

2. In same skillet, melt remaining salted butter, add chicken livers, and cook over quite high heat for 3 to 4 minutes, stirring and tossing the chicken livers almost constantly, until they are brown on outside but still

slightly pink within. Pour Cognac over them, ignite, and let the flame burn out.

3. Empty liver into blender. Add 2 tablespoons of the cream, cover, and blend on HIGH speed, stopping to stir down if necessary. If mixture is too thick to purée, add a couple more tablespoons of the cream and blend until mixture is smooth.

4. With blades spinning, remove cover, add sherry, salt, and curry powder, and gradually slice in the sweet butter, slice by slice, stopping to stir down if necessary.

5. Pack the pâté into a 1-quart pottery dish, smooth top with a spatula, and cover tightly with transparent film. Refrigerate and serve well chilled.

Other Savory Appetizers

CHOPPED CHICKEN LIVER

Makes 2 cups, serves 4 to 6

½ pound chicken livers, cleaned and quartered	2 hard-cooked eggs, quartered
1 medium onion, diced	½ teaspoon salt
4 tablespoons chicken fat or butter (½ stick)	¼ teaspoon pepper
	Pinch of thyme

1. Sauté the chicken livers and onion in the chicken fat or butter for about 8 minutes, or until livers are cooked through and onion is golden. Cool.

2. Put chicken liver mixture with drippings into container. Add eggs, salt, pepper, and thyme. Cover and blend on HIGH speed for about 10 seconds, stopping to stir down if necessary.

3. Chill and serve on pumpernickel bread or in lettuce cups.

NOTE: For a smooth spread, add 3 tablespoons chicken broth and blend for 30 seconds.

COTTAGE CHEESE DUMPLINGS
WITH SOUR CREAM

Makes 16 to 24 dumplings

1	cup cottage cheese (8 ounces)	Pinch of salt
2	eggs	1 tablespoon heavy cream
2	egg yolks	3 tablespoons flour
	Thin strip of lemon rind	Butter
4	tablespoons melted butter	Sour cream
	(½ stick)	

1. Put cottage cheese, eggs, egg yolks, lemon rind, melted butter, salt, and heavy cream into container. Cover and blend on HIGH speed until smooth.

2. Empty cheese mixture into a bowl and add 3 tablespoons flour.

3. Form into small dumplings, adding a little more flour if necessary.

4. Sauté the dumplings in butter until golden brown on all sides.

5. Serve hot with a topping of sour cream.

EGG AND SHRIMP APPETIZER

Serves 6

1	pound cooked shrimp,	2 green onions, coarsely cut
	peeled and deveined	¼ teaspoon Tabasco sauce
	Blender mayonnaise (page 27)	6 hard-cooked eggs, halved
¼	cup parsley clusters	Shredded lettuce or romaine
½	teaspoon salt	

1. Make blender mayonnaise and leave in container. Add parsley, salt, green onions, Tabasco, and half the shrimp. Cover and blend on HIGH speed for 20 seconds, or until smooth, stopping to stir down if necessary.

2. Arrange the eggs on a bed of shredded, crisp lettuce. Spoon the shrimp mayonnaise over them and garnish with the whole shrimp. Keep cold until ready to serve.

LOW-CALORIE SALMON CHEESE SALAD

Serves 2

½ small onion	1 medium cucumber, peeled,
1 clove garlic, halved	seeded, and chopped
⅓ cup cottage cheese	One 7½-ounce can salmon, drained
2 tablespoons milk	and flaked
2 tablespoons lemon juice	Romaine leaves

1. In container, put onion, garlic, cottage cheese, milk, and lemon juice. Cover and blend on MEDIUM speed until mixture is smooth, or about 1 minute.

2. In a mixing bowl, combine cucumber and salmon. Add cottage cheese mixture and toss lightly.

3. Serve on romaine leaves.

CLAMS ROCKEFELLER

Serves 6. The marvelous purée of spinach and watercress in this recipe was the inspiration of Michael Field. He used it as a topping for Clams Rockefeller (you can use oysters, of course, if you prefer), because he felt it was a little too aggressive for the more delicate oyster. However, it is so good in itself that you will want to use it in many other ways. Try it on poached eggs, for example, or as a sandwich filling for bread, which should be sliced paper thin.

One 10-ounce package frozen	1 teaspoon lemon juice
chopped spinach, defrosted	1½ sticks butter, melted and
½ cup parsley clusters	cooled
½ cup watercress leaves	¼ cup Pernod
¼ cup coarsely chopped celery	¼–½ teaspoon Tabasco sauce
½ cup coarsely chopped green	* 1 cup blender dry bread crumbs
onions, including part of	3 dozen Little Neck or
the tops	Cherrystone clams
1 small clove garlic	

1. Squeeze as much liquid out of the spinach as possible and put it into blender container. Add parsley, watercress, celery, green onions, garlic,

lemon juice, melted butter, Pernod, Tabasco, and salt. Cover and blend on HIGH speed until reduced to a smooth purée, stopping to stir down if necessary.

2. Empty the purée into a mixing bowl and stir in 6 tablespoons of the bread crumbs. If mixture is too juicy, add a couple more tablespoons of crumbs.

3. If clams are not open, open them now, reserving the shells.

4. Preheat oven to 500° F.

5. Wash the deep half of each shell carefully, place it on a baking sheet and place a clam in each. Spread a thin layer of the vegetable purée over each clam, masking it completely and spreading the purée to the edges of the shell.

6. Sprinkle each clam lightly with a little of the remaining crumbs and bake in the hot oven for 8 to 10 minutes, or until crumbs are lightly browned.

NOTE: If possible, have your fish dealer open the clams, and pack them in their juice, wrapping the shells separately.

CAVIAR CHEESE MOLD

Makes 1 pint

2	tablespoons lemon juice		Good dash of Tabasco sauce
1	envelope plain gelatin	1	clove garlic, peeled
½	cup simmering water	1	teaspoon Worcestershire sauce
1	cup cream-style cottage cheese	1	cup sour cream
	(8 ounces)	One	4-ounce jar red caviar
¼	teaspoon salt		

1. Put lemon juice and gelatin into container. Add simmering water. Cover and blend on HIGH speed for 40 to 60 seconds.

2. Add cottage cheese, salt, Tabasco, garlic, Worcestershire sauce, and sour cream. Cover and blend on HIGH speed for 20 seconds, or until mixture is smooth.

3. Remove container from blender and stir in the caviar. Pour into an oiled 1-pint mold and chill for 6 hours, or overnight.

4. Unmold onto a serving plate and serve with buttered toast or melba toast.

DEVILED HAM BALL

Makes a 4-inch ball

Two	4½-ounce cans deviled ham	2	tablespoons mayonnaise
6	large stuffed green olives	One	8-ounce package cream cheese
1	tablespoon prepared mustard	2	teaspoons milk or light cream
¼	teaspoon Tabasco sauce		

1. Put deviled ham, olives, mustard, Tabasco, and mayonnaise into container. Cover and blend on HIGH speed until smooth, stopping to stir down if necessary.

2. Form the mixture into a ball on a serving plate and chill.

3. Soften cream cheese and beat in milk until fluffy. Frost the ball with the cream cheese and keep cold until serving time.

4. Garnish with parsley and serve with buttered rye bread fingers.

STUFFED CUCUMBER APPETIZER

Serves 4

1	firm medium cucumber	1	onion, coarsely cut
	Salt	¼	green pepper, coarsely cut
One	8-ounce package cream cheese, cubed	1	teaspoon paprika
¼	cup sour cream	1	teaspoon Worcestershire sauce

1. Peel cucumber and cut in half lengthwise. Scoop out the seeds rather deeply with a teaspoon, leaving a center hollow. Sprinkle with salt and set aside.

2. Put cream cheese and sour cream into container. Add remaining ingredients. Cover and blend on HIGH speed until the cheese is smooth and vegetables are finely chopped.

3. Dry cucumber halves, pack the hollows firmly with the cheese mixture, and press the halves back together. Chill.

4. To serve, cut crosswise into thin slices.

CHEESE ROLLS

Makes 2 rolls

3   tablespoons milk
2   teaspoons Worcestershire
     sauce
1   clove garlic
     Dash of cayenne pepper
¼   pound sharp Cheddar cheese,
     diced

¼   pound pimiento cheese, diced
One 3-ounce package cream cheese,
     diced
* ¼ cup dried beef or pecans,
     blender-grated
½   cup finely chopped parsley

1. Put all ingredients, except dried beef or pecans and parsley into container. Cover and blend on HIGH speed for 30 seconds, or until smooth. If necessary, stop blender and stir down ingredients in container.

2. Empty cheese mixture out of container onto waxed paper and divide in half. Shape each half into a roll about 1 inch in diameter. Coat one roll with dried beef or pecans, the other with parsley. Wrap in waxed paper and refrigerate for at least 2 hours.

3. To serve, slice about ⅛ inch thick and serve the slices on melba toast rounds.

TRIPLE CHEESE BALL

Makes a 4-inch ball

* 1 cup walnut meats,
     blender-grated
* ½ cup parsley clusters,
     blender-chopped
2   tablespoons brandy
¼   cup milk

2   teaspoons Worcestershire
     sauce
One 8-ounce package cream cheese,
     diced
½   cup crumbled blue cheese
1   cup diced Cheddar cheese

1. Grate walnut meats and empty out onto a sheet of waxed paper.

2. Chop parsley clusters, empty onto waxed paper, and mix with the nuts.

3. Put brandy, milk, and Worcestershire sauce into container. Cover and begin blending on HIGH speed. Remove cover, and with blades spinning, gradually drop in the cream cheese, blue cheese, and Cheddar cheese. Continue blending until mixture is smooth, stopping to stir down if necessary.

4. Scrape cheese out of container with a slim rubber spatula onto the ground nuts and parsley. Put hands under waxed paper and shape cheese

into a ball, coating it with the nuts and parsley. Wrap in foil and chill for 3 to 4 hours, or overnight.

5. Remove foil and serve with crackers.

DEVILED EGGS

Serves 6

6 hard-cooked eggs, shelled and halved lengthwise	¼ teaspoon Tabasco sauce
¼ cup mayonnaise	One 3-ounce package soft cream cheese or 6 tablespoons soft butter (¾ stick)
½ teaspoon salt	Parsley for garnish
½ teaspoon dry mustard	
1 teaspoon lemon juice	

1. Remove egg yolks from egg whites and put yolks into container. Add remaining ingredients except parsley. Cover and blend on HIGH speed for 30 seconds, stopping to stir down if necessary.

2. Heap egg yolk mixture onto egg whites and garnish with sprigs of parsley.

CHEESED HAM SQUARES

Makes 48 squares

One 3-ounce package cream cheese, cubed	2 tablespoons mayonnaise
5 large stuffed green olives	½ teaspoon dry mustard
	4 thin slices boiled ham

1. Put cream cheese, olives, mayonnaise, and mustard in container. Cover and blend on HIGH speed until mixture is smooth, stopping to stir down if necessary.

2. Spread one-third of the mixture on a ham slice and cover with a second ham slice. Spread this with another one-third of the cheese mixture, cover with a ham slice, spread again with remaining third of the cheese mixture, and top with remaining slice of ham.

3. Wrap the "sandwich" firmly in foil and refrigerate for 2 hours or longer.

4. Cut the sandwich in half, then slice each half thinly across the layers of cheese and ham, or cut into bite-size squares.

VARIATIONS: Use sliced bologna, liverwurst, or salami in place of the ham.

Dips

The basic recipe for a cheese dip is included in the Mini-Course in Blender Cooking (page 19). Remember, in blending heavy mixtures such as dips and spreads, to stop the motor when necessary to stir down the ingredients in the container.

THE GOOD EGG DIP

Makes 2 cups

1½	tablespoons lemon juice	¼	teaspoon white pepper
	Thin slice of a small onion	½	cup mayonnaise
2	teaspoons mustard	6	hard-cooked eggs
½	teaspoon Tabasco sauce	One	4-ounce package pimiento
½	teaspoon salt		cream cheese, cubed

1. Put lemon juice, onion, mustard, Tabasco, salt, pepper, and mayonnaise into container. Cover and blend on HIGH speed for 10 seconds.

2. With motor on, remove cover and drop in eggs, one at a time, blending until mixture is smooth after each addition.

3. Add cream cheese and continue to blend until smooth, stopping to stir down if necessary.

4. Chill and serve with assorted chips and crackers or raw vegetables.

CHEDDAR CHEESE DIP

Makes about 2 cups

1 cup sour cream
½ pound Cheddar cheese, diced
1 small clove garlic
1 garlic dill pickle, quartered

1. Put sour cream, cheese, and garlic into container. Cover and blend on HIGH speed, stopping to stir down as often as necessary. Blend for 20 seconds, or until smooth.

2. Add pickle, stir to combine, cover, and blend for 5 seconds longer.

TRIPLE CHEESE DIP

Makes about 3 cups

1 cup diced Cheddar cheese	1 teaspoon dill weed
1 8-ounce package cream cheese, diced	½ teaspoon Tabasco sauce
	1 small clove garlic
1 cup creamy cottage cheese (8 ounces)	½ cup milk or water

Put all ingredients into container and blend on HIGH speed until smooth, stopping to stir down if necessary.

SHRIMP DIP

Makes about 2 cups

1 cup chopped cooked shrimp	½ teaspoon paprika
½ pint sour cream (1 cup)	½ teaspoon thyme
¼ cup bourbon	¾ teaspoon salt
1 teaspoon chopped onion	¼ teaspoon pepper
1 teaspoon chopped parsley	

Put all ingredients into blender and blend on HIGH speed until smooth. Remove from blender and chill. Serve as a dip for raw vegetables, shrimp, or crackers.

CRAB MEAT DIP

Makes 1 pint

½ cup water	1 teaspoon salt
2 tablespoons lemon juice	¼ teaspoon pepper
1 strip lemon peel	½ teaspoon dill weed
1 cup cottage cheese (8 ounces)	One 6½-ounce can crab meat, drained and flaked
1 sliver garlic	
1 tablespoon Worcestershire sauce	

1. Into container put the water, lemon juice, lemon peel, cottage cheese, garlic, Worcestershire sauce, salt, pepper, and dill. Cover and blend on HIGH speed for 10 seconds.

2. Remove cover, and with motor on, gradually add crab meat. Continue blending for 20 seconds, or until smooth, stopping to stir down if necessary. Chill.

3. Serve as a dip for raw vegetables or with crackers.

SOUR CREAM AND CRAB MEAT DIP

Makes 2 cups

1 cup sour cream	¼ cup mayonnaise
One 6½-ounce can crab meat, drained and flaked	1 tablespoon lemon juice
	¼ teaspoon salt
1 thin slice onion	1 tablespoon capers

Put all ingredients except capers into container. Cover and blend on HIGH speed until smooth. With motor on, remove cover and add capers. Turn motor off as soon as the last caper is drawn down into the blades. Chill before serving.

GUACAMOLE

1 avocado, peeled, seeded, and sliced
1 large clove garlic
½ teaspoon hot red pepper flakes
3 tablespoons lemon or lime juice
4 tablespoons olive oil
¼ teaspoon salt

Into container put all ingredients. Cover and blend on HIGH speed for 60 seconds. Should mixture stop blending, turn off motor, stir mixture with a rubber spatula, then continue blending. Serve as a dip for cucumber sticks or crackers.

HAWAIIAN DIP

Makes 1 cup

One 3-ounce package cream cheese, diced
¼ cup milk or pineapple juice
4 tablespoons peanut butter
1 teaspoon curry powder
2 green onions, coarsely cut

Put all ingredients into container. Cover and blend on HIGH speed for 20 seconds, or until smooth.

HAM DIP

Makes 1¾ cups

1 cup creamy cottage cheese (8 ounces)
¼ cup water or milk
One 2¼-ounce can deviled ham
1 tablespoon coarsely cut chives or green onion tops
One 3-ounce package cream cheese, diced

Put all ingredients into container. Cover and blend on HIGH speed for 15 seconds, or until smooth. Chill.

TERITUAR
(Cucumber Dip)

Makes about 1 pint

1 clove garlic
1 cup walnut meats
1 teaspoon salt
2 tablespoons vinegar

½ cup olive oil
2 small cucumbers, peeled and diced

1. Put garlic, walnut meats, salt, vinegar, and olive oil into container. Cover and blend on HIGH speed for about 12 minutes, or until mixture is fairly smooth.

2.　Pour the mixture over the cucumbers and mix well. Chill.

3.　Serve in a bowl surrounded by crisp romaine leaves and other crisp vegetables for scooping.

SARDINE DIP

Makes about 1½ cups

¼　cup milk
4　drops Tabasco sauce
1　tablespoon coarsely cut green onions with tops
1　cup creamy cottage cheese (8 ounces)
One　3¾-ounce can boneless sardines in olive oil
1　tablespoon lemon juice (juice of ½ lemon)

Put all ingredients into container. Cover and blend on HIGH speed for 6 seconds. Break surface with rubber spatula, or stop motor and stir down. Continue to blend for 15 seconds, or until smooth. Serve with raw vegetables or potato chips.

VARIATIONS: Shrimp, herring, or smoked salmon may be substituted for the sardines.

BABA GHANNOUJ
(Eggplant Dip)

Makes about 1 pint

1　large eggplant
⅓　cup lemon juice
⅓　cup sesame or salad oil
1　large clove garlic
½　teaspoon salt

Olive oil
* 2　tablespoons blender-chopped parsley
1　tablespoon sesame seeds

1.　Cut stem and green hull from top of eggplant. Place in a baking pan and bake in a 400° F. oven for about 1 hour, or until soft.

2.　Scoop pulp out of skin into container. Cover and turn blender on LOW speed, then switch to HIGH.

3.　Remove cover or inner cap, and gradually pour in lemon juice and oil. Add garlic and salt and blend until smooth.

4. Empty the eggplant mixture into a serving bowl and sprinkle with a little olive oil, chopped parsley, and sesame seeds. Chill until ready to serve.

5. Serve with crisp radishes, green onions, and crackers.

HUMMUS BI TAHEENI
(Chick Pea Purée)

Serves 6

⅓   cup salad or sesame oil
½   cup lemon juice
1   large clove garlic
½   teaspoon salt
1   cup canned chick peas (garbanzos), drained
3–4   parsley clusters

Put oil, lemon juice, garlic, and salt into container. Cover and start blending on HIGH speed. When blades reach full speed, remove cover or inner cap, and add chick peas and parsley. Blend until smooth. Serve with crackers or toast.

CHILI CON QUESO
(Cheese and Hot Pepper Dip)

Makes 2½ cups

½   cup milk
One   4-ounce can green chili peppers, drained and stemmed
1   clove garlic
One   2-ounce can pimientos, drained
1   pound American cheese, diced

1. Put milk, chili peppers, garlic, and pimientos into container. Cover and blend on HIGH speed until smooth.

2. Empty into a saucepan, add cheese, and heat, stirring constantly, until cheese is melted.

3. Serve in chafing dish.

HOT MEXICAN BEAN DIP

Makes 2½ cups

One	1-pound can garbanzos or kidney beans with liquid	½	teaspoon salt
1	clove garlic	2	teaspoons vinegar
4–6	canned hot chili peppers, stemmed	1	teaspoon Worcestershire sauce
1	cup diced Cheddar cheese	4	slices bacon, cooked and crumbled

1. Put all ingredients except bacon into container. Cover and blend on HIGH speed until well blended, stopping to stir down if necessary.

2. Empty into a saucepan, and heat, stirring constantly, until hot and smooth.

3. Pour into a chafing dish and sprinkle with bacon.

MYSTERY DIP

Makes 2 cups

One 10½-ounce can condensed black bean soup
Two 3-ounce packages cream cheese, cubed
4 drops Tabasco sauce
1 teaspoon Worcestershire sauce
½ teaspoon salt
1 clove garlic

Put all ingredients into container. Cover and blend on HIGH speed until smooth, stopping to stir down if necessary.

DIP FOR CHIPS

Makes 1¼ cups

¾	cup cottage cheese	½	teaspoon Tabasco sauce
½	cup mayonnaise	1	tablespoon chili sauce
½	teaspoon dry mustard	½	teaspoon curry powder
1	small clove garlic		

Put all ingredients into container. Cover and blend on HIGH speed until smooth, stirring down if necessary. Chill before serving.

Spreads

CHICKEN ALMOND SPREAD

Makes 1 cup

2 tablespoons water
⅓ cup blanched almonds
½ teaspoon curry powder
¼ cup mayonnaise
1 cup coarsely diced cooked chicken

1. Put water and almonds into container. Cover and blend on HIGH speed until smooth.

2. Add remaining ingredients and continue blending until smooth. Chill until ready to use.

PRUNE-NUT SPREAD

Makes 1¾ cups

½ cup pitted, cooked prunes (or soaked overnight and drained)
1 tablespoon lemon juice
3 tablespoons milk
¼ teaspoon powdered ginger
One 8-ounce package cream cheese, cubed
⅓ cup walnut meats

1. Put prunes, lemon juice, milk, and ginger into container. Cover and blend on HIGH speed for 5 seconds.

2. Leave motor on, remove lid, and gradually add the cream cheese and walnuts. Continue blending until smooth, stopping to stir down if necessary. Chill.

EGG AND OLIVE SPREAD

Makes 1 cup

2	tablespoons milk	¼	teaspoon Tabasco sauce
3	tablespoons mayonnaise	4	hard-cooked eggs, yolks and
½	teaspoon salt		whites separated
½	teaspoon dry mustard	6	large stuffed olives
	Thin slice of onion		

1. Put all ingredients except eggs and olives into container. Cover and blend on HIGH speed for 10 seconds.

2. With motor on, remove cover and drop in the egg yolks.

3. Drop in egg whites and olives and turn motor off as soon as they are coarsely chopped.

SHRIMP SPREAD

Makes ¾ cup

2	teaspoons chili sauce
2	teaspoons mayonnaise
2	teaspoons lemon juice
⅛	teaspoon curry powder
One	5-ounce can shrimp, drained
	Watercress for garnish

1. Put all ingredients into container. Cover and blend on HIGH speed until smooth(about 30 seconds), stopping to stir down after 15 seconds.

2. Spread on bits of bread, toast, or crackers for hors d'oeuvres. Garnish with a sprig of watercress.

SALMON SPREAD

Makes 1 cup

2	tablespoons vinegar	¼	teaspoon pepper
2	tablespoons coarsely chopped green onion tops	¼	teaspoon paprika
		6–8	parsley clusters
¼	teaspoon tarragon		Dash of salt
¼	teaspoon oregano	1	7¾-ounce can salmon, drained

Put all ingredients into container, cover, and blend on HIGH speed for 40 seconds, or until smooth, stopping to stir down if necessary. Excellent for spreading on toasted English muffins.

Homemade Butters

IT'S a real thrill to be able to serve truly fresh sweet butter on a slice of homemade bread still hot from the oven. Your electric blender can churn cream to butter in less than 5 minutes. Herbs or garlic can be blended into the butter for use as a spread on slices of toasted French bread or as a final savory touch to broiled fish or meats.

Cream which has been refrigerated for a couple of days turns into butter faster than fresh cream.

SWEET BUTTER

Makes 6 ounces

1 cup whipping cream
½ cup cold water
2 ice cubes, cracked

1. Pour cream into container. Cover and turn motor on HIGH speed. Remove cover and blend until cream is whipped. No special precautions are needed to prevent the cream from curdling for this is the beginning of butter.

2.   To the whipped cream, add the cold water and ice cubes. Cover and blend on HIGH for 1 to 2 minutes. The blending time will depend on the age of the cream. The water increases the amount of liquid in the container which allows the butter particles to form above the blades. The ice chills the butter so that it is fairly firm.

3.   When the butter particles have formed, pour contents of container into a small sieve to drain. Knead the butter in the sieve with the back of a wooden spoon to press out any bubbles of water trapped in it.

4.   Spoon into a small crock, cover tightly, and chill.

GARLIC BUTTER

Add 1 or 2 cloves garlic along with the water and ice cubes.

HERB BUTTER

Add 1 tablespoon fresh herbs or 1 teaspoon dried herbs along with the water and ice cubes.

WATERCRESS BUTTER

Makes about 1 cup

Put ¾ cup (6 ounces) soft sweet butter into container. Add the leaves from ½ bunch watercress, 1 tablespoon lemon juice, and a small amount of salt and pepper. Don't oversalt. Cover and blend on HIGH speed for 30 seconds, stopping to stir down as often as necessary. Marvelous for paper thin tea sandwiches.

ANCHOVY BUTTER

Makes about ¾ cup

Put ¾ cup (6 ounces) soft sweet butter into container. Add 1 teaspoon lemon juice and 8 anchovies. Cover and blend on HIGH speed for 30 seconds, stopping to stir down as often as necessary.

EGG & CHEESE DISHES

Egg & Cheese Dishes

You don't have to buy a blender to beat eggs, but if you have one, use it. For scrambled eggs, a couple of forks will do, but your blender will beat the eggs faster and will give a new light texture and fluffiness to the finished dish. In addition, you can use whole eggs or egg yolks as the liquid medium in which to finely grate crisp vegetables, poultry, meat, or fish for omelets and soufflés which normally would have to be finely chopped or shredded by hand.

To grate hard cheese for spaghetti dishes and casserole toppings, see page 13. To shred Cheddar and Swiss cheese, see page 14, and to make a perfect velvet-smooth cheese sauce in seconds, see page 171. For Hollandaise Sauce to serve over poached eggs (Eggs Benedict), see pages 166–167.

We'll begin this chapter with some easy scrambled eggs and omelets and progress to more elaborate quick supper and luncheon dishes made from cheese, eggs, or a combination of these and other ingredients.

Scrambled Eggs

BASIC SCRAMBLED EGGS

Serves 2

4   eggs
¼   cup water, milk, or cream
½   teaspoon salt
    Dash of white pepper
1   tablespoon butter
2   slices hot buttered toast

1. Put eggs, liquid, salt, and pepper into container. Cover and blend on LOW speed for 6 seconds.

2. Melt butter in a skillet. When butter is hot and before it begins to brown, add egg mixture. Stir over low heat until eggs are set but still creamy.

3. Serve on or with the buttered toast.

CREAM CHEESE EGGS

Serves 3

6	eggs	½	teaspoon salt
½	cup light cream		Dash of white pepper
One	3-ounce package cream cheese,	2	tablespoons butter
	quartered	3	slices hot, buttered toast

1. Put eggs, cream, cheese, salt, and pepper into container. Cover and blend on HIGH speed for about 6 seconds, or until smooth.

2. Melt butter in skillet. When butter is hot, but before it begins to brown, add egg mixture. Stir over low heat until eggs are set but still creamy.

3. Serve on or with the toast.

SCRAMBLED EGG VARIATIONS:

You may add infinite variety to either of the preceding recipes for scrambled eggs by the addition of cooked meat, vegetables, herbs, and spices. For instance:

HAM 'N' EGGS

Add to blended eggs ½ cup diced cooked ham and 1 thin slice onion. Cover and blend on HIGH speed for 6 seconds.

MEXICAN EGGS

Use tomato juice for liquid. Blend ½ teaspoon chili powder with the eggs.

CURRIED EGGS WITH CHICKEN

Add to blended eggs ½ cup diced cooked chicken, ½ teaspoon curry powder, and 3–4 parsley clusters. Cover and blend on HIGH speed for 6 seconds.

MUSHROOM EGGS

Omit liquid from recipe. Add to blended eggs a 4-ounce can mushrooms with liquid and 1 green onion, coarsely cut. Blend on HIGH speed for 6 seconds.

SPANISH SCRAMBLE

Omit liquid from recipe. Add to blended eggs, 2 strips green pepper, 1 slice medium onion, ½ ripe tomato. Cover and blend on HIGH speed for 6 seconds.

COTTAGE CHEESE SCRAMBLE

Omit liquid from recipe. Add to blended eggs, 1 thin slice small onion, and ¼ cup cream-style cottage cheese. Cover and blend on HIGH speed for 6 seconds.

SCRAMBLED HERBED EGGS

Add to eggs in container, 3–4 parsley clusters and ¼ teaspoon dry dill weed or tarragon (or use fresh herbs, which are sensational).

CHEDDAR CHEESE SCRAMBLED EGGS

Serves 2

¼ cup sour cream
½ cup diced Cheddar cheese
4 eggs
   Pinch each of salt and pepper

Put all ingredients into container. Cover and blend on HIGH speed for 6 seconds. Cook as for Basic Scrambled Eggs.

SHRIMP OR CRAB MEAT SCRAMBLED EGGS

Serves 2

¼ cup tomato juice or stewed tomatoes
½ cup diced, cooked shrimp or flaked crab meat
1 thin slice onion
   Dash of Tabasco sauce
4 eggs
   Pinch of salt

Put all ingredients into container. Cover and blend on HIGH speed for 6 seconds. Cook as for Basic Scrambled Eggs.

Omelets

OMELETS are* nothing more or less than quickly scrambled eggs! The blended egg mixture is stirred rapidly over quite a brisk heat until barely set. The soft scrambled eggs are then smoothed evenly on top, and the bottom of the eggs is allowed to set to a thin casing. The skillet is then removed from the heat, and a teaspoon of butter is put in the center of the omelet. A rubber spatula is used to turn the upper one-third of the omelet over onto the center, then the two layers of egg are turned onto the lower one-third, the skillet tipped over the serving dish, and the omelet gently eased out with the spatula. Presto! There it is in all its golden glory. Dione Lucas used to say in her classes that if it takes longer than 1 minute to cook an omelet, it will be tough!

Any of the recipes given for scrambled eggs may be made into omelets— just cook and roll them quickly.

The above method of making an omelet is known as the French method and is considered the ONLY way to make an omelet by expert cooks and chefs. There are other ways, however, to cook an omelet in a more leisurely fashion and still turn out an excellent family lunch or supper dish.

CHEESE OMELET

Serves 3–4

⅓ cup milk or water
1 cup diced American cheese
6 eggs
 Pinch each of salt and pepper
3 tablespoons butter

1. Put liquid, cheese, eggs, salt, and pepper into container. Cover and blend on HIGH speed for 6 seconds.

2. Melt butter in a 9-inch skillet. When hot, but before it begins to brown, pour in egg mixture and cook over moderate heat, lifting the edges gently with a spatula to let the uncooked portion run underneath.

3. When just set, but not dry, fold and serve on a warm platter.

WESTERN OMELET

Serves 3–4

¼	cup diced cooked ham	6	eggs
½	green pepper, cut into strips		Salt and pepper
1	thick slice medium onion	3	tablespoons butter
½	large ripe tomato		

1. Put all ingredients except butter into container. Cover and blend on HIGH speed for 6 seconds.

2. Melt butter in a 9-inch skillet. When hot, but before it begins to brown, pour in egg mixture and cook over moderate heat, lifting the edges gently with a rubber spatula to let the uncooked portion run underneath.

3. When set, but not dry, fold and turn out on a warm plate.

CHICKEN OR SHRIMP OMELET

Serves 3–4

⅓	cup milk	1	cup coarsely diced, cooked
¼	teaspoon celery salt		chicken or shrimp
	Dash of Tabasco sauce	6	eggs
6–8	parsley clusters	3	tablespoons butter for cooking

Follow directions in recipes above.

SAVORY CREAM SAUCE TO SERVE WITH OMELETS

Makes about 1 cup

1	thin slice onion	¼	teaspoon salt
3–4	parsley clusters		Dash of pepper
1	tablespoon butter	1	cup hot milk
1	tablespoon flour		

1. Put onion, parsley, butter, flour, salt, pepper, and ¼ cup of the milk into container. Cover and blend on HIGH speed.

2. With blades spinning, remove cover or inner cap and gradually pour in remaining hot milk.

3. Pour into small saucepan and bring to a boil, stirring constantly. Keep warm and serve over an omelet.

EGGS FOO YUNG

Serves 4

6	eggs	1	tablespoon dry sherry
1	cup coarsely cut, cooked shrimp, chicken, or flaked crab meat	1	tablespoon soy sauce
		1	tablespoon flour
One	4-ounce can water chestnuts, drained	½	teaspoon salt
		¼	teaspoon pepper
1	stalk celery with leaves, coarsely cut	One	1-pound can bean sprouts, drained
2	green onions, coarsely cut		Cooking oil

1. Put into container the eggs, the chicken or seafood, water chestnuts, celery, onions, sherry, soy sauce, flour, salt, and pepper. Cover and blend on HIGH speed for 6 seconds.

2. Turn motor off and stir in bean sprouts.

3. Pour enough cooking oil into a 6-inch skillet to just coat the bottom. Heat. Then pour in about one-fourth of the egg mixture and cook over low heat until browned on under side. Turn carefully and cook for 2 or 3 minutes longer, or until golden.

4. Turn out on warm serving platter and keep warm while cooking the remaining egg mixture.

STILL A THIRD TYPE of omelet, and a very popular one, is the puffy omelet in which the eggs are separated. Your blender will not beat egg whites to sufficient volume to make the omelet mixture really puffy, so beat the whites with a rotary beater or whisk, and fold them into the egg yolk mixture.

Any of the previous omelets may be converted to puffy omelets by simply separating yolks from whites first and then folding the whites into the yolk mixture.

PUFFY OMELET

Serves 4

⅓ cup milk
1 cup diced Swiss or Cheddar
   cheese
½ teaspoon salt

¼ teaspoon white pepper or
   Tabasco sauce
6 egg yolks
6 egg whites
3 tablespoons butter

1. Preheat oven to 325° F.

2. Put milk, cheese, salt, pepper, and egg yolks into container. Cover and blend on MEDIUM speed for 6 seconds.

3. In a mixing bowl, beat egg whites until stiff but not dry. Pour the egg-yolk mixture over the egg whites and fold together gently until blended.

4. In a 9-inch skillet or omelet pan, melt the butter until hot but not brown. Pour in egg mixture and cook over low heat for about 5 minutes, or until omelet is puffed on top and lightly browned beneath.

5. Transfer to preheated oven and bake for 15 minutes, or until set and brown.

Soufflés

BLENDER CHEESE SOUFFLÉ

Serves 4

1 cup diced Cheddar cheese
3 tablespoons butter
4 tablespoons flour
¼ teaspoon dry mustard

½ teaspoon salt
5 egg yolks
1 cup hot milk
6 egg whites, stiffly beaten

1. Preheat oven to 375° F. Butter a 1½-quart soufflé dish.

2. Into container put cheese, butter, flour, mustard, salt, egg yolks, and milk. Cover and blend on MEDIUM speed for 15 seconds. Stir down with rubber spatula. Cover and blend on LOW speed for 15 seconds.

3. Pour into saucepan and cook over low heat, stirring constantly, until mixture is thick. Remove from heat and let cool for 5 minutes.

4. Fold in beaten egg whites. Turn into prepared soufflé dish and bake in preheated oven for 30 minutes.

FOR SHRIMP SAUCE TO SERVE WITH THE SOUFFLÉ: Make Savory Cream Sauce (page 84) and 1 minute before serving, stir in ½ cup chopped, cooked shrimp.

BLENDER CHEESE-BREAD SOUFFLÉ

Serves 4

3 tablespoons butter	1 cup diced Cheddar cheese
1 cup milk	4 egg yolks
1 thin slice white bread	5 egg whites
½ teaspoon dry mustard	* 1 tablespoon blender-grated
½ teaspoon salt	Parmesan cheese
Pinch of nutmeg or cayenne pepper	

1. Preheat oven to 375° F. Butter a 1½-quart soufflé dish.

2. In a small saucepan, heat butter and milk until steaming.

3. Into container put bread, mustard, salt, and nutmeg or cayenne pepper. Cover and blend on HIGH speed for 5 seconds. Remove cover, and with motor on, pour in hot milk mixture. Gradually add cheese and continue blending until mixture is smooth.

4. Add egg yolks and blend for 10 seconds longer.

5. In a large mixing bowl, beat egg whites with rotary beater until stiff but not dry. Gradually pour cheese mixture over egg whites, folding cheese into whites gently with a rubber spatula until lightly blended. Spoon into prepared dish and sprinkle with grated Parmesan.

6. Bake in preheated oven for 30 minutes, or until set to taste.

SOUFFLÉ VARIATIONS:

In either of the Cheese Soufflé recipes you may substitute for the cheese any one of the following ingredients:

1 cup diced, cooked ham plus 2 tablespoons tomato paste.

1 cup diced, cooked chicken meat plus 1 teaspoon curry powder.
1 cup diced, cooked lobster or shrimp or flaked crab meat.
1 cup corn kernels, fresh or canned.
1 cup drained, cooked spinach, plus pinch of nutmeg.
1 cup (7¾-ounce can) salmon, plus ½ teaspoon dry mustard, 1 teaspoon Worcestershire sauce, and a dash of cayenne pepper.

CRAB OR LOBSTER SOUFFLÉ

Serves 3

One	6½-ounce can crab meat or lobster	½	teaspoon curry powder
		½	teaspoon salt
3	tablespoons butter	¼	teaspoon oregano
1	cup cream	2	tablespoons sherry
2	thin slices bread	4	eggs
1	small onion, halved	6–8	parsley clusters
½	teaspoon mustard	1	additional egg white
⅛	teaspoon cayenne pepper		

1. Pick over crab or lobster meat, discarding any sinews.

2. Preheat oven to 375° F.

3. In a small saucepan, heat butter and cream until butter is melted and mixture is hot.

4. Tear the bread into container and add onion, seasonings, and sherry. Cover and blend on HIGH speed until bread is crumbed.

5. Add hot cream mixture and blend on HIGH speed for 30 seconds.

6. Separate eggs, dropping whites into a 1½-quart soufflé dish and adding the yolks to the mixture in the container. Cover and blend on HIGH speed for 10 seconds. Add parsley and crab meat or lobster and blend for just 4 seconds longer.

7. Add additional egg white to soufflé dish and beat with rotary beater until eggs are stiff but not dry. Fold in crab mixture lightly but thoroughly.

8. Bake in preheated oven for 35 minutes. Serve immediately.

HAM SOUFFLÉ

Serves 3–4

3 tablespoons butter	Good pinch of cayenne pepper
1 cup cream	4 eggs
¼ cup milk	* 1 cup blender-shredded ham
2 slices bread	1 additional egg white
1 teaspoon dry mustard	Blender Cheese Sauce (page
⅛ teaspoon nutmeg	171)
¼ teaspoon marjoram	

1. Preheat oven to 375° F.

2. In a small saucepan, heat butter, cream, and milk until butter is melted and mixture is hot.

3. Tear bread into container. Add seasonings and blend on HIGH speed for 5 seconds. With blades spinning, remove cover and pour in hot milk mixture.

4. Separate eggs, dropping whites into a 1½-quart soufflé dish and adding the yolks to the mixture in container. Cover and blend on HIGH speed for 10 seconds. Add ham and blend on HIGH until well mixed, stopping to stir down if necessary.

5. Add additional egg white to soufflé dish and beat with rotary beater until eggs are stiff but not dry. Fold in ham mixture lightly but thoroughly.

6. Bake in preheated oven for 35 minutes, and serve with Blender Cheese Sauce.

Egg & Cheese Dishes

CHEESE PIE

Serves 4 to 6

9-inch Savory Crumb Crust (pages 56–57)	½ teaspoon salt
3 eggs	2 tablespoons soft butter
½ pound diced Swiss or Cheddar cheese	2 green onions, coarsely cut
	1 cup hot cream

1. Make Savory Crumb Crust. Preheat oven to 350° F.

2. Put eggs, cheese, salt, butter, and onions into container. Cover and blend on LOW speed for 5 seconds.

3. With blades spinning, remove cover or inner cap and pour in hot cream.

4. Pour cheese custard into prepared pie plate and bake in preheated oven for 35 minutes. Serve hot or warm.

SCALLOPED EGGS

Serves 4

```
2    cups Blender Medium Cream Sauce (page 170)
½    teaspoon dry mustard
6    hard-cooked eggs, peeled and sliced
* 1  cup fresh blender bread crumbs
2    tablespoons butter
```

1. Preheat oven to 350° F. Butter a 1-quart casserole.

2. Make Blender Cream Sauce, adding dry mustard along with the salt and pepper.

3. In a casserole, arrange alternate layers of sauce, eggs, and crumbs.

4. Dot with butter and bake in preheated oven for 25 minutes.

EGGS LYONNAISE

Serves 4

8 eggs	3 tablespoons flour
* 2 ounces Parmesan cheese,	1 teaspoon salt
blender-grated	¼ teaspoon pepper
1½ cups hot milk	1 small onion, quartered
3 tablespoons soft butter	

1. Hard boil eggs. Cool just long enough to handle, then peel and slice into a 1½-quart shallow, buttered baking dish. Set aside.

2. Preheat oven to 375° F. Blender-grate the cheese.

3. Put ½ cup of the hot milk into container. Add butter, flour, salt, pepper, and onion. Cover and blend on HIGH speed for 20 seconds.

4. With blades spinning, remove lid or inner cap and gradually pour in remaining hot milk.

5. Pour sauce over eggs and sprinkle with grated Parmesan.

6. Bake in preheated oven for 25 minutes.

CURRIED EGG CASSEROLE

Serves 4

8 hard-cooked eggs, peeled and sliced	2 tablespoons flour
* ½ cup blender buttered bread crumbs	2 tablespoons soft butter
1 cup hot milk	4 green onions, coarsely cut
1 cup diced Cheddar cheese	1 tablespoon good curry powder
	1 teaspoon salt

1. Butter a 1½-quart shallow baking dish. Arrange sliced eggs in it and set aside. Preheat oven to 400° F.

2. Make blender crumbs and set aside.

3. Put remaining ingredients into container. Cover and blend on LOW speed for 15 seconds.

4. Pour sauce over eggs and sprinkle with bread crumbs.

5. Bake in preheated oven for 20 minutes, or until sauce is bubbling and crumbs are brown.

BELGIAN EGGS

Serves 4

1 tablespoon soft butter	1½ cups hot heavy cream
5–6 parsley clusters	2 cups cooked shrimp or diced lobster meat
½ teaspoon mustard	6 hard-cooked eggs, peeled and chopped
1 teaspoon salt	
1½ teaspoons paprika	

1. Preheat oven to 375° F. Butter a 2-quart casserole.

2. Put butter, parsley, mustard, salt, paprika, and ½ cup of the heavy cream into container. Cover and turn blender on LOW speed.

3. With blades spinning, remove cover and gradually pour in remaining hot cream. Turn blender off.

4. Add shrimp or lobster meat. Cover and blend on LOW speed for 10 seconds, or until seafood is coarsely chopped.

5. Combine eggs and seafood mixture. Mix well and empty into prepared casserole.

6. Bake in preheated oven for 20 minutes, or until top is lightly browned.

WELSH RABBIT

Serves 2

1 tablespoon flour	1 cup diced Cheddar cheese
¼ teaspoon dry mustard	Dash of cayenne pepper
½ teaspoon salt	1 tablespoon soft butter
1 cup hot milk	Hot toasted crackers
1 egg	

1. Put all ingredients except crackers into container. Cover and blend on HIGH speed for 10 seconds.

2. Empty into saucepan and heat over simmering water. Serve on the crackers.

SWISS FONDUE

Serves 3–4

2 cups diced imported Swiss or Gruyère cheese	Pinch of nutmeg
1 small clove garlic	¾ cup hot Chablis or other dry white wine (do not let wine boil)
1½ tablespoons flour	
¼ teaspoon salt	2 tablespoons kirsch
¼ teaspoon freshly ground pepper	French bread, cut into chunks

1. Put cheese, garlic, flour, salt, pepper, and nutmeg into container. Cover and turn blender on HIGH speed. With blades spinning, remove cover or inner cap and pour in the hot wine.

2. Pour mixture into a saucepan and add the kirsch. Keep hot over simmering water, stirring frequently. Serve in a chafing dish or casserole with chunks of French bread.

CHEESE MONKEY

Serves 2

2	slices bread	1	egg
1	cup hot milk	½	teaspoon salt
1	tablespoon soft butter		Dash of cayenne
1	cup diced Cheddar cheese	4	slices buttered toast

1. Put bread and milk into container. Add butter, cheese, egg, salt and cayenne. Cover and blend on HIGH speed for 10 seconds.

2. Empty into saucepan and cook over simmering water, stirring occasionally, until thick and smooth. Serve on toast.

RINKTUM DIDDIE

Serves 4

2	tablespoons butter	½	teaspoon paprika
2	tablespoons flour		Dash of cayenne pepper
¾	cup hot cream		Pinch of nutmeg
1½	cups canned tomatoes, drained	2	cups diced Cheddar cheese
⅛	teaspoon baking soda	2	eggs
1	teaspoon salt		Buttered, salted crackers

1. Put butter, flour, and hot cream into container. Cover and blend on HIGH speed for 5 seconds.

2. Add remaining ingredients except crackers. Cover and blend on HIGH speed for 20 seconds.

3. Empty into saucepan and cook over hot water, stirring constantly, until smooth and thickened. Serve on crackers.

CHEESE BAKE

Serves 6

12 slices bread, trimmed and cubed	2½ cups hot milk
½ pound American cheese, diced	½ teaspoon mustard
4 eggs	1 thin slice medium onion
2 tablespoons soft butter	½ teaspoon salt
	¼ teaspoon pepper

1. Butter a 2-quart casserole. Arrange half the bread in it.

2. Put cheese, eggs, hot milk, mustard, onion, salt, and pepper into container. Cover and blend on HIGH speed for 20 seconds.

3. Pour half the cheese mixture over bread in baking pan. Top with remaining bread slices and pour over remaining cheese mixture. Let stand for 1 hour before baking.

4. Bake in a preheated 325° F. oven for 1 hour, or until custard is set.

CHEESE PUFF

Serves 4

2 tablespoons soft butter	¼ teaspoon pepper
2 tablespoons flour	¼ teaspoon paprika
1½ cups hot milk	1 cup cooked rice
1 cup diced Cheddar cheese	3 eggs, separated
¾ teaspoon salt	

1. Preheat oven to 350° F. Butter a 1½-quart casserole.

2. Put butter, flour, milk, cheese, salt, pepper, paprika, rice, and egg yolks into container. Cover and blend on HIGH speed for 20 seconds, or until well blended.

3. In a mixing bowl, beat egg whites with rotary beater until stiff but not dry. Pour cheese mixture over egg whites and fold together gently but thoroughly.

4. Empty into prepared casserole, place casserole in a pan of hot water, and bake in preheated oven for 1 hour.

PASTA & RICE DISHES

Pasta & Rice Dishes

Your electric blender can be an invaluable aid in the preparation of spaghetti sauces and noodle, macaroni, and rice dishes. You know, if you have used a blender for any length of time, how efficiently it grates hard cheeses (page 13) and shreds semisoft cheeses (page 14) to include in a casserole or to sprinkle on top of a steaming dish of spaghetti or linguini. It is just as efficient and timesaving in the making of healthful, nourishing combinations of vegetables, rice, or pasta, that can rescue the weekly food budget and still supply adequate complete proteins through the eggs and cheese included in the recipes. If meat, chicken, or fish are added, these high-priced protein foods can be stretched into remarkably economical family dishes.

I'm going to begin this chapter with some quick spaghetti sauces, followed by some extraordinarily good luncheon or supper dishes.

For a good dish of macaroni and cheese, see page 25.

Spaghetti Sauces

FRENCH SPAGHETTI SAUCE

Makes about 3 cups

2	tablespoons olive oil	¼	teaspoon pepper
1	large onion, coarsely cut	½	teaspoon basil
1	clove garlic	¼	teaspoon thyme
2	cups water	6–8	parsley clusters
1	teaspoon salt	One	6-ounce can tomato paste

1. Put all ingredients into container except tomato paste. Cover and blend on HIGH speed for 15 seconds.

2. Empty into a saucepan, add tomato paste, bring to a boil, and simmer for 45 minutes, stirring occasionally.

SPAGHETTI MEAT SAUCE

Makes about 4 cups

1	tablespoon olive oil	1	teaspoon salt
1	pound ground beef	¼	teaspoon black pepper
Two	8-ounce cans tomato sauce	½	teaspoon oregano
1	large onion, coarsely cut	½	teaspoon sweet basil
6–8	parsley clusters	1	cup water
2	cloves garlic		

1. In a large skillet, heat the olive oil, and in it brown the beef well, stirring occasionally.

2. Into container put remaining ingredients except the water. Cover and blend on HIGH speed. As soon as blades reach full speed, remove cover and pour in the water.

3. Empty into skillet with the meat, bring to a boil, and simmer for 30 minutes, stirring occasionally.

MEAT SAUCE VIENNOISE

Makes about 4 cups

1	tablespoon cooking oil or shortening	½	cup water
		1½	teaspoons salt
1	pound ground beef	1	teaspoon celery seed
1	large onion, coarsely cut	1	teaspoon dry mustard
1	green pepper, seeded and cut in strips		Dash of pepper
		1	teaspoon drained horseradish
2	cloves garlic	One	4-ounce can sliced mushrooms
Three	8-ounce cans tomato sauce		

1. In a heavy skillet or saucepan, heat oil or shortening and in it brown beef well, stirring occasionally.

2. Into container put onion, green pepper, garlic, 1 can tomato sauce, water, salt, celery seed, mustard, and pepper. Cover and blend on HIGH speed for 15 seconds.

3. Pour over meat in skillet or saucepan. Add remaining 2 cans tomato sauce. Bring to a boil and simmer for 30 minutes, stirring occasionally.

4. Stir in mushrooms and horseradish, cover, and simmer for 30 minutes longer.

MARINARA SAUCE

Makes about 2½ cups

One	1-pound, 13-ounce can tomatoes	1 teaspoon sweet basil
½	cup olive oil	½ teaspoon oregano
2	cloves garlic	1 teaspoon salt
6–8	parsley clusters	½ teaspoon black pepper
		Dash of cayenne pepper

1. Put all ingredients into blender container. Cover and begin blending on LOW speed. When blades reach full speed, switch to HIGH and blend for 15 seconds.

2. Empty into a saucepan, bring to a boil, and simmer for 25 minutes.

20-MINUTE MEATLESS SPAGHETTI SAUCE

Makes about 1½ cups

¼	cup olive oil	One 6-ounce can tomato paste
1	large onion, coarsely cut	3–4 parsley clusters
1	clove garlic	½ teaspoon oregano
¼	pound mushrooms, washed and halved	1 teaspoon salt
One	1-pound, 4-ounce can Italian tomatoes	¼ teaspoon black pepper

1. Put all ingredients into blender container. Cover and blend on HIGH speed for 20 seconds.

2. Empty into saucepan, bring to a boil, and simmer for 20 minutes.

SPAGHETTI SAUCE PESTO

Makes enough sauce for ½ pound spaghetti.   In summer and early fall, when fresh sweet basil is available beg, borrow, or steal enough to make this delicious sauce for spaghetti. If you like it, make lots and freeze in freezer bags for wintertime use. Try adding a tablespoon of this sauce to vegetable soups and stews.

```
   18   large, fresh sweet basil leaves
   ½    cup olive oil
*  ½    cup blender-grated, aged Parmesan cheese
   ½    teaspoon salt
   ⅓    cup pine nuts
   4    cloves garlic
```

1. Put all ingredients into container. Blend on HIGH speed for 30 seconds, or to a thick smooth sauce, stopping to stir down if necessary.

2   Empty into mixing bowl or freeze in double plastic bags.

FOR SPAGHETTI:

Cook ½ pound thin spaghetti in rapidly boiling salted water for 10 minutes, or until just tender. Fork the spaghetti directly from the pot into mixing bowl with the sauce. Add 3 tablespoons hot spaghetti water and a chunk of butter and toss until butter is melted. Serve with grated Parmesan cheese.

IF FROZEN:

Remove from bag and defrost in mixing bowl set over a saucepan of hot, not boiling, water.

Cannelloni, Manicotti
& Spaghetti Dishes

CANNELLONI AU GRATIN

Serves 4

* 2 ounces Parmesan cheese,
    blender-grated
  1 small onion, halved
  1 large stalk celery
  1 small carrot   blender-shredded *
    A small handful parsley
    clusters
  2 tablespoons oil
  2 cups ground cooked chicken
    or flaked salmon
½ teaspoon oregano
¼ cup sherry
  4 tablespoons butter (½ stick)
  4 tablespoons flour

  1 teaspoon salt
⅛ teaspoon pepper
    Dash of cayenne pepper
  2 cups scalding hot milk
  8 cannelloni or Crêpes
    (page 282)
¾ cup heavy cream

1. Blender-grate the Parmesan cheese and set aside.

2. Blender-shred the onion, celery, carrot, and parsley, shredding each vegetable separately and emptying out onto waxed paper.

3. Heat oil in skillet and in it sauté the shredded vegetables for 5 minutes, or until vegetables are tender. Add half the salt and the oregano, salmon or chicken, and sherry. Simmer for 3 minutes. Set aside.

4. Put into container the butter, flour, remaining salt, pepper, cayenne, and ½ cup of the hot milk. Cover and start blending on HIGH speed. With motor on, remove cover and gradually pour in remaining hot milk. Empty into saucepan and stir over low heat for 5 minutes. Stir ½ cup of the sauce into chicken or salmon mixture.

5. If using cannelloni, cook in plenty of boiling salted water for 8 minutes. Drain and rinse in cold water.

6. Preheat oven to 450° F. Grease a shallow casserole or lasagne dish.

7. Put ¼ cup of the filling on each cannelloni, or crêpe, and roll up. Arrange side by side in the prepared baking dish.

8. Stir the cream into the remaining sauce and pour over the cannelloni. Sprinkle with the grated Parmesan.

9. Bake in the preheated oven for 10 minutes, or until sauce is bubbling and cheese is lightly browned.

MANICOTTI WITH RED WINE TOMATO SAUCE

Serves 4 to 6

* 2 ounces Parmesan cheese, blender-grated
  2 cloves garlic
  1 small onion, halved
  ½ teaspoon sweet basil
  ½ teaspoon oregano
  3–4 parsley clusters
  ¼ pound mushrooms, halved

  ½ cup dry red wine
  One 6-ounce can tomato paste
  One 1-pound can stewed tomatoes
  12 manicotti or Crêpes (page 282)
  1 pound ricotta cheese
  1 pound Mozzarella cheese, shredded
  2 eggs

1. Blender-grate the Parmesan cheese and set aside.

2. Put into container garlic, onion, basil, oregano, parsley, mushrooms, dry red wine, and tomato paste. Cover and blend on LOW speed for 10 seconds. Switch to HIGH speed, uncover and pour in the stewed tomatoes. Blend for 10 seconds longer.

3. If using manicotti, cook in plenty of boiling salted water for 8 minutes. Drain and rinse in cold water.

4. Combine ricotta, Mozzarella, and eggs for the filling.

5. Preheat oven to 350° F. Oil a 13 x 9½ x 2-inch baking dish.

6. Spread manicotti or crêpes generously with filling. Roll up and arrange in prepared pan.

7. Pour tomato sauce over the manicotti and sprinkle with the reserved grated cheese.

8. Bake in preheated oven for 30 minutes.

TURKEY TORTA

Serves 6

  8 ounces spaghetti
  2 eggs
  ½ cup milk
  ¼ cup coarsely diced onion
  ¼ cup parsley clusters
  ½ teaspoon salt

  ¼ pound American cheese, diced
* ½ cup blender-grated Parmesan cheese
  Creamed turkey, chicken, ham, fish, or eggs

1. Break spaghetti into short lengths and cook according to package directions. Drain and rinse.

2. Grease a shallow 10 x 6-inch baking dish. Preheat oven to 350° F.

3. Put eggs, milk, onion, parsley, salt, and American cheese into container. Add spaghetti. Cover and blend on HIGH speed until spaghetti is finely chopped, about 1 minute, stirring down once if necessary.

4. Pour blended mixture into baking dish and sprinkle with Parmesan cheese. Bake in preheated oven for about 1 hour, or until firm.

5. Cut in squares and top with creamed poultry, ham, fish, or eggs.

Macaroni Dishes

MACARONI RING

Serves 6.   Fill with creamed vegetables or fish.

1½	cups cooked elbow macaroni	1 small onion, halved
* 1	cup blender-grated Parmesan cheese	3 tablespoons soft butter
		1 egg
* 1	cup blender-crumbed soft bread	1 teaspoon salt
		¼ teaspoon pepper
3–4	parsley clusters	1 cup scalding hot milk
1	canned pimiento	

1. Preheat oven to 375° F. Oil an 8-inch ring mold.

2. In a mixing bowl, combine macaroni, cheese, and bread crumbs.

3. Put into container the parsley, pimiento, onion, butter, egg, salt, and pepper. Cover and blend on LOW speed for a couple of seconds.

4. With blades whirling, remove cover and gradually pour in the hot milk. Without turning off blender, switch to HIGH speed and blend for 10 seconds.

5. Pour the sauce over the macaroni mixture and mix well. Pack into prepared mold and bake in preheated oven for 35 minutes.

6. Let stand for 5 minutes, then unmold onto serving dish.

MACARONI AND CHIPPED BEEF CASSEROLE

Serves 6

1 small onion, halved	One 10½-ounce can condensed
1 cup diced Cheddar cheese	cream of mushroom soup
¾ pound chipped beef	4 hard-cooked eggs, diced
1 teaspoon dry mustard	4 cups cooked elbow macaroni
1 cup hot scalding milk	

1. Preheat oven to 350° F. Butter a 2-quart casserole.

2. In a mixing bowl combine macaroni and eggs.

3. Put into container onion, cheese, chipped beef, dry mustard, and hot milk. Cover and blend on HIGH speed for 15 seconds. With blades whirling, remove cover and add mushroom soup. Continue to blend for 5 seconds.

4. Pour the sauce over the macaroni mixture, mix well, and empty into prepared casserole.

5. Bake in preheated oven for 30 minutes.

CHESTERFIELD PIE

Serves 4

1 cup cooked elbow macaroni	1½ cups light cream
* 1 cup blender-shredded sharp	3 eggs, separated
Cheddar cheese	1 teaspoon salt
* 1 cup blender-crumbed	¼ teaspoon pepper
soft bread	Quick Mushroom Sauce #2
½ green pepper, cut into strips	(page 182)
1 canned pimiento	

1. Preheat oven to 350° F. Oil a 1½-quart baking dish.

2. In a mixing bowl, combine macaroni, cheese, and bread crumbs.

3. Into container put the green pepper, pimiento, cream, egg yolks, salt, and pepper. Cover and begin blending on LOW speed. When blades have reached full speed, switch to HIGH and blend for 10 seconds.

4. Pour sauce over macaroni mixture and mix well.

5. Beat egg whites until stiff but not dry and fold into macaroni mixture.

6. Empty into prepared casserole and bake in preheated oven for 50 minutes.

7. Serve with Mushroom Cream Sauce.

CHEESE AND HAM MACARONI LOAF

Serves 6

8	ounces elbow macaroni, cooked, rinsed, and drained	¼	teaspoon salt
* 1	cup blender fresh bread crumbs	2	green onions, sliced
		2	strips green pepper
		3–4	parsley clusters
3	eggs	½	pound diced Cheddar cheese
One	4-ounce can deviled ham	1½	cups hot milk
2	tablespoons soft butter		

1. Preheat oven to 325° F. Butter a 9 × 5 × 3-inch loaf pan.

2. In a mixing bowl, combine macaroni and bread crumbs.

3. Put eggs, ham, butter, salt, onions, green pepper, parsley, and cheese into container. Cover and blend on LOW speed for 10 seconds.

4. With blades spinning, remove cover or inner cap and gradually pour in hot milk. Continue to blend for 20 seconds.

5. Pour cheese mixture over macaroni mixture and mix well.

6. Empty into prepared loaf pan and bake in preheated oven for 1 hour, or until firm.

7. Cool for 10 minutes, then unmold, and serve hot or cold.

SHRIMP AND MACARONI BAKE

Serves 4

2	cups cooked elbow macaroni	½	teaspoon salt
¼	cup sliced stuffed olives	½	teaspoon dry mustard
1	thin slice medium onion	¼	teaspoon paprika
2	clusters parsley	1½	cups hot milk
3	tablespoons flour	1	cup diced cooked shrimp or a
3	tablespoons butter		5-ounce can, drained

1. Preheat oven to 375° F. Butter a 10 × 6-inch baking dish. Spread the macaroni evenly over bottom of the dish and sprinkle with the olives.

2. Put into container the onion, parsley, flour, butter, salt, mustard, paprika, and hot milk. Cover and blend on HIGH speed for about 15 seconds.

3. Stop blender. Add shrimp, cover, and blend for 2 seconds longer, or until shrimp are coarsely chopped.

4. Pour shrimp mixture over macaroni and bake in the preheated oven for 30 to 35 minutes.

GREEN CHEESE CASSEROLE

Serves 4

1	cup parsley clusters	1	teaspoon salt
4	egg yolks	¼	teaspoon pepper
¼	small onion	8	ounces elbow macaroni,
1½	cups diced Cheddar cheese		cooked, rinsed, and drained
½	cup melted butter (1 stick)	4	egg whites

1. Preheat oven to 350° F. Butter a 2-quart casserole or baking dish.

2. Put parsley, egg yolks, onion, cheese, melted butter, salt, and pepper into container. Cover and blend on LOW speed for 20 seconds, or until well blended, stopping to stir down if necessary.

3. Mix the parsley sauce with the macaroni.

4. Beat egg whites until stiff, but not dry, and fold into macaroni mixture. Empty into prepared baking dish and bake in preheated oven for 30 minutes.

Noodle Dishes

BAKED NOODLES YUKON

Serves 6

2 tablespoons soft butter	½ teaspoon salt
2 tablespoons flour	8 ounces medium noodles,
1 cup hot milk	cooked, rinsed, and drained
One 1-pound can salmon with liquid	* 1 cup buttered blender bread crumbs
Dash of Tabasco sauce	

1. Preheat oven to 350° F. Butter a 2-quart casserole.

2. Put butter, flour, and hot milk into container. Cover and blend on LOW speed for 10 seconds. Switch to HIGH speed.

3. With blades spinning, remove cover and add salmon, Tabasco, and salt. Turn off blender as soon as ingredients are blended.

4. Pour over cooked noodles and mix lightly. Empty into prepared casserole and sprinkle top with buttered bread crumbs.

5. Bake in preheated oven for 30 minutes.

NOODLES ROMANOFF

Serves 6

8 ounces medium egg noodles	1 small clove garlic
* ½ cup blender buttered bread crumbs	½ teaspoon salt
	Dash of Tabasco sauce
½ cup heavy cream	One 8-ounce package soft cream cheese, quartered
1 small onion, halved, or 2 tablespoons coarsely cut chives	

1. Cook noodles according to package directions until just barely tender. Drain.

2. While noodles are cooking, make blender buttered crumbs. Empty out onto waxed paper and set aside.

3. Into container put cream, onion, garlic, salt, and Tabasco. Cover

and turn motor on HIGH speed. Remove cover, and with blades spinning, gradually drop in soft cream cheese. Continue to blend until smooth.

4. Toss cream cheese mixture and noodles together and turn into buttered baking dish. Top with buttered crumbs.

5. Bake in a preheated 350° F. oven for 20 minutes, or until crumbs are brown and sauce is bubbling.

NOODLE PUDDING

Serves 6

2	cups cream-style cottage cheese (16 ounces)	½	teaspoon salt
1	cup sour cream	8	ounces medium noodles, cooked, rinsed, and drained
4	egg yolks		Dash of pepper
½	cup melted butter (1 stick)	4	egg whites

1. Preheat oven to 325° F. Butter a 2½-quart casserole.

2. Put cottage cheese, sour cream, egg yolks, butter, salt, and pepper into container. Cover and blend on HIGH speed for 20 seconds.

3. Empty cheese mixture into mixing bowl and add noodles. Mix well and correct seasoning with salt and pepper.

4. In another mixing bowl, beat egg whites until stiff but not dry. Fold into noodle mixture.

5. Empty into prepared casserole and bake in the preheated oven for 50 minutes.

NOODLES BAKED WITH DRIED BEEF

Serves 8

2   cups blender Thin Cream Sauce (page 24)
1   cup diced Cheddar cheese
¼   teaspoon salt
¼   teaspoon pepper
8   ounces fine noodles, cooked, rinsed, and drained
½   pound dried beef, coarsely cut

1. Preheat oven to 350° F. Butter a 2½-quart casserole.

2. Make blender Thin Cream Sauce. Add cheese and pepper and blend on HIGH speed for 20 seconds.

3. In a mixing bowl, combine cheese sauce, noodles, and beef.

4. Empty into prepared casserole and bake in preheated oven for 30 minutes.

NOODLE DELIGHT

Serves 4 to 6

1½ cups hot milk	¼ teaspoon pepper
4 tablespoons soft butter	1 teaspoon salt
(½ stick)	2 cups diced Cheddar cheese
4 tablespoons flour	8 ounces noodles, cooked,
¼ cup chopped chives or green onion tops	rinsed, and drained

1. Preheat oven to 350° F. Butter a 2-quart baking dish.

2. Put all ingredients except noodles into container. Cover and blend on LOW speed for 20 seconds, or until well blended.

3. Mix sauce with noodles. Empty into prepared baking dish and bake in preheated oven for 30 minutes.

SPANISH EGG AND NOODLE CASSEROLE

Serves 6

6 ounces medium noodles, cooked, rinsed, and drained	4 tablespoons soft butter (½ stick)
* 1 cup blender-shredded Cheddar cheese	4 tablespoons flour
	1 small clove garlic
One 1-pound, 4-ounce can tomatoes	½ teaspoon chili powder
1 medium onion, quartered	½ teaspoon salt
½ green pepper, cut in strips	6 hard-cooked eggs, sliced

1. Preheat oven to 350° F. Butter a 2-quart casserole.

2. Blender-shred cheese and set aside.

3. Heat tomatoes with juice until bubbling and empty into container. Add onion, green pepper, butter, flour, garlic, chili powder, and salt. Cover and blend on LOW speed until vegetables are coarsely chopped.

4. Arrange half the noodles in casserole and cover with half the eggs. Cover eggs with half the tomato mixture. Repeat layers ending with tomato sauce.

5. Sprinkle with shredded cheese and bake in the preheated oven for 30 minutes.

OYSTERS TETRAZZINI

Serves 4

2 cups fine egg noodles	1 teaspoon salt
1 pint oysters, freshly shucked	¼ teaspoon pepper
* 1 slice bread, blender-crumbed	1 teaspoon Worcestershire sauce
* 2 ounces Parmesan cheese, blender-grated	About 1½ cups hot milk
	½ teaspoon paprika
4 tablespoons butter (½ stick)	2 tablespoons sherry
2 tablespoons flour	

1. Preheat oven to 400° F. Butter a 1½-quart casserole.

2. Cook noodles according to package directions, drain, rinse in cold water, and spread in bottom of baking dish.

3. Drain oysters, reserving oyster liquid, and arrange oysters on top of the noodles.

4. Blender-crumb bread and grate cheese. Combine and set aside.

5. Put half the butter into the container. Add flour, salt, pepper, Worcestershire, and hot milk. Cover and blend on HIGH speed for 10 seconds. With blades spinning, remove cover or inner cap and pour in reserved oyster liquid, paprika, and the sherry.

6. Pour sauce over oysters and sprinkle with crumb-cheese mixture. Dot with butter and bake in the preheated oven for 30 minutes, or until sauce is bubbling and crumbs are golden.

CHICKEN NOODLE CASSEROLE

Serves 5 to 6

6	ounces medium noodles	1	medium onion, quartered
2	cups diced, cooked chicken	½	green pepper, cut in strips
4	tablespoons butter (½ stick)	2	tablespoons flour
* ½	cup blender buttered bread crumbs	1	cup chicken broth
		½	pound American cheese, diced
2	stalks celery, coarsely cut	One	8-ounce can mushrooms

1. Preheat oven to 350° F. Butter a 2-quart baking dish.

2. Cook noodles according to package directions. Drain, empty into baking dish, and mix with the chicken and half the butter.

3. Make buttered bread crumbs and set aside.

4. Into container put remaining butter, celery, onion, green pepper, flour, chicken broth, cheese, and mushrooms. Cover and blend on HIGH speed for 15 seconds, or until all ingredients are blended and cheese and vegetables are shredded.

5. Pour sauce over noodles and sprinkle with the buttered bread crumbs.

6. Bake in preheated oven for 35 to 40 minutes, or until crumbs are golden.

Rice Dishes

ARROZ CON POLLO

Serves 8

Two	3-pound frying chickens, cut in serving portions	½	cup coarsely diced green pepper
½	cup salad oil	1	teaspoon salt
1⅔	cups rice	¼	teaspoon pepper
3	chicken bouillon cubes	2	pinches saffron
1	clove garlic	3	cups water
½	cup coarsely diced onion		

1. Preheat oven to 350° F.

2. Sauté chicken pieces in salad oil over moderate heat until browned on all sides and transfer to a 3-quart casserole.

3. Add rice to oil in pan and cook, stirring frequently, until golden brown. Pour rice over the chicken in casserole.

4. Put remaining ingredients in container and blend on HIGH speed for 10 seconds, or until contents are finely cut.

5. Empty into saucepan and bring to a boil, then pour over chicken.

6. Cover casserole, and bake in the preheated oven for 30 minutes; then remove cover and continue baking until chicken is tender, or about 45 minutes longer.

INDIAN RICE

Serves 6

1	medium onion, quartered	½	teaspoon ginger
2	tart apples, peeled, cored, and quartered	¼	teaspoon red pepper
		½	teaspoon turmeric
1	stalk celery with leaves, coarsely cut	3	tablespoons tomato paste
		3	cups well-flavored chicken broth
½	green pepper, cut in strips		
2	teaspoons curry powder	¼	cup olive oil
1	clove garlic	1½	cups raw rice
1	teaspoon mustard seeds	½	cup grated coconut
8	peppercorns		

1. Put first 12 ingredients into container and add as much of the chicken broth as needed to just cover. Cover container and blend on HIGH speed for 2 seconds, or just until the last piece of vegetable takes a nose dive down into the blades.

2. In a large skillet or heavy saucepan, heat the olive oil. Add rice and cook, stirring, until rice is coated with the oil. Add contents of container and remaining chicken broth. Bring to a boil over high heat. Cover tightly, reduce heat to lowest point, and cook without removing cover for 20 minutes.

3. Remove cover and fluff rice with a fork. Leave over low heat to steam for 10 minutes, or until ready to serve.

4. Just before serving, stir in the coconut.

SPANISH RICE CASSEROLE

Serves 6

One 1-pound can tomatoes
1 small onion, halved
1 small clove garlic
One 4-ounce can pimientos,
    drained
1 green pepper, seeded and cut
    in strips

¼ teaspoon Tabasco sauce
1½ teaspoons salt
2 tablespoons soft butter
4 cups cooked rice

1. Preheat oven to 350° F. Butter a 1½-quart casserole.

2. Put all ingredients except rice into container. Cover and blend on HIGH speed for 20 seconds.

3. Combine contents of container with the rice. Empty into prepared casserole and bake in preheated oven for 45 minutes.

BRAZILIAN RICE

Serves 4

½ cup diced onion
½ cup diced carrots
½ cup diced celery
¼ diced green pepper
1 cup water
1 cup tomato sauce

One 3-ounce can chopped
    mushrooms
½ teaspoon salt
½ teaspoon sugar
⅛ teaspoon pepper
1 cup converted rice

1. Put onion, carrots, celery, green pepper, and water in container. Cover and blend on HIGH speed for 3 seconds or until vegetables are finely chopped.

2. Pour blended mixture into a saucepan and add tomato sauce, mushrooms, seasonings, and rice.

3. Bring to boil, cover, reduce heat to low, and cook for about 20 minutes until rice is tender and most of liquid is absorbed.

MEXICAN RICE

Serves 4

1	small onion, halved	Two	10½-ounce cans beef
¼	green pepper, cut in strips		consommé
¾	teaspoon cumin seeds	2	tablespoons butter
½	teaspoon chili powder	1¼	cups raw rice
¾	teaspoon salt		

1. Put onion, green pepper, cumin seeds, chili powder, salt, and 1 can of the beef consommé in container. Cover and blend on HIGH speed for 2 to 3 seconds.

2. In a heavy saucepan, melt butter and in it sauté the rice until lightly browned, stirring frequently.

3. Add contents of container and remaining beef consommé and bring to a rapid boil. Cover tightly, reduce heat to very low, and cook without removing the lid, for 20 minutes.

4. Remove cover, flake rice with a fork, and leave over low heat for 10 to 15 minutes before serving.

RICE CRAB CAKES

Serves 6

* 2	slices bread, blender-crumbed	1	teaspoon salt
1	egg	½	teaspoon dry mustard
½	small onion, halved	⅛	teaspoon cayenne pepper
One	6½-ounce can crab meat, drained and flaked	2	cups cooked rice
		4	tablespoons butter
¼	cup parsley clusters		Hollandaise Sauce (page 166)

1. Crumb 1 slice of bread at a time. Empty onto waxed paper and reserve.

2. Put egg, onion, crab meat, parsley, salt, mustard, and cayenne into container. Cover and blend on HIGH speed for 10 seconds, stopping to stir down if necessary.

3. Combine the crab mixture and rice. Shape into 6 flat patties and press bread crumbs into patties on both sides to coat completely. Chill patties for at least 30 minutes.

4. To cook, melt butter in a large skillet and sauté the crab cakes in it for 3 to 4 minutes on each side, or until golden. Serve with Hollandaise Sauce.

CRAB RICE CASSEROLE

Serves 4 to 6

1 slice bread, trimmed	2 tablespoons soft butter
1 cup diced Cheddar cheese	1 teaspoon salt
1 medium green pepper, cut in strips	¼ teaspoon Tabasco sauce
	1 cup hot milk
2 carrots, coarsely cut	3 cups cooked rice
1 medium onion, quartered	One 6½-ounce can crab meat,
½ cup parsley clusters	drained and flaked
2 tablespoons flour	

1. Preheat oven to 375°F. Butter a 2-quart casserole.

2. Tear bread into container. Add half the cheese. Cover and blend on HIGH speed for 6 seconds. Empty mixture out onto waxed paper and set aside for topping.

3. Put remaining cheese, green pepper, carrots, onion, parsley, flour, butter salt, Tabasco, and milk into container. Cover and blend on HIGH speed for 15 seconds, or until vegetables are finely chopped.

4. Combine rice and crab meat in a mixing bowl. Pour ingredients in the container over rice and crab meat and mix lightly. Empty into prepared casserole and sprinkle with the reserved topping.

5. Bake in preheated oven for 25 to 30 minutes, or until sauce is bubbling and topping is lightly browned.

MAIN DISHES— HOT & COLD

Main Dishes—Hot & Cold

WHAT can a blender do for roasts, chops, and other main-course dishes? If you get into the blender habit, it can do plenty! For instance, it can add that final touch of Yorkshire Pudding to a prime roast of beef and assure you of a velvet-smooth gravy. It can blend all kinds of savory marinades for pot roasts and barbecue and basting sauces for steak, fish, and chicken. It can crumb a loaf of bread in about a minute, then chop onion, celery, and mixed herbs with melted butter to make enough stuffing for an 8-pound bird in less than another minute. Blender crumbs, made of bread or crackers, give you the crisp coating for fried chicken or fish or croquettes, for au gratin toppings, or to use as extenders for loaves and casserole dishes. The blender virtually eliminates the need for a food mill or sieve by purée-ing the flavor vegetables of a recipe—which otherwise are often discarded—right with the pan liquid to make exquisite sauces. These are only a few of the ways your blender simplifies the preparation of entrées and improves the final flavor of the dish.

Main-dish recipes in which the blender plays a major role are numerous and varied. But, in addition, many recipes can be adapted to blender techniques that save countless minutes of preparation time, even when the blending process itself may be only a minor aspect of the recipe. All I can do within the confines of a single chapter, although it is a long one, is to give you examples of both kinds of recipes that together encompass a great many types of dishes. You take it from there!

Beef Dishes

BEEF STROGANOFF

Serves 4

1½   pounds round steak, in slab
        cut 1 inch thick
  4   tablespoons butter (½ stick)
  ¼   pound fresh mushrooms,
        wiped clean and halved
  2   small onions, quartered

     3   tablespoons flour
One   10½-ounce can beef
          consommé
     2   teaspoons prepared mustard
     1   teaspoon tomato paste
     ½   cup water
     1   teaspoon salt
     ½   teaspoon coarsely cracked
          pepper
     1   cup sour cream

1. Slice meat slantwise into strips as thin as possible. (If partially frozen, the meat will be easier to slice.)

2. In a large heavy skillet, melt the butter and in it brown meat quickly on both sides.

3. Put into container the mushrooms, onion, flour, consommé, mustard, and tomato paste. Cover and blend on HIGH speed for 6 seconds, or until vegetables are chopped.

4. Pour over meat. Add water, salt, and pepper, cover, and cook over low heat until meat is tender. Liquid should only simmer, not boil, or meat is apt to be tough.

5. Just before serving, combine sour cream with a little of the hot pan sauce. Stir into remaining sauce and heat just to serving temperature.

6. Serve with cooked rice, and a colorful, buttered vegetable.

SWISS STEAK

Serves 4

1½   pounds chuck steak, in slab
         cut 1 inch thick
¼   cup flour
2   tablespoons cooking oil
One 1-pound can stewed tomatoes
2   medium onions, quartered
1   green pepper, seeded and
         cut in strips
1   large clove garlic
¼   pound mushrooms, wiped
         clean and halved

1   teaspoon salt
½   teaspoon coarsely cracked
         black pepper
½   teaspoon thyme
1   tablespoon Worcestershire
         sauce
One 10½-ounce can beef
         consommé
* 3–4   parsley clusters,
         blender-chopped

1. Place steak on waxed paper on work table and sprinkle with the flour. Rub well into steak on all sides. Reserve any remaining flour.

2. In a heavy 12-inch skillet, heat cooking oil and in it brown the meat well on both sides.

3. Put tomatoes and reserved flour into container. Add onions, pepper, garlic, and mushrooms. Cover and blend on HIGH speed for 4 to 6 seconds, or until vegetables are finely chopped.

4. Pour mixture in container over steak. Add salt, pepper, thyme, Worcestershire, and consommé. Cover skillet, turn heat to very low, and simmer for 2 to 2½ hours, turning steak occasionally and spooning some of the pan sauce over it.

5. To serve, cut steak into 4 equal portions, or slice and transfer to serving platter. Pour sauce over meat and sprinkle with chopped parsley.

SAUERBRATEN

Serves 8

2	tablespoons fat	2	cloves garlic
4	pounds rolled top, eye, or bottom round of beef	2	stalks celery with leaves, coarsely cut
1	teaspoon salt	2	carrots, coarsely cut
¼	teaspoon coarsely ground black pepper		Handful of parsley clusters
1	large bay leaf	¼	teaspoon clove
1½	cups dry red wine or water	¼	teaspoon nutmeg
2	slices lemon	Two	10½-ounce cans beef consommé
1	large onion, coarsely cut	1	tablespoon cornstarch
1	cup red wine vinegar	2	teaspoons water

1. In a heavy kettle, heat the fat and in it brown the meat well on all sides. When brown, sprinkle with 1 teaspoon salt and the coarsely ground black pepper. Add the bay leaf.

2. Put into container the red wine or water, lemon slices, and onion. Cover and blend on HIGH speed for 3 seconds, or until onion is chopped. Pour over meat and bring to a boil.

3. Put vinegar, garlic, celery, carrots, and parsley into container. Cover and blend on HIGH speed for 3 seconds, or until vegetables are chopped.

Pour mixture into kettle. Cover tightly and cook over very low heat for 1½ hours. The liquid should not boil actively, just barely simmer.

4. Add clove, nutmeg, and the consommé, cover, and continue to braise the roast for 1½ hours longer.

5. Place meat on a hot serving platter. Remove fat from surface of liquid. Combine the cornstarch and 2 teaspoons water and bring liquid to a boil. Stir in the cornstarch mixture and cook, stirring constantly, for 1 minute. Pour a little of the gravy over the roast, and serve the rest separately.

6. Serve with boiled or mashed potatoes. I like the mashed, to sop up the wonderful gravy.

HUNGARIAN GOULASH

Serves 6

4 slices bacon, diced	1 tablespoon paprika
2 pounds beef, chuck or top round, cut in 1-inch cubes	One 6-ounce can tomato paste
	1 teaspoon salt
2 large onions, quartered	¼ teaspoon pepper
4 cloves garlic	1 large green pepper, seeded and cut in coarse strips
Two 12-ounce cans beer or ale	
½ teaspoon thyme	1 cup sour cream

1. In a heavy 12-inch skillet, sauté the bacon for 2 to 3 minutes, or until fat is rendered from bacon and bacon is lightly browned. Add beef and cook over high heat until meat is browned on all sides.

2. Into container put onions, garlic, one can of the beer or ale, and the thyme. Cover and blend on HIGH speed for 5 seconds, or until onions are finely chopped. Empty into skillet, bring to a boil, cover and simmer for 1½ hours.

3. Put into container the remaining can of beer or ale, paprika, tomato paste, salt, pepper, and green pepper. Cover and blend on HIGH speed for 3 to 4 seconds, or until green pepper is chopped. Add to skillet, cover, and simmer for 30 minutes, or until meat is tender.

4. Before serving, blend together the sour cream and ½ cup of the sauce in skillet. Stir into meat mixture and heat to serving temperature. Do not boil after sour cream is added.

5. Serve with cooked noodles or boiled potatoes.

CHILI CON CARNE

Serves 6. This is my favorite chili. Serve it with cooked rice and canned kidney beans, heated in their own liquid and drained. Bowls of shredded lettuce and chopped onion are a refreshing accompaniment to sprinkle over the chili.

6	tablespoons cooking oil	1	teaspoon cumin seeds
2	pounds round steak, cubed	1	teaspoon oregano
Two 13¾-ounce cans beef broth		1	teaspoon salt
6	tablespoons flour	3	cloves garlic
6	tablespoons chili powder		

1. In a heavy 12-inch skillet, heat cooking oil and in it cook the steak, stirring and tossing the meat in the hot oil until it loses all red color.

2. Put into container 1 can beef broth and remaining ingredients. Cover and blend on HIGH speed for 15 seconds.

3. Pour blended mixture over meat, add remaining can of broth, and bring to a simmer. Cover and cook over very low heat for 2 to 4 hours, or until ready to serve, stirring occasionally. The longer it cooks (without boiling) the better it is.

CHINESE PEPPER STEAK

Serves 4

1½	pounds round steak, in slab 1 inch thick	4	tablespoons soy sauce
2	tablespoons cooking oil	1	cup water
1	clove garlic	2	green peppers, seeded and coarsely cut
1	medium onion, coarsely cut		
½	pound fresh mushrooms, halved	1	tablespoon cornstarch
One 8-ounce can tomato sauce		1	cup canned bean sprouts, drained
½	teaspoon salt	4	green onions, with tops, thinly sliced

1. Slice steak as thinly as possible into slanting pieces. This is easy to do if the steak is partially frozen.

2. In a heavy 12-inch skillet, heat oil and in it brown meat lightly on all sides.

3. Put into container the garlic, onion, mushrooms, tomato sauce, salt, soy sauce, and half the water. Cover and blend on HIGH speed for 10 seconds. Pour mixture over meat.

4. Cover skillet and cook over low heat for 1 hour, or until meat is tender.

5. Put into container the green pepper, cornstarch, and remaining water. Cover and blend on HIGH speed for 10 seconds. Add to meat with the bean sprouts. Cover and cook for 5 minutes longer, stirring frequently. Do not overcook. The green peppers and bean sprouts should be crisp.

6. Sprinkle with sliced onions and serve with cooked rice.

BISTECCA ALLA FIORENTINA
(Steak with Garlic Sauce)

Serves 4

1	cup olive oil	4	rib steaks, each 1 inch thick
4	cloves garlic	4	lemon slices
½	cup parsley clusters		Butter
3	tablespoons lemon juice		Parsley for garnish
2	teaspoons salt		
1	teaspoon freshly ground black pepper		

1. Put olive oil, garlic, parsley clusters, lemon juice, salt, and pepper into container. Blend on HIGH speed for 1 minute.

2. Place steaks in a large shallow dish, and pour contents of blender over them, turning the steaks over in the marinade. Set steaks aside in a cool place to marinate for 2 to 3 hours, turning occasionally.

3. Broil under high heat for 3 minutes on each side, or until done to taste.

4. Serve hot from the grill, garnishing each steak with a nut of butter, a slice of lemon, and a sprig of parsley.

BEEF IN BEER

Serves 4

1½	pounds chuck steak, in slab 1½ inches thick	¼	teaspoon pepper
One	12-ounce can beer	¼	teaspoon Tabasco sauce
1	large onion, coarsely cut	½	teaspoon oregano
¼	cup parsley clusters	¼	cup flour
1	bay leaf	3	tablespoons cooking oil
1½	teaspoons salt	2	stalks celery, coarsely cut

1. Slice steak as thinly as possible into slanting pieces. This is easy to do if steak is partially frozen. Put meat into a mixing bowl.

2. Put into container the beer, onion, parsley, bay leaf, salt, pepper, Tabasco, and oregano. Cover and blend on HIGH speed for 8 seconds, or until onion is chopped. Pour over meat, stir to mix, and let marinate in refrigerator for 6 hours, or overnight.

3. Drain meat, reserving the marinade. Pat meat dry with paper towels and coat with flour.

4. In a 12-inch skillet, heat the oil and in it sauté the meat until well browned, stirring and scraping bottom of skillet frequently.

5. Return marinade to container, add celery, cover, and blend on HIGH speed for 6 seconds, or until celery is chopped. Pour over meat in skillet and bring to a boil. Cover and cook over low heat for 1 hour, or until meat is tender, stirring occasionally and adding a little water if the sauce becomes too thick.

BEEF KABOBS

Serves 4

½	cup red wine	¼	cup parsley clusters
2	tablespoons oil	1	pound beef sirloin, cut in 2-inch cubes
1	teaspoon salt		
¼	teaspoon pepper	¼	pound mushroom caps
1	tomato, quartered	1	green pepper, seeded and cut in 2-inch cubes
¼	teaspoon Tabasco sauce		
½	clove garlic	8	cooked, whole, small white onions
¼	teaspoon dry mustard		
1	small onion		

1. Put into container, red wine, oil, salt, pepper, tomato, Tabasco, garlic, dry mustard, onion, and parsley clusters. Cover and blend on HIGH speed for 15 seconds.

2. In a shallow dish, arrange the cubed sirloin, mushroom caps, green pepper, and onions.

3. Pour marinade over meat and vegetables. Marinate overnight in refrigerator, turning meat and vegetables occasionally.

4. Arrange meat and vegetables on 4 skewers and broil or cook on outdoor grill for 4 to 5 minutes on each side, or until desired degree of doneness, brushing frequently with marinade.

Lamb, Pork & Veal Dishes

MINTED LAMB CHOPS

Serves 6

1　cup red wine vinegar
1　cup fresh mint leaves
1　medium onion, quartered
2　cloves garlic
6　double lamb chops
1　lemon, sliced, and fresh mint for garnish

1. In container combine vinegar, mint leaves, onion, and garlic. Cover and blend on HIGH speed for about 1 minute, or until mint is finely chopped.

2. Empty mixture into a saucepan, bring to a boil, and simmer for 3 minutes. Cool.

3. Pour the cooled marinade over the chops and refrigerate for 2 hours, or longer, turning chops occasionally in the marinade.

4. Broil chops on rack about 4 inches from source of heat for 3 to 4 minutes on each side, or until done to taste. Garnish each chop with a slice of lemon and a sprig of mint.

BRAISED LAMB SHANKS

Serves 4

½	cup olive oil	2	stalks celery with leaves,
4	lamb shanks		quartered
1	bay leaf	½	teaspoon oregano
3	cloves garlic	½	teaspoon thyme
2	carrots, coarsely cut	1	cup water
1	large onion, peeled and	One	1-pound can plum tomatoes
	coarsely cut		

1. Heat olive oil in a heavy skillet and in it brown lamb shanks on all sides. When brown, transfer to a heavy casserole or Dutch oven. Add the bay leaf.

2. Put garlic, carrots, onion, celery, oregano, thyme, and water into container. Cover and blend on HIGH speed for 6 seconds, or until vegetables are chopped.

3. Pour mixture in container over lamb shanks. Add the can of tomatoes with liquid. Cover casserole or Dutch oven tightly and braise on top of stove or in a 350° F. oven for 2 to 2½ hours, checking occasionally to make sure the liquid is not cooking too rapidly. It should just simmer.

4. Skim off all fat from top of liquid and serve one shank per person with plenty of pan sauce and boiled potatoes.

BEST BARBECUED SPARERIBS

Serves 2 for dinner, 4 as an appetizer

2	pounds spareribs	4	tablespoons soy sauce
	Salt and coarsely ground	½	teaspoon ground ginger
	pepper	3	tablespoons chili sauce
2	cloves garlic	1	tablespoon honey
4	tablespoons chutney		

1. Preheat oven to 350 ° F. Line shallow baking pan with a piece of foil long enough to fold over the spareribs. Place spareribs on the foil and

sprinkle generously with salt and pepper. Bring foil up and over spareribs and seal tightly with a double fold. Bake in preheated oven for 1 hour.

2. Put remaining ingredients into container. Cover and blend on HIGH speed for 10 seconds, or until smooth.

3. Remove baking dish from oven. Increase oven temperature to 375° F. Open foil and roll back around ribs. With bulb baster, remove melted fat that has collected in foil wrapping. Spread ribs with the mixture in the container.

4. Bake for 1 hour longer, basting several times with sauce in baking pan.

PORK CHOW MEIN

Serves 2

¾ pound lean loin of pork	¼ teaspoon pepper
2 tablespoons butter or cooking oil	½ cup each canned bean sprouts, sliced mushrooms, and sliced water chestnuts
1 medium onion, quartered	
2 stalks celery, quartered	1 tablespoon cornstarch
1 cup beef consommé	2 tablespoons water
2 tablespoons soy sauce	Chinese noodles
½ teaspoon salt	

1. Cut pork into 1-inch cubes.

2. In a skillet, heat butter or oil, and in it brown pork on all sides over moderate heat.

3. Put into container the onion, celery, consommé, soy sauce, salt, and pepper. Cover and blend on HIGH speed for just 5 seconds, or until onion and celery are chopped.

4. Pour mixture from container over pork, bring to a boil, cover, and simmer for 1 hour.

5. Add bean sprouts, mushrooms, and water chestnuts.

6. Combine cornstarch and water. Stir into pork mixture and cook, stirring constantly, until sauce is clear and thickened.

7. Serve over Chinese noodles.

HAM OR CHICKEN AND EGG HASH

Serves 6

4	slices bread	¼	cup milk
* ¼	diced Cheddar cheese, blender-shredded	¼	cup parsley clusters
		1	small onion, halved
* 3	cups diced, cooked ham or chicken, blender-shredded	½	green pepper, seeded and cut in strips
7	eggs	¼	teaspoon salt
½	cup tomato catsup or chili sauce	½	teaspoon dry mustard
		2	tablespoons butter

1. Prepare topping by blender-shredding 1 slice of bread with the cheese. Empty onto waxed paper and set aside.

2. Preheat oven to 350° F. Butter a shallow baking dish.

3. Blender-shred the ham, ½ cup at a time with ½ slice bread and empty into prepared baking pan.

4. Put into container 1 egg, the tomato catsup or chili sauce, milk, parsley, onion, green pepper, salt, and mustard. Cover and blend on HIGH speed for 8 seconds, or until vegetables are chopped. Pour over ham and crumbs and mix lightly.

5. Make 6 indentations with back of spoon in ham mixture and break an egg into each hole. Sprinkle with bread-cheese topping.

6. Dot with butter and bake in preheated oven for 25 minutes.

POTATO-HAM SCALLOP

Serves 4

2	cups milk	2	cups coarsely diced cooked ham
2	tablespoons flour		
½	cup coarsely diced onion	4	cups thinly sliced raw potatoes
1	teaspoon salt	¼	teaspoon paprika
⅛	teaspoon pepper		

1. Preheat oven to 375° F. Oil a 2-quart casserole.

2. Put into container the milk, flour, onion, salt, pepper, and ham. Cover and blend on HIGH speed until ham is coarsely chopped, or about 10 seconds.

3. Arrange half the potatoes in a layer in the prepared casserole. Pour half the blended mixture over the potatoes. Repeat with remaining potatoes and remaining blended mixture. Sprinkle with paprika.

4. Cover and bake in moderately hot oven until potatoes are tender, or about 45 minutes. Remove cover and continue baking for 15 minutes longer.

STUFFED PORK TENDERLOIN

Serves 6

* 4 slices bread, blender-crumbed
1 small onion, quartered
3 tablespoons soft butter
¼ cup parsley clusters
½ teaspoon salt
⅛ teaspoon pepper

½ teaspoon sage
¾ cup hot water
2 large pork tenderloins
1 tablespoon shortening or
    bacon drippings

1. Preheat oven to 350° F. Grease a small baking pan.

2. Blender-crumb bread, and empty into a mixing bowl.

3. Put into container the onion, butter, parsley, salt, pepper, sage, and ¼ cup of the water. Cover and blend on HIGH speed for 5 seconds, or until smooth. Mix with crumbs.

4. Trim and wipe tenderloins. Slash them lengthwise, almost but not quite through. Fill tenderloins with stuffing and tie securely with string. Place in greased baking pan. Spread with shortening. Add remaining water to pan and bake in preheated oven for 50 to 60 minutes, basting every 10 minutes with pan juices.

VEAL CHOPS PROVENÇALE

Serves 2

2 tablespoons flour
½ teaspoon salt
¼ teaspoon pepper
2 veal chops, about ½ inch
    thick

3   tablespoons butter or olive oil
1   cup canned tomatoes with
       juice
1   small onion, halved
¼   teaspoon oregano
6–8 parsley clusters
    Pinch of thyme

1. Combine flour, salt, and pepper. Coat veal chops with the flour mixture.

2. In a skillet, heat butter or olive oil, and in it brown the chops on both sides.

3. For tomato sauce, put remaining ingredients into container. Cover and blend on HIGH speed for 10 seconds.

4. Pour tomato sauce over chops and cover. Simmer for 30 minutes.

VEAL CHOPS PAPRIKASH

Serves 2

2   tablespoons flour
½   teaspoon salt
¼   teaspoon pepper
2   veal chops, about ½ inch thick
3   tablespoons butter
½   cup chicken broth
½   cup dry white wine or
       vermouth

1   small onion, halved
1   stalk celery, quartered
¼   green pepper, seeded and cut
       in strips
1   tablespoon paprika
½   cup sour cream
    Chopped parsley for garnish

1. Combine flour, salt, and pepper. Coat chops with the mixture.

2. In a skillet, heat butter and in it brown chops on both sides.

3. Put remaining ingredients, except sour cream and parsley, into container. Cover and blend on HIGH speed for 10 seconds.

4. Pour sauce over chops, cover, and simmer for 30 minutes.

5. Arrange chops on serving plate. Stir sour cream into pan juices and cook, stirring, until sauce it hot.

6. Pour sauce over veal chops and sprinkle with parsley.

ITALIAN STUFFED VEAL

Serves 6

One 2-pound leg or shoulder of veal, boned and rolled
* 2 slices bread, 1½ slices blender-crumbed
* ½ cup diced cooked ham, blender-shredded
1 egg
½ small onion
¼ cup parsley clusters
¼ cup pitted ripe olives
3 tablespoons oil

1 teaspoon salt
¼ teaspoon pepper
3 cups chicken stock
½ pound mushrooms, washed and quartered
4 green onions, coarsely cut
1 cup dry white wine or vermouth
1½ tablespoons cornstarch
2 tablespoons water

1. Cut a pocket in the veal, wipe with a damp cloth, and set aside.

2. Blender-crumb 1½ slices bread. Use remaining bread to blender-shred ham. Combine bread crumbs and ham in a mixing bowl.

3. Put into container the egg and onion. Cover and blend on HIGH speed for 5 seconds, or until onion is liquefied. Add parsley, olives, 1 tablespoon of the oil, salt, and pepper. Cover and blend on HIGH speed for 6 seconds or until olives are chopped. Pour into bowl with crumbs and ham and mix well.

4. Stuff the veal with this dressing and sew or skewer opening closed.

5. In a heavy saucepan, put remaining 2 tablespoons oil and in it brown the veal well on all sides.

6. Put into container half the chicken stock, the mushrooms, and green onions. Cover and blend on HIGH speed for 5 seconds, or until mushrooms and onions are chopped. Add to veal with remaining chicken stock and the wine. Bring to a boil, cover, and simmer for 1½ hours or until veal is tender.

7. Remove veal from liquid, discard skewers or string, and arrange on serving platter.

8. Combine cornstarch and water. Stir into liquid in saucepan and cook over low heat until sauce is thickened, stirring constantly.

9. Spoon a little of the sauce over the veal and serve the rest separately.

BONELESS BIRDS

Serves 4

2	pork sausages	2	tablespoons cooking oil
* 1	slice bread, blender-crumbed	1	medium onion, quartered
1	cup quartered mushrooms	2	tablespoons flour
1	small onion, halved	½	teaspoon oregano
6–8	parsley clusters	¼	teaspoon thyme
1	egg	1	tablespoon tomato paste
1	teaspoon salt	One	10½-ounce can beef
¼	teaspoon pepper		consommé
2	tablespoons melted butter		
8	very thin slices veal or lean beef, about 1¼ pounds		

1. For stuffing, first remove skins from sausages and crumble meat into mixing bowl.

2. Blender-crumb bread and add to sausage meat.

3. Put into container the mushrooms, small onion, parsley, egg, salt, pepper, and melted butter. Cover and blend on HIGH speed for 6 seconds. Pour over sausage meat and combine all ingredients well.

4. Spread each slice of meat with a layer of the stuffing. Roll each jelly-roll fashion and secure with a wooden pick.

5. Heat cooking oil in skillet and in it sauté the "birds" until brown on all sides.

6. Pour remaining ingredients into container. Cover and blend on HIGH speed for 6 seconds. Pour over meat rolls and bring liquid to a boil. Cover and cook over low heat for 1 hour, stirring occasionally. Remove wooden picks before serving.

NOTE: If desired, ½ cup cream may be stirred into pan juices before serving.

Meat Loaves & Timbales

SAVORY MEAT LOAF

Serves 8

¾	pound ground raw beef or veal	2	eggs
¾	pound ground lean pork or ham	1½	teaspoons salt
		¼	teaspoon pepper
¾	cup oatmeal, quick-cooking or regular	¼	teaspoon thyme
		1	small onion, halved
		6	parsley clusters

1. Preheat oven to 350° F. Oil an 8 × 4-inch loaf pan.

2. Place meats in mixing bowl.

3. Put the oatmeal into container, cover, and blend on HIGH speed until oatmeal is like coarse meal. Pour blended oatmeal over meat.

4. Put remaining ingredients into container, cover, and blend on HIGH speed for 15 seconds. Pour blended mixture into bowl with meat and mix thoroughly with hands or wooden spoon.

5. Pack lightly into prepared pan and bake in preheated oven until well done, about 1½ hours.

LIVER LOAF

Serves 6

* 2	slices bread, blender-crumbed	¼	teaspoon pepper
½	cup milk	1½	pounds calves liver or young beef liver, cut into 2-inch pieces
1	egg		
1	small clove garlic		
1	medium onion, quartered	½	pound ground pork
¼	cup parsley clusters	6	slices bacon
1½	teaspoons salt		Parsley for garnish

1. Preheat oven to 350° F. Grease 9 × 5-inch loaf pan.

2. Pat blender-crumbed bread in a mixing bowl and set aside.

3. Put into container, milk, egg, garlic, onion, parsley clusters, salt, and pepper. Cover and blend on HIGH speed for 5 seconds, or until smooth. Turn blender to LOW and gradually add liver, piece by piece. When about half the liver has been added, switch to HIGH speed, and continue blending until all the liver has been added and mixture is smooth. Turn into mixing bowl with the crumbs. Add pork and mix well.

4. Arrange 3 slices of bacon in bottom of prepared loaf pan. Fill with liver mixture and top with remaining bacon slices.

5. Place loaf pan in shallow pan containing 1 inch of hot water. Bake in preheated oven for 1½ hours. Let stand for 5 minutes, then unmold, and garnish with parsley, if desired.

CHEESE MEAT LOAF

Serves 8

* 4	slices bread, blender-crumbed	2	eggs
1	pound ground beef	2	teaspoons salt
½	pound ground veal	¼	teaspoon pepper
½	pound ground pork	1	tablespoon Worcestershire
One	8-ounce can tomato sauce		sauce
¼	cup parsley clusters	½	teaspoon basil or tarragon
1	medium onion, quartered	1	cup diced Cheddar cheese
½	green pepper, seeded and cut in strips		

1. Preheat oven to 350° F. Grease a 9-inch loaf pan.

2. In a mixing bowl, combine bread crumbs, beef, veal, and pork.

3. Put remaining ingredients into container. Cover and blend on HIGH speed for 10 seconds. Pour over meat and mix well.

4. Pack mixture into a loaf pan and bake in preheated oven for 1½ hours.

5. Let stand for 5 minutes, drain off excess liquid, and turn out onto serving dish.

DEVILED HAM LOAF

Serves 6

* 1½ cups diced, cooked ham,
    blender-shredded
* 10 slices bread, blender-crumbed
  1 medium onion, quartered
  1 stalk celery
  ½ cup parsley clusters

3 eggs
2 teaspoons Worcestershire
  sauce
2 teaspoons prepared mustard
¼ teaspoon pepper

1. Preheat oven to 350° F. Line bottom of a 9-inch loaf pan with waxed paper and oil the paper.

2. Blender-shred ham, ½ cup at a time, using ½ slice of the bread with each ½ cup ham. Empty ham into mixing bowl. Blender-crumb remaining bread and empty into mixing bowl.

3. Put remaining ingredients into container, cover, and blend on HIGH speed for 15 seconds, or until blended. Add to ham mixture and mix well.

4. Pack ham mixture into loaf pan and bake in preheated oven for 1 hour and 15 minutes.

5. Cool loaf for 5 minutes, then unmold onto serving dish. Remove waxed paper and serve hot or cold.

DELICATE TIMBALES, made of vegetables, poultry, seafood, or cheese, were once extremely popular as a luncheon dish for special occasions. In this day of high food cost, a revival of timbales might be welcomed, for they make a little go a long way, yet are high in protein and exquisite in flavor. With a blender they are now very convenient to make.

OLD-FASHIONED SALMON TIMBALES

Serves 4

* 2 slices fresh bread, blender-
    crumbed
  ¾ cup hot milk
  4 tablespoons soft butter
    (½ stick)

    1   small onion, halved
  4–6   parsley clusters
  One   1-pound can salmon including
            liquid or 2 cups diced
            cooked ham or chicken
    4   eggs
    2   tablespoons sherry
   ¼   teaspoon salt
   ⅛   teaspoon pepper
         Mushroom Sauce (page 182)

1. Preheat oven to 350°F. Butter a 4-cup timbale mold or 6 individual custard cups.

2. Blender-crumb bread and leave crumbs in container. You should have about 1 cup.

3. Add milk, butter, onion, and parsley. Cover and blend on HIGH speed for 10 seconds.

4. Add remaining ingredients, cover, and blend on HIGH speed for 15 seconds longer, or until ingredients are smooth, stopping to stir down if necessary.

5. Pour salmon mixture into the mold or cups. Set cups or mold in a shallow pan containing about 1 inch hot water, and bake in the preheated oven for 1½ hours for large mold and 30 minutes for individual cups, or until custard is set. To test, insert a silver knife near the center of the custard and if knife comes out clean the cream is ready to be served.

6. Run a knife around edge of mold and invert on serving platter or plates. Serve with Mushroom Sauce and small buttered peas.

CHICKEN LIVER TIMBALES

Serves 8

    2   tablespoons soft butter   2   eggs
    2   tablespoons flour   2   egg yolks
    1   cup hot milk   6   tablespoons heavy cream
   ½   teaspoon salt   2   tablespoons port or Cognac
   ⅛   teaspoon white pepper   Sauce Béarnaise (page 134)
   ½   pound chicken livers, cleaned
            and halved

1. Preheat oven to 350° F. Butter 8 small ramekins, each about 4 ounces in capacity.

2. Put butter, flour, hot milk, salt, and pepper into container. Cover and blend on LOW speed for 10 seconds. Switch to HIGH speed.

3. With blades spinning, remove cover or inner cap and drop in chicken livers, one by one. Add eggs, egg yolks, cream, and port or Cognac, and continue to blend on HIGH speed for 1 minute.

4. Pour into prepared ramekins, filling each almost to the top.

5. Set ramekins into a shallow pan containing about 1 inch hot water. Bake in preheated oven for 30 minutes, or until knife inserted in middle comes out clean.

6. Let cool 5 minutes, then turn timbales out onto serving plates and serve with Béarnaise Sauce.

Poultry Dishes

BAKED CHICKEN BREASTS

Serves 4

One	4-ounce can mushrooms	¼	teaspoon pepper
½	medium onion, halved	⅛	teaspoon saffron
1	stalk celery, coarsely cut	1	tablespoon soft butter
1	tablespoon lemon juice	¼	teaspoon Tabasco sauce
1	teaspoon salt	4	chicken breasts, skinned
2	tablespoons milk		

1. Preheat oven to 350° F. Butter a shallow baking pan.

2. Drain mushrooms, reserving liquid.

3. Put into the container the mushroom liquid, onion, celery, lemon juice, salt, milk, pepper, saffron, butter, and Tabasco. Cover and blend on HIGH speed for 10 seconds. Leave motor on, remove lid, and add reserved mushrooms. Continue blending only until mushrooms are chopped.

4. Arrange chicken breasts in baking dish. Pour mushroom sauce over chicken. Bake in preheated oven for 1 hour, or until chicken is tender.

CHICKEN BAKED IN CURRANT SAUCE

Serves 6

4	pound roasting chicken, cut in serving pieces		Thin orange rind from 1 orange
6	tablespoons flour	½	cup currant jelly
¼	cup bacon drippings	1½	teaspoons salt
2	cups chicken broth	¼	teaspoon pepper
¼	green pepper, cut in strips		

1. Preheat oven to 300° F. Grease a 3-quart baking dish.

2. Dip pieces of chicken in water, then coat with flour. Reserve any remaining flour.

3. Melt bacon drippings in a large skillet and brown chicken well on all sides. Arrange in baking dish.

4. Put chicken broth and reserved flour into container. Add remaining ingredients. Cover and blend on HIGH speed for 20 seconds. Empty into skillet and bring to a boil, stirring constantly.

5. Pour sauce over chicken and bake in preheated oven for 2 hours, basting occasionally with the pan juices.

BAKED CHICKEN BARBECUE

Serves 8

1	teaspoon salt	⅓	cup lemon juice
½	teaspoon pepper	1	tablespoon Worcestershire sauce
1	tablespoon paprika		
1	tablespoon sugar	¼	cup cooking oil
1	clove garlic	5	pounds chicken parts
1	medium onion, quartered		Seasoned flour
1	cup catsup		Fat for frying
½	cup water		

1. Put all ingredients, except chicken, seasoned flour, and fat for frying, into container. Cover and blend on HIGH speed for 15 seconds.

2. Empty into a saucepan and bring to a boil. Makes 2½ cups sauce.

3. Preheat oven to 325° F.

4. Coat chicken with flour.

5. In a skillet, melt enough fat to bring it to a depth of about ½ inch, and in this brown chicken on all sides.

6. Arrange chicken, one layer deep in shallow baking pan. Spoon barbecue sauce over.

7. Bake in preheated oven for 45 to 60 minutes.

CHICKEN CURRY À L'INDIENNE

Serves 4

1	fresh coconut	1	teaspoon each poppy seeds, cumin seeds, and coriander
2	cups boiling water		
6	tablespoons butter	2	or 3 pieces fresh, canned, or candied ginger root
3½	pound chicken, cut in serving pieces		
		4	dried hot chili peppers
1	teaspoon ground tumeric	6	whole cloves
2	cloves garlic	1	bay leaf
1	medium onion, quartered	2	cups water

1. MAKE COCONUT MILK AND CREAM: Crack the coconut and remove all the meat from the shell. Cut meat into chunks and pile into container of blender. Add 2 cups boiling water. (If it won't all fit, divide coconut and water and blend half at a time.) Cover container and blend on HIGH speed for 1 minute. Pour ground coconut and liquid into a sieve lined with cheese cloth and let the coconut milk drip through into a bowl, pressing the coconut with back of a wooden spoon to extract as much liquid as possible. Let the extracted milk stand undisturbed so that the cream will rise to the top. You will be able to spoon off about 1 cup coconut cream, leaving about 1 cup coconut milk.

2. In a skillet, melt the butter and in it sauté chicken until nice and brown on one side. Sprinkle with turmeric, turn, and sauté until golden brown on other side.

3. Put into container the garlic, onion, seeds, ginger root, chili peppers, cloves, bay leaf, and 1 cup of the water. Cover and blend on HIGH speed for 30 seconds. Pour mixture over chicken, add remaining cup of water, and bring to a boil. Partially cover skillet and simmer the chicken for 30 minutes.

4. Skim and set aside the coconut cream. Add coconut milk to chicken, cover, and simmer for 20 minutes longer.

5. Season the curry sauce with salt to taste and turn heat to very low. Stir in coconut cream, turn off heat, cover skillet, and let the curry stand for 10 minutes before serving.

6. Serve with cooked rice and chutney.

CHICKEN IN WHITE WINE

Serves 4

3½	pound chicken, cut in serving portions	½	teaspoon tarragon
1	tablespoon olive oil	1	teaspoon salt
1	tablespoon butter	¼	teaspoon pepper
1	small onion, halved	One	1-pound can whole tomatoes, drained and coarsely cut, or 2 ripe tomatoes, peeled and chopped
1	clove garlic		
½	chicken broth		
½	cup dry vermouth or white wine	1	teaspoon cornstarch
1	tablespoon tomato paste	2	teaspoons cold water
1	bay leaf		Chopped parsley for garnish

1. Wash and dry chicken pieces.

2. In a large heavy skillet, heat the olive oil and butter and in it brown chicken pieces on all sides over moderate heat.

3. Put onion, garlic, chicken broth, white wine, and tomato paste into container. Cover and blend on HIGH speed for 4 to 5 seconds, or until vegetables are finely chopped. Pour over chicken in skillet.

4. Add bay leaf, tarragon, salt, and pepper. Cover skillet and simmer for 30 minutes.

5. Add tomatoes and simmer for 2 minutes, or until tomatoes are just heated through.

6. Combine cornstarch and water, stir into sauce in skillet and cook, stirring for 2 minutes longer.

7. Spoon sauce and tomatoes over chicken and sprinkle with chopped parsley.

CHICKEN IN SOUR CREAM SAUCE

Serves 4

½	pound mushrooms	½	cup dry white wine
1	lemon	2	green onions, coarsely cut
3½	pound chicken, cut in serving portions	1½	cups sour cream
		½	teaspoon salt
4	tablespoons butter (½ stick)	¼	teaspoon black pepper

1. Wash, trim and quarter the mushrooms. Put on absorbent paper to dry.

2. Remove thin yellow rind from lemon and set aside. Squeeze lemon and set juice aside.

3. Wash and dry chicken portions.

4. In a heavy skillet, melt butter and in it sauté chicken pieces until golden brown on all sides.

5. Meanwhile, put into container the mushrooms and dry white wine. Cover and blend on HIGH speed for 6 seconds, or until mushrooms are finely chopped. Add mixture to skillet and cook, stirring in all the brown bits from bottom and sides of pan.

6. Put sour cream, lemon rind, lemon juice, and green onions into container. Cover and blend on HIGH speed for 6 seconds, or until lemon rind and onions are finely chopped. Stir in with chicken in skillet and sprinkle with the salt and pepper. Cover and cook over low heat for 35 to 40 minutes, or until chicken is tender, stirring occasionally.

7. Correct seasoning with salt and serve with rice pilaf and a colorful vegetable.

CHICKEN IN RED WINE

Serves 4

3½	pound chicken, cut in serving pieces	½	green pepper, seeded and cut in strips
2	tablespoons olive oil	2	cloves garlic
2	tablespoons butter	½	teaspoon tarragon
One	1-pound can stewed tomatoes	1	teaspoon pepper
1	large onion, coarsely cut	¾	cup dry red wine

1. Wash and dry chicken pieces well.

2. In a heavy skillet, heat olive oil and butter and in it brown pieces of chicken over moderate heat.

3. Put into container the tomatoes, onion, green pepper, and garlic. Cover and blend on HIGH speed for 4 to 6 seconds, or until vegetables are finely chopped.

4. Pour mixture in container over chicken. Cover and cook over low heat, at a simmer, for 20 minutes, stirring occasionally.

5. Add the tarragon, salt, pepper, and wine. Cover and simmer for 20 minutes longer.

6. Correct seasoning with salt and serve with cooked rice or buttered noodles.

CHICKEN CANTONESE

Serves 6

½	cup flour	1	cup chicken broth
2	teaspoons salt	1	clove garlic
¼	teaspoon pepper	½	cup chutney with syrup
6	serving portions of chicken	1	tablespoon lemon juice
¼	cup cooking oil	1	tablespoon cornstarch
2	tablespoons butter	6–8	parsley clusters

1. Combine flour, salt, and pepper. Coat chicken pieces with the flour mixture.

2. Heat oil and butter in large skillet. Arrange chicken pieces in the hot fat and cook for about 20 minutes, or until lightly browned on all sides.

3. Into container put chicken broth and garlic. Cover and blend on HIGH speed for 6 seconds. Pour over chicken in skillet, cover, and cook over low heat for 30 minutes, or until chicken is tender.

4. Remove chicken to serving platter and keep warm. Return pan juices to container. Add remaining ingredients. Cover and blend on HIGH speed for 10 seconds. Return sauce to skillet and cook, stirring, over moderate heat until sauce is thickened.

5. Ladle sauce over chicken and serve with cooked rice.

CHILI CON POLLO

Serves 4

	4-pound roasting chicken, cut in serving pieces	4	tablespoons flour
One	13¾-ounce can chicken broth	2	cloves garlic
Two	1-pound cans whole tomatoes	2	large onions, coarsely cut
4	tablespoons chili powder		Juice of ½ lemon
1	teaspoon cumin seeds	1	teaspoon salt
1	teaspoon oregano	¼	teaspoon pepper

1. Put chicken pieces into a heavy saucepan with the chicken broth, salt, and pepper. Bring liquid to a boil.

2. Put into container 1 can tomatoes with juice, the chili powder, cumin seeds, oregano, flour, garlic, and onions. Cover and blend on HIGH speed for 6 seconds, or until onion is chopped.

3. Add blended mixture to chicken, add remaining can tomatoes, bring to a simmer, and cook over low heat for 1½ hours, or until chicken is tender, stirring occasionally.

4. Correct seasoning with salt and stir in lemon juice.

5. Serve with cooked rice and top with shredded lettuce.

CHICKEN PAPRIKASH

Serves 4

3	tablespoons cooking oil	2	tablespoons flour
	3-pound chicken, cut into serving portions	1	tablespoon paprika
1½	cups chicken broth	1½	teaspoons salt
	(13¾-ounce can)	½	teaspoon rosemary
1	medium onion, quartered	¼	teaspoon pepper
	Yellow rind of ½ lemon	½	cup sour cream

1. In a large heavy skillet, heat oil and in it sauté chicken pieces until golden on all sides.

2. Put into container the chicken stock, onion, lemon rind, flour,

paprika, salt, rosemary, and pepper. Cover and blend on HIGH speed for 15 seconds, or until onion and rind are finely chopped. Pour mixture over chicken and bring to a simmer, stirring occasionally. Cover and simmer for 40 minutes, stirring occasionally.

3.   Combine sour cream with ½ cup of the sauce from skillet. Stir into remaining sauce in skillet and heat to serving temperature without letting it boil.

4.   Serve with noodles.

DUCKLING BIGARADE

Serves 4

1	Long Island duckling, about 5 pounds	1	teaspoon lemon juice
	Rinds of 1 lemon and 1 orange	2	tablespoons cornstarch
1½	cups orange juice	½	teaspoon salt
1	teaspoon coarsely diced onion	½	teaspoon ginger

1.   Quarter duckling and roast in uncovered roasting pan in preheated 350° F. oven for 1 hour. Transfer to a covered baking dish or casserole.

2.   Put remaining ingredients into container. Cover and blend on HIGH speed for 1 minute, then pour into a saucepan. Bring to a boil, stirring constantly.

3.   Pour sauce over duckling in baking dish, cover, and continue baking for about 30 minutes longer, or until duckling is tender.

CURRIED CHICKEN LIVERS

Serves 2

12	ounces fresh or thawed chicken livers	½	tablespoon curry powder
2	tablespoons butter	½	teaspoon salt
½	cup chicken broth	1	tablespoon flour
1	small onion, quartered		Freshly ground black pepper
		½	cup heavy cream

1.   Remove connecting tissues between the two lobes of each liver and cut each lobe in half.

2. In a skillet, heat butter and in it sauté livers for 5 to 8 minutes, stirring frequently.

3. Put chicken broth, onion, curry powder, salt, and flour into container. Cover and blend on HIGH speed for 6 seconds. Pour mixture over livers and bring to a boil, stirring constantly.

4. Sprinkle generously with pepper and stir in the heavy cream. Cook over low heat for 2 minutes.

5. Serve with cooked rice or rice pilaf.

Poultry Stuffings

QUICK CHICKEN STUFFING

Enough for 1 roasting chicken

* ½ loaf bread, blender-crumbed
  2 medium onions, quartered
  ½ cup melted butter (1 stick)
  1 teaspoon salt
  ¼ teaspoon pepper
  1 teaspoon mixed dry herbs

1. Blender-crumb bread 2 slices at a time. Empty crumbs into bowl.

2. Into container put remaining ingredients. Cover and blend on HIGH speed for 6 seconds.

3. Mix with crumbs and correct seasoning to taste.

MATZO-PRUNE STUFFING FOR CHICKEN

Enough for 1 roasting chicken

8	prunes	3	tablespoons chicken fat
* 4	matzos, blender-crumbed	½	medium onion, coarsely cut
1	cup hot water	3	tablespoons sugar
3	eggs	¼	teaspoon cinnamon
1½	teaspoons salt		

1. Pour boiling water over prunes, let soak 15 minutes, then drain and pit.

2. Blender-crumb matzos coarsely, 1 at a time. Empty the crumbs into a bowl. Add hot water and mix.

3. Put into container remaining ingredients, including the prunes. Cover and blend on HIGH speed for 8 seconds. Empty over matzos and mix lightly. Stuff chicken, leaving room for the filling to expand, and roast in the usual manner.

MATZO BALLS FOR CHICKEN SOUP OR STEW

Makes 12 balls

3 tablespoons chicken fat
3 eggs
1 teaspoon salt
1 cup matzo meal

1. Into container put chicken fat, eggs, and salt. Cover and turn motor on HIGH speed. Remove cover, and with motor on, gradually pour in the matzo meal.

2. With thin rubber spatula or bottle scraper, remove mixture to a bowl, cover, and refrigerate for 30 minutes.

3. Bring a large pot of lightly salted water to a boil. Reduce heat and into the just simmering water drop balls formed from the chilled mixture. Cover and cook for 40 to 45 minutes.

4. Have soup at room temperature, or warmer, and remove matzo balls from water to soup pot. When ready to serve, bring soup to a boil and simmer for about 5 minutes.

POTATO STUFFING

Enough for a 10-pound bird

½ cup melted butter (1 stick)   2 medium onions, quartered
2 teaspoons salt   ¼ cup parsley clusters
½ teaspoon pepper   6 cups diced, cooked potatoes
½ teaspoon sage

1. Into container put melted butter, salt, pepper, sage, onions, and parsley clusters. Cover and blend on HIGH speed for 20 seconds, or until smooth.

2. Pour into mixing bowl and mix lightly with the diced cooked potatoes.

APPLE AND PRUNE STUFFING FOR GOOSE

Enough for a 10-pound goose

1	cup prunes
* 10	slices bread, blender-crumbed
3	medium apples, peeled and sliced
2	medium onions, quartered
3	stalks celery, coarsely cut
½	teaspoon marjoram
¼	pound soft butter or margarine (1 stick)
2	teaspoons salt
¼	teaspoon pepper
½	teaspoon thyme

* water-chopped in blender

1. Cook prunes in boiling water to cover for 15 minutes; drain and cool. Remove pits and reserve prunes.

2. Blender-crumb bread 2 slices at a time and empty into mixing bowl.

3. Loosely pack into container half the apples, onions, and celery and water-chop. Drain and empty into mixing bowl with crumbs. Repeat until all vegetables are chopped.

4. Put butter, salt, pepper, thyme, marjoram, and prunes into container. Cover and blend on high speed for 15 seconds, or until prunes are chopped. Empty into mixing bowl with crumbs and vegetables. Mix lightly.

NUT STUFFING FOR TURKEY

Enough for a 12-pound bird

* 16 slices bread, blender-crumbed
  2 cups nut meats
  1 cup melted butter (2 sticks)
  3 stalks celery, coarsely cut
  2 medium onions, quartered
  ½ cup hot water

  1 teaspoon thyme
  1 teaspoon mixed dried herbs
  2 teaspoons salt
  ½ teaspoon coarsely ground pepper
  ½ cup parsley clusters

1. Crumb bread in container, 2 slices at a time, and empty crumbs into large mixing bowl.

2. Grate the nuts, 1 cup at a time, and empty into bowl with crumbs.

3. Put remaining ingredients into container. Cover and blend on HIGH speed for 15 seconds. Pour over bread crumbs and mix until all the crumbs are moistened with the blended mixture.

Fish & Seafood Dishes

PESCADO DORADO

Serves 6 to 8

Whole baking fish, weighing about 4 pounds, ready to cook
2 large limes
2 teaspoons salt
½ teaspoon pepper
2 medium onions, quartered
12 pitted green olives
1 tablespoon capers

1 tablespoon juice from jar of capers
½ cup water
½ cup olive oil
2 cloves garlic
2 bay leaves
One 1¼-pound can whole tomatoes, drained
1 canned pimiento, sliced

1. Preheat oven to 500° F.

2. Wash fish inside and out. Cut 2 shallow gashes on both sides and place in buttered baking dish. Squeeze juice of the limes over fish and sprinkle with salt and pepper.

3. Put into container the onion, olives, capers and juice, water, olive oil, and garlic. Cover and blend on HIGH speed for 4 seconds.

4. Pour mixture in container over fish. Add bay leaves and tomatoes.

5. Bake in the preheated oven for 15 minutes. Reduce oven temperature to 425° F. and bake for 25 minutes longer, basting occasionally with pan juices.

6. Garnish with canned pimiento before serving.

FILLETS OF SOLE DUGLÉRÉ

Serves 4

4	fillets of sole or flounder	2	fresh tomatoes, peeled, or 2
2	tablespoons butter		canned tomatoes
¼	cup chicken broth	1	tablespoon flour
½	cup dry white wine	½	teaspoon salt
2	slices medium onion	¼	teaspoon coarsely ground
1	clove garlic		black pepper
6–8	parsley clusters		Parsley for garnish

1. Cut each fillet in half lengthwise and roll each half like a fat jelly roll. Secure with wooden pick.

2. In a skillet, melt half the butter. Arrange rolls in pan, curled side up. Add chicken broth, white wine, onion, garlic, parsley, and tomatoes. Bring liquid to a simmer, cover skillet, and let the fish poach for 5 minutes. Turn the rolls and poach for 5 minutes longer.

3. Remove fish to a warm serving platter and discard wooden picks. Empty liquid in skillet into blender container and add the flour, salt, pepper, and remaining tablespoon butter. Cover and blend on HIGH speed for 15 seconds.

4. Return sauce to skillet and cook over moderate heat, stirring constantly, for 2 minutes. Pour over fish rolls and tuck a sprig of parsley into center of each.

FISH MOUSSE WITH SHRIMP SAUCE

Serves 6. This mousse recipe is a classic French dish which, if made in the traditional manner, requires much beating and mashing and rubbing of the fish through a fine hair sieve. Your electric blender does it all in a matter of minutes, and the result is an epicurean dish of unbelievable delicacy and texture.

1	pound fillet of pike, red snapper, or halibut, or boneless fresh cod or salmon (very cold)	2	cups heavy cream (very cold)
		2	ice cubes, cracked
		1	teaspoon salt
		½	teaspoon white pepper
2	egg whites	¼	teaspoon nutmeg

1. Butter a 1-quart plain ring mold. Preheat oven to 350° F.

2. Cut the fish into strips ½ inch wide, making sure all bones have been discarded.

3. Put half of all the ingredients into container. Cover and blend for 20 seconds, or until smooth, stopping to stir down if necessary.

4. Empty into prepared mold and repeat the process with remaining ingredients. Empty into mold.

5. Cover mold with aluminum foil, place in a shallow pan containing 1 inch hot water, and bake in preheated oven 25 to 30 minutes, or until firm to the touch.

6. Remove mold from oven and let cool for 5 minutes. Then turn out and cover with Shrimp Sauce.

SHRIMP SAUCE

Makes about 3 cups

1	cup heavy cream	½	teaspoon white pepper
½	cup chicken stock or clam juice	½	teaspoon dry tarragon or 1 tablespoon fresh dill
½	cup dry white wine	6–8	parsley clusters
4	tablespoons soft butter (½ stick)	1	cup cooked, cleaned shrimp (½ pound)
2	tablespoons flour	1	teaspoon lemon juice
1	teaspoon salt		

1. Put cream, chicken stock or clam juice, wine, half the butter, flour, salt, pepper, and tarragon or dill into container. Cover and blend on LOW speed.

2. When blades reach full speed, switch to HIGH. With blades spinning, remove cover, and add parsley and shrimp. Turn motor off the second that the last shrimp is pulled down into the blades.

3. Empty into saucepan and cook over moderate heat, stirring constantly, until sauce is slightly thickened and steaming hot.

4. Just before serving, add remaining butter and lemon juice, and stir until butter is just melted.

GEFILTE FISH

Makes about 3 dozen, to serve 6 to 8

4 pounds fresh fish (white fish, carp, or pike) with skin, heads, and bones

STOCK:

- 2 medium onions, quartered
- 2 carrots, coarsely cut
- 1 stalk celery with leaves, coarsely cut
- 2 teaspoons salt
  Cold water

FISH BALLS:

- 2 eggs
- ½ cup water
- 2 teaspoons salt
- ¼ teaspoon pepper
- 1 medium onion, quartered
- 1 carrot, coarsely cut
- ¼ cup matzo meal

1. Fillet fish, reserving heads, bones, and skins. Dice fish and set aside for fish balls (about 3 cups diced). Place fish remains in large saucepan.

2. To prepare stock: Into container put onions, carrots, celery, and salt. Cover to within 1 inch from top of container with cold water. Cover and blend on HIGH speed for 2 to 3 seconds, or until vegetables are chopped. Empty into saucepan and add 1 quart water. Cover and simmer for 30 minutes.

3. Prepare fish balls: Into container put 1 egg, ¼ cup water, salt, pepper, and half the onion. Cover and turn motor on HIGH speed. With motor on, remove cover and gradually add half the fish and half the carrot; continue to blend for about 1 minute or until smooth, stopping to stir down if necessary. Empty into a small bowl. Into container put remaining egg, ¼ cup water, and onion, cover, and turn motor on HIGH speed. With blades

spinning, remove cover and gradually add remaining fish and carrot. Blend for 1 minute, or until smooth, stopping to stir down, if necessary. Empty into bowl with rest of fish mixture and stir in matzo meal. Chill 30 minutes.

4. With wet hands, shape mixture into small balls (using 1 tablespoon mixture for each). Place balls in simmering stock. Cover and simmer for 1½ to 2 hours.

5. Carefully remove fish balls from stock. Strain stock over fish balls and chill until liquid is slightly jellied. Serve with red horseradish.

RED HORSERADISH

Makes about 2 cups

1   cup diced fresh horseradish root
3   small cooked or canned beets
½   cup vinegar
1   teaspoon salt
1   tablespoon sugar

1. Put all ingredients into container. Cover and blend on HIGH speed for about 30 seconds. Empty into a preserving jar, and add more vinegar if necessary to cover.

2. Cover and store in refrigerator.

SALMON CASSEROLE SOUFFLÉ

Serves 4. Here is a quick, economical, and very good main course for lunch or supper. Serve it with a tossed salad.

4	slices bread, trimmed	½	teaspoon dry mustard
1	cup milk	1	thin slice medium onion
4	eggs	One	7¾-ounce can salmon
¼	teaspoon salt		

1. Preheat oven to 325° F. Butter a 1½-quart casserole.

2. Tear bread into container. Add remaining ingredients. Cover and blend on HIGH speed for 20 seconds.

3. Pour into prepared casserole and bake in preheated oven for 40 to 45 minutes. Serve hot.

SALMON DIVAN PROVENÇALE

Serves 4

* 4	tablespoons blender buttered crumbs	½	small clove garlic
One	1-pound can salmon	5	tablespoons flour
	Milk	½	teaspoon salt
Two	10-ounce packages frozen broccoli spears	¼	teaspoon pepper
		1	cup diced Cheddar cheese
4	tablespoons butter (½ stick)	2	whole tomatoes, peeled, fresh, or canned, cut in chunks

1. Make buttered bread crumbs and set aside.

2. Drain salmon into a measuring cup and add milk to make a total of 1½ cups liquid. Pour into a saucepan and heat to simmering.

3. Flake salmon into large chunks and set aside.

4. Cook broccoli half as long as directed on package and drain thoroughly.

5. Arrange broccoli in an 8-inch baking dish, 2 inches deep. Spread salmon over broccoli.

6. Put into blender container the butter, garlic, flour, salt, pepper, and half the hot milk-salmon mixture. Cover and blend on HIGH speed. As soon as blades reach full speed, remove cover, and pour in remaining milk. Add cheese and tomatoes and blend for 6 seconds, or until cheese is shredded.

7. Pour sauce over salmon and broccoli and sprinkle with bread crumbs.

8. Bake in preheated 400° F. oven for 20 to 25 minutes or until crumbs are lightly browned.

SALMONBURGERS

Serves 4

One 1-pound can salmon
  1 medium onion, quartered
  4 tablespoons melted butter
       (½ stick)
  1 slice bread
  2 eggs
  ¼ cup parsley clusters

  1 teaspoon dry mustard
  ½ teaspoon salt
* ½ cup blender-crumbed dry
       bread
  ½ cup cooking oil
       Lemon wedges for garnish

1. Drain liquid from salmon into blender container. Add onion, butter, bread, eggs, parsley, mustard, and salt. Cover container and blend on HIGH speed for 10 seconds.

2. Empty mixture from container into mixing bowl. Add salmon and mix well.

3. Shape into 4 large cakes and roll in dry bread crumbs. Sauté the cakes in the hot oil for 5 minutes on each side, or until golden.

4. Drain on absorbent paper and serve hot with lemon wedges.

CRAB OR SHRIMP CASSEROLE

Serves 4

* 1 slice bread, blender-crumbed
  3 tablespoons butter
  3 tablespoons flour
  ½ teaspoon salt
  1 teaspoon dry mustard
  ½ teaspoon paprika

1½ cups hot light cream
6–8 parsley clusters
  2 cups crab meat or 1 pound
       cleaned shrimp
       Butter

1. Preheat oven to 375° F. Butter a 1-quart shallow baking dish.

2. Blender-crumb bread, empty onto waxed paper, and set aside.

3. Put into container the butter, flour, salt, mustard, paprika, cream, and parsley clusters. Cover and blend on MEDIUM speed for 10 seconds.

4. With blades spinning, remove cover and dump in crab meat or

shrimp. Turn off motor the second that the last piece of seafood is pulled down into the blades.

5. Empty into a saucepan and cook over moderate heat, stirring constantly until sauce is thickened.

6. Empty into prepared baking pan and sprinkle with crumbs. Dot with butter and bake in the preheated oven for 25 to 30 minutes.

LOBSTER, CRAB, OR SHRIMP NEWBURG

Serves 4

2	cups hot milk	1	tablespoon brandy
4	tablespoons soft butter (½ stick)	2	cups cooked lobster, shrimp, or crab meat
6	tablespoons flour	½	cup heavy cream
½	teaspoon salt	2	egg yolks
⅛	teaspoon white pepper	3	tablespoons sherry

1. Put milk into container. Add butter, flour, salt, pepper, and brandy. Cover and blend on MEDIUM speed for 10 seconds.

2. With blades spinning, remove cover and add seafood. Turn off motor the second that the last piece of seafood is pulled down into the blades.

3. Empty into a saucepan and bring to a simmer, stirring constantly until sauce is thickened.

4. Combine cream, egg yolks, and sherry. Gradually stir into seafood mixture and cook over low heat for 2 minutes, stirring constantly. Do not let mixture boil.

5. Correct seasoning and serve on hot buttered toast.

DEVILED CRAB CAKES

Makes 4 cakes

* 4	slices bread, blender-crumbed	3	eggs
1	medium onion, quartered	One	6½-ounce can crab meat,
½	cup melted butter (1 stick)		flaked
½	teaspoon salt		Flour
1	teaspoon dry mustard		Butter
6–8	parsley clusters		Tartar Sauce (page 168)

1. Blender-crumb bread and empty into mixing bowl.

2. Into container put onion, butter, salt, mustard, parsley, and eggs. Cover and blend on HIGH speed for 15 seconds.

3. Empty into bowl with crumbs, add crab meat, and mix lightly.

4. Shape mixture into flat cakes, roll in flour, and brown in skillet in a little hot butter until golden on both sides.

5. Serve with Tartar Sauce.

CRAB MEAT LOUIS

Serves 2

1½	cups hot light cream		Dash of Tabasco sauce
2	tablespoons butter	¼	cup diced Cheddar or Swiss
2	green onions, coarsely cut		cheese
2	strips green pepper	3–4	parsley clusters
3	tablespoons flour	One	6½-ounce can crab meat
½	teaspoon dry mustard		

1. Into container put hot cream, butter, onions, green pepper, flour, mustard, Tabasco, cheese, and parsley. Cover and blend on HIGH speed for 15 seconds.

2. Empty into a saucepan and bring to a boil, stirring constantly. Cook over low heat for 2 minutes, stirring occasionally.

3. Add crab meat and heat to serving temperature.

NOB HILL SHRIMP

Serves 4

1	cup chicken broth	$\frac{1}{8}$	teaspoon hot red pepper flakes
1	small clove garlic	2	tablespoons dry sherry
$\frac{1}{2}$	teaspoon salt	$\frac{1}{2}$	cup cream
1	bay leaf	$1\frac{1}{2}$	pounds shrimp, shelled and
$\frac{1}{4}$	cup parsley clusters		deveined
2	tablespoons cornstarch		Cooked wild rice
2	tablespoons soft butter		

1. Put into container the chicken broth, garlic, salt, bay leaf, parsley, cornstarch, butter, pepper flakes, and sherry. Cover and blend on HIGH speed for 10 seconds, or until smooth. With blades spinning, remove lid and gradually pour in cream.

2. Pour into saucepan and bring to a boil, stirring occasionally. Simmer for 2 minutes.

3. Add shrimp, cover, and simmer for 10 minutes, or until shrimp are tender, stirring occasionally. Serve on bed of wild rice.

SHRIMP OR SCALLOPS AU GRATIN

Serves 4

*	$\frac{1}{2}$	cup blender-crumbed bread	6	tablespoons butter
*	$\frac{1}{4}$	cup blender-grated Parmesan cheese	3	green onions, coarsely cut
	1	cup dry white wine	2	strips green pepper
		Small bay leaf	2	tablespoons flour
	1	stalk celery, coarsely cut	6–8	parsley clusters
	1	teaspoon salt	1	cup cream
	$\frac{1}{4}$	teaspoon peppercorns	2	egg yolks
	2	pound shrimp, shelled and deveined, or scallops, washed and quartered		

1. Combine bread crumbs and grated cheese and set aside.

2. Preheat oven to 375° F. Butter a shallow 2-quart baking dish.

3. In a saucepan, combine wine, bay leaf, celery, salt, and peppercorns. Bring to a simmer, add shrimp or scallops, and cook over low heat for 10 minutes. Do not let liquid boil. Remove seafood to prepared dish with slotted spoon. Strain liquid from seafood, return to saucepan, and cook over high heat until reduced to ½ cup.

4. Empty reduced liquid into container. Add half the butter, green onions, green pepper, flour, and parsley. Cover and blend on HIGH speed for 15 seconds. Empty into saucepan, and cook over moderate heat, stirring constantly, until sauce is thickened. Cook over low heat for 5 minutes, stirring occasionally.

5. Combine cream and egg yolks and stir into the sauce. Remove from heat and pour over seafood in baking dish. Sprinkle with bread crumbs and cheese and dot with remaining butter.

6. Bake in preheated oven for 15 minutes, or until sauce is bubbling.

SCALLOPS POULETTE

Serves 3

1 pound fresh or thawed sea scallops	3 tablespoons flour
3 tablespoons soft butter	½ teaspoon salt
1 slice medium onion	⅛ teaspoon white pepper
½ cup dry white wine	3–4 parsley clusters
½ bay leaf	½ cup heavy cream
¼ pound mushrooms, washed and quartered	2 egg yolks
	1 teaspoon lemon juice

1. Wash scallops under cold running water, slice, and set aside.

2. Put onion and white wine into a saucepan and bring just to a simmer.

3. Into container put butter, bay leaf, mushrooms, flour, salt, pepper, and parsley. Pour in hot wine and onion. Cover and blend on HIGH speed for 4 seconds.

4. Empty into saucepan and bring to a boil, stirring constantly, until sauce is thickened. Add scallops and cook over low heat for 2 minutes, stirring occasionally.

5. Combine cream, egg yolks, and lemon juice with a little of the hot sauce. Stir gradually into mixture in saucepan and cook over very low heat, stirring constantly, for 3 minutes. Do not let the sauce boil.

CLAMS AU GRATIN

Serves 3

6	tablespoons butter (¾ stick)	Pinch of tarragon
* 4	slices bread, blender-crumbed	Dash of white pepper
One	9-ounce can minced clams	Salt, if necessary
1	cup hot milk	1 egg
3	tablespoons flour	

1. Heat half the butter in a small skillet.

2. Crumb bread one slice at a time and empty into the hot butter. Sauté crumbs, stirring constantly, until golden brown. Set aside.

3. Put remaining butter into container. Drain liquid from minced clams into container and add hot milk, flour, tarragon, and white pepper. Cover and blend on HIGH speed for 15 seconds.

4. Empty into saucepan and cook, stirring constantly, until sauce is thickened and smooth. Add a little salt, if needed, and remove from heat.

5. Combine the egg with a little of the hot sauce. Stir egg mixture gradually into sauce in pan. Cool a little, then stir in the clams.

6. Preheat oven to 350° F.

7. Sprinkle a little crumb mixture into bottom of shallow au gratin dish. Empty in the clam mixture and sprinkle with the remaining crumbs.

8. Bake in preheated oven for 15 minutes, or until sauce is bubbling.

Cold Entrées & Savory Mousses

In this section are molded warm-weather dishes in which cooked diced chicken, ham, corned beef, tongue, turkey meat are all interchangeable, one meat for another. Cooked crab meat, lobster, salmon, or shrimp may also be changed at will in those recipes specifying fish as the main ingredient.

First, however, is a very special, famous cold Italian dish for which the sauce is quite a lot of trouble to make unless you have a blender. The combination sounds incredible, but actually it is delicious.

VEAL WITH TUNA SAUCE
(Vitello Tonnato)

Serves 6 to 8

FOR THE MEAT AND VEAL STOCK:

One	2-ounce can anchovies	1	bay leaf
1	clove garlic, cut in thin slivers	1	small carrot, quartered
3	pounds of boned leg of veal	1	stalk celery, quartered
2	quarts water	6–8	parsley clusters
1	medium onion, quartered	6	peppercorns
2	cloves	1	teaspoon salt

FOR THE SAUCE:

One	3-ounce can Italian tuna fish, drained		Pinch of cayenne pepper
¾	cup olive oil	¼	cup heavy cream
1	egg yolk		About ¼ cup cold meat stock from veal
2	tablespoons lemon juice	2	tablespoons capers, drained

FOR GARNISH:

* Blender-chopped parsley and chives
4 ripe tomatoes, peeled and sliced
2 hard-cooked eggs, quartered
2 lemons, cut in wedges
 Black olives

1. Drain anchovies and reserve half of them. Cut remaining anchovies into slivers. Make small incisions along length of veal with a small pointed

knife and insert in each a piece of anchovy and a thin sliver of garlic. Tie the meat securely with string.

2. Put water into a large saucepan and add onion, cloves, bay leaf, carrot, celery, parsley, peppercorns, and salt. Bring to a boil. Place the veal in the saucepan, cover, and simmer for 1½ hours, or until meat is tender but still firm. Remove saucepan from heat and let the veal cool in the stock.

3. To make the sauce: Put into container the tuna fish, olive oil, egg, lemon juice, cayenne, and the reserved anchovy fillets. Cover and blend on HIGH speed for about 12 seconds, or until smooth. With blades spinning, remove cover and gradually pour in cream and ¼ cup veal stock. The sauce should just be the consistency of heavy cream. If too thick, blend in a little more veal stock. Add capers, and blend for just 1 second, or until capers are drawn down into blades.

4. Remove meat from stock, wipe dry, and carve into thin slices, discarding any fat or gristle.

5. Spread bottom of a shallow serving platter with a thin layer of the tuna sauce and in it place the slices of veal, side by side. Pour the rest of the sauce over the slices, and spread with a spatula so that each piece of meat is lightly coated with the sauce. Cover platter with transparent film and chill overnight.

6. Remove veal from refrigerator a couple of hours before serving. Sprinkle with chopped parsley and chives.

7. Before serving, garnish platter with tomatoes, hard-cooked eggs, lemon sections, and black olives.

CHICKEN MOUSSE

Serves 4. A delicate and delicious warm weather luncheon dish is ready to chill in 1½ minutes. Serve with a cool glass of dry white wine.

1	envelope plain gelatin	3–4	parsley clusters
2	tablespoons sherry	1	teaspoon tarragon
1	small slice onion	1	cup heavy cream
½	cup boiling chicken broth		Watercress
½	cup mayonnaise		Sliced cucumber
3	cups diced cooked chicken		Radishes

1. Put gelatin into container. Add sherry, onion, and boiling stock. Cover and blend on HIGH speed for 60 seconds.

2. Add mayonnaise, chicken, parsley, and tarragon. Cover and blend on HIGH speed for 10 seconds, stopping to stir down if necessary.

3. With blades spinning, remove cover, gradually pour in heavy cream, and blend until mixture is smooth.

4. Pour into a 4-cup ring mold and chill for several hours, or until firm.

5. Turn out onto chilled serving platter and fill center with watercress. Garnish platter with sliced cucumbers and radishes.

SALMON MOUSSE

Use a 1-pound can salmon, drained, in place of the chicken.

HAM MOUSSSE

Use 3 cups diced ham in place of chicken.

JELLIED CHICKEN OR TURKEY ROYAL

Serves 6 to 8

2	tablespoons sherry	1/4	teaspoon dry mustard
1	envelope plain gelatin		Dash of cayenne pepper
1/2	cup hot chicken broth	2	cups diced cooked chicken
3/4	cup cool chicken broth	1	egg white, stiffly beaten
1	egg yolk	1	cup heavy cream, whipped
1/2	small onion		Salad greens and cherry
1/4	cup parsley clusters		tomatoes for garnish
1	teaspoon salt		

1. Put sherry, gelatin, and the hot chicken broth into container. Cover and blend on HIGH speed for 50 seconds.

2. Add to mixture in container, the cool chicken broth, egg yolk, onion, parsley, salt, mustard, and cayenne. Cover and turn blender on HIGH. With blades spinning, remove cover and gradually add the chicken. Continue blending until mixture is smooth.

3. Empty into a mixing bowl and fold in egg white and whipped cream. Turn into an oiled 1-quart mold and chill until firm.

4. When set, unmold onto cool serving plate and garnish with salad greens and tomatoes.

HAM MOUSSE

Serves 6

½ cup hot water	½ teaspoon Tabasco sauce
2 envelopes plain gelatin	3 cups diced cooked ham
1 cup chicken broth	2 egg whites, beaten stiff
2 egg yolks	1 cup heavy cream, whipped
¼ cup dry sherry	Tomato slices for garnish
½ small onion	

1. Into container put the hot water and plain gelatin. Cover and blend on HIGH speed for 50 seconds.

2. Add the chicken broth, egg yolks, sherry, onion, and Tabasco. Cover and blend on HIGH speed. Remove lid and gradually add the cooked diced ham.

3. Continue blending until smooth. Fold into egg whites and heavy cream.

4. Turn into an oiled 1½-quart mold. Chill until set. Unmold and garnish with tomato slices.

CRAB MEAT MOUSSE

Serves 4

½ cup hot water	¼ cup parsley clusters
1 envelope plain gelatin	1 cup sour cream
1 thin slice medium onion	¼ teaspoon Tabasco sauce
1 7½-ounce can crab meat, drained and cartilage removed	½ teaspoon salt
	Tomato wedges

1. Put gelatin and boiling water into container. Cover and blend on HIGH speed for 50 seconds.

2. Add remaining ingredients. Cover and blend on HIGH speed for 30 seconds, or until smooth.

3. Turn into 3-cup mold. Chill until set. Unmold and garnish with tomato wedges.

CREAM CHEESE AND SHRIMP LOAF

Serves 6

* 9 zwieback, blender-crumbed
1¼ teaspoons salt
3 tablespoons melted butter
2 tablespoons lemon juice
1 envelope plain gelatin
1 green onion, coarsely cut
⅓ cup boiling water

1 pound cream cheese, sliced
¼ cup parsley clusters
1 pound shrimp, cooked,
   shelled, and deveined
Lettuce
Tomatoes for garnish

1. Blender-crumb half zwieback, then the remainder. In a small bowl, mix zwieback crumbs with ¼ teaspoon of the salt and the melted butter. Press mixture onto bottom and sides of a 1-quart loaf or spring-form pan.

2. Put lemon juice, gelatin, green onion, and boiling water into container. Cover and blend on HIGH speed for 60 seconds. With blades spinning, remove cover and add cream cheese, slice by slice. Blend until smooth.

3. Add remaining salt, parsley, and shrimp. Cover and blend on HIGH speed for 15 seconds, or until smooth, stopping to stir down if necessary.

4. Turn into crumb-coated pan and chill until set.

5. Turn out onto chilled platter and garnish with lettuce greens and tomato sections.

HAM OR CORNED BEEF AND EGG LOAF

Serves 6

2 tablespoons lemon juice
2 envelopes plain gelatin
1 thin slice onion
½ cup boiling water
½ cup blender mayonnaise
   (page 27)
1 cup diced celery
1½ cups diced cooked ham or a
   12-ounce can corned beef
½ cup cream

½ teaspoon salt
Dash of pepper
½ teaspoon dry mustard
½ cup hot chicken broth
1 cup cool chicken broth
1 green onion, coarsely cut
4 hard-cooked eggs
1 small dill pickle, quartered
Salad greens, olives, and
   radishes for garnish

1. Put lemon juice and 1 envelope plain gelatin into container with onion and boiling water. Cover and blend on HIGH speed for 50 seconds.

2. Add mayonnaise, celery, ham or corned beef, and cream. Cover and blend on HIGH speed for 5 seconds, or until meat and celery are coarsely cut, stopping to stir down if necessary.

3. Empty into a 5-cup loaf pan and chill until set.

4. Put salt, pepper, mustard, hot chicken broth, and remaining envelope gelatin into container. Blend on HIGH speed for 50 seconds. With blades spinning, remove cover, and pour in the cool chicken broth.

5. Drop eggs, one at a time, then the pickle into the blending mixture and turn motor off the instant the last piece of pickle is pulled down into blades.

6. Pour egg mixture on top of ham mixture and chill until firm. Unmold on bed of salad greens and garnish with olives and radishes. Cut into slices to serve.

JELLIED HAM-VEGETABLE RING

Serves 6

1 envelope plain gelatin	1 cup diced cooked potatoes
⅓ cup hot water	1 cup chopped celery
2 10½-ounce cans beef consommé with gelatin	4 tablespoons chopped parsley
	½ cup chopped green onions
½ pound boiled ham, thinly sliced	½ teaspoon salt
	¼ teaspoon pepper
1 cup cooked peas	Salad greens or watercress for garnish
1 cup diced cooked carrots	

1. Put gelatin and hot water into container. Cover and blend on HIGH speed for 50 seconds. With blades spinning, remove cover, and pour in the beef consommé.

2. Coat bottom of a 6-cup ring mold with blended consommé and chill until set. Reserve remaining consommé; do not chill.

3. Dip ham slices, one at a time, into the consommé and line the mold with the ham, overlapping each slice slightly. Chill again until set.

4. Meanwhile, combine vegetables, salt, pepper, and remaining consommé, and chill until mixture is just beginning to set. Pour into the prepared mold and chill until set.

5. When ready to serve, unmold on serving platter and fill center with salad greens or watercress. Serve with a mayonnaise salad dressing.

CREAMED HAM MOLD

Serves 4

1 cup beef stock or consommé	¼ cup parsley clusters
1 envelope plain gelatin	1 teaspoon Worcestershire sauce
½ small onion	Dash of pepper
One 4½-ounce can deviled ham	
One 3-ounce package cream cheese, cubed	

1. In a small saucepan, heat to boiling ½ cup beef stock or consommé. Pour into container and add envelope gelatin. Cover and blend on HIGH speed for 50 seconds.

2. Add onion, deviled ham, cream cheese, parsley clusters, Worcestershire sauce, and pepper. Cover and blend on HIGH speed for 30 seconds, or until smooth. With blades spinning, remove lid, and gradually add the remaining cold stock or beef consommé.

3. Turn into a 3-cup mold. Chill until set. Unmold and garnish with pimiento strips and salad greens.

SAVORY SAUCES

Savory Sauces

THE FIRST of these is Hollandaise, that tricky combination of eggs, butter, and lemon juice that is so marvelous to serve over broccoli or asparagus, on top of poached eggs, or with poached fish or savory mousses.

It is one of the great classic recipes that can be made in an electric blender better than by any other method, all the others being time-consuming and difficult if you are not an experienced cook. With a blender there is no worry that the Hollandaise may not thicken or may curdle, and it may be stored in the refrigerator for at least a week, or even frozen for longer life, and reheated over hot water. It is a real boon to fine cooking, for a few spoonfuls of Hollandaise stirred into a cream or velouté sauce before serving adds an indefinable touch of quality to the dish.

Blender Hollandaise is one of my few claims to fame and was simply an amplification of the basic recipe for making blender mayonnaise. If a blender would homogenize oil, egg, and vinegar, it seemed logical that it would do the same for melted butter, egg, and lemon juice. It did, and it did it beautifully. The only precaution I advise is to make sure the butter is really hot and not just melted. When melted butter begins to bubble, it does not mean it is boiling—the water contained in the butter is simply evaporating. When the bubbling stops and the butter becomes still, BUT BEFORE IT BEGINS TO BROWN, is the perfect moment to add it to the eggs and lemon juice in the container.

Hollandaise & Mayonnaise
& Their Variations

HOLLANDAISE SAUCE TO SERVE SIX

Makes 1 1/4 cups

½ pound butter (2 sticks)
4 egg yolks
2 tablespoons lemon juice
   Pinch of salt
   Good pinch of cayenne pepper

1. In a small saucepan, heat the butter until very hot, but do not let it begin to brown.

2. Put egg yolks, lemon juice, salt, and cayenne into container. Cover container and turn on MEDIUM speed.

3. As soon as the blades have reached full speed, remove cover, and pour in the hot butter in a steady stream.

NOTE: Serve Hollandaise sauce immediately or keep it warm by setting the container in a deep saucepan of hot water. Should the sauce become too thick while standing, add 1 tablespoon hot water and blend briefly.

HOLLANDAISE SAUCE TO SERVE FOUR

Makes ¾ cup

¼ pound butter (1 stick)
3 egg yolks
2 tablespoons lemon juice
   Pinch of salt
   Good pinch of cayenne pepper

Follow same directions as in previous recipe.

SAUCE BÉARNAISE

Makes about 1 cup.   For grilled or sautéed meats.

2 tablespoons white wine
1 tablespoon tarragon vinegar
1 tablespoon chopped fresh tarragon or 1 teaspoon dried
1 tablespoon chopped green onions or shallots
¼ teaspoon freshly ground black pepper

1. Put white wine, vinegar, tarragon, onions or shallots, and pepper into a small saucepan. Bring to a boil and cook rapidly until almost all liquid has evaporated.

2. Scrape remaining mixture into container with ¾ cup blender Hollandaise. Stir to combine, cover, and blend on HIGH speed for 6 seconds.

SAUCE AURORIAN

Makes 1½ cups. Especially good on poached fish or cold fish mousse in aspic.

Into ¾ cup blender Hollandaise fold 3 tablespoons mayonnaise and ½ cup whipped cream. Store in refrigerator.

AFTER Hollandaise, Mayonnaise is the next most important sauce in a cook's repertoire. It is truly a basic sauce for everyone, and the recipe is given in the Mini-Course in Blender Cooking, on page 27. Herewith are a few savory sauces made from a mayonnaise base. And, a group of mayonnaise-based salad dressings begins on page 27.

SAUCE TARTAR

Makes 1½ cups. For fried fish or seafood.

	Blender Mayonnaise (page 27)
3–4	parsley clusters
2	cloves garlic
5	sweet gherkin pickles
3	pitted green olives
¼	teaspoon pepper

1. Make Blender Mayonnaise and leave in container.

2. Add remaining ingredients, stir to combine, cover, and blend on HIGH speed for 6 seconds.

SAUCE RAVIGOTE

Makes 1½ cups. For sautéed fish fillets or trout.

2	tablespoons capers	1	tablespoon lemon juice
6–8	parsley clusters	1¼	cup Blender Mayonnaise
1	clove garlic		(page 27)
2	tablespoons coarsely cut onion	1	hard-cooked egg
⅓	cup white wine		

1. In a saucepan, combine capers, parsley, garlic, onion, white wine, and lemon juice. Bring to a boil and simmer for 15 minutes.

2. Make mayonnaise, and when thick, stop motor and add the cooked vegetable mixture. Stir to combine, cover, and blend on HIGH speed for 3 seconds. Stop blender, stir, and blend again for 5 seconds.

3. Poke the hard-cooked egg gently down into the spinning blades with a rubber spatula, and turn off blender immediately.

COLD "HOT" SAUCE

Makes ¾ cups.   For green beans, asparagus, or other vegetables.

	Blender Mayonnaise (page 27)	1	tablespoon Worcestershire
4	hard-cooked eggs, quartered		sauce
1–3	teaspoons Tabasco sauce, to	1	teaspoon prepared mustard
	taste	2	teaspoons olive oil
2	small cloves garlic		

1. Make mayonnaise and leave in container.

2. Add remaining ingredients, stir to combine, cover, and blend on HIGH speed for 15 seconds, or until smooth.

GREEN MAYONNAISE

Makes 1½ cups.   For fish or eggs.

1	egg	1	cup salad oil
½	teaspoon dry mustard	¼	cup parsley clusters
½	teaspoon salt	1	sweet gherkin
2	tablespoons vinegar	2	green onions, coarsely cut
½	clove garlic		

1. Put in container the egg, mustard, salt, vinegar, garlic, and ¼ cup oil. Cover and turn motor on HIGH. With blades spinning, remove center cover and add remaining oil in a steady stream.

2. Add parsley, gherkin, and green onions and blend for 15 seconds, or until vegetables are finely chopped.

SKORDALIA

Makes 1½ cups. This is the Greek version of the heavily garlicked mayonnaise sauce, called Aïoli (page 204) made in France. It's wonderfully gutsy served with boiled beef and its accompanying vegetables, or with cooked artichokes, fried eggplant, cold boiled lobsters, or hard-cooked eggs.

```
      Blender Mayonnaise (page 27)
 ½    cup blanched almonds
 2    cloves garlic
 6–8  parsley clusters
```

Make mayonnaise and leave in container. Add remaining ingredients, stir to combine, cover, and blend on HIGH speed for 15 seconds.

Cream or White Sauces

NEXT are cream or white sauces, those bugaboos for the novice homemaker, which are so easy to make in an electric blender that no one need ever fear a lumpy sauce or gravy again. The basic recipe is included in the Mini-Course in Blender Cooking, on page 23, but I repeat it here in brief with its many variations for easy reference.

BASIC MEDIUM WHITE SAUCE

Makes 2 cups

```
 2    cups hot milk
 4    tablespoons flour
 4    tablespoons soft butter (½ stick)
 ½    teaspoon salt
 ⅛    teaspoon white pepper
```

1. Pour 1 cup of the hot milk into container and add the flour, butter, salt, and pepper. Cover and turn blender on LOW speed.

2. As soon as blades have reached full speed, switch to HIGH. Remove cover and gradually pour in remaining hot milk.

3. Pour into a saucepan and cook over low heat for 3 minutes, stirring occasionally, or pour immediately over other ingredients in a casserole or baking dish to be baked.

THIN WHITE SAUCE FOR SOUPS

Use only half the amount of flour and butter in basic recipe.

THICK WHITE SAUCE FOR CROQUETTES OR LOAVES

Use 6 tablespoons each flour and butter.

CHEESE SAUCE

Add to White Sauce in container 1 cup diced Cheddar, Gruyère, or Swiss cheese, ½ teaspoon dry mustard, and a dash of Tabasco sauce, and continue blending until cheese is finely grated.

CHICKEN À LA KING SAUCE

Makes 3 cups

Make Thick White Sauce, substituting 1 cup hot chicken broth for 1 cup of the hot milk. Gradually pour into ingredients in container 1 cup cream and 2 to 3 tablespoons dry sherry.

TOMATO SAUCE

Makes 2¾ cups

Make Medium White Sauce. With blades revolving, add ¾ cup (6 ounces) tomato paste, and continue to blend until thoroughly blended.

CHICKEN VELOUTÉ SAUCE

Makes 2 cups

Make Medium White or Thick White Sauce, substituting hot chicken broth for all or part of the hot milk.

CREAM SAUCE

Makes 3 cups

Make Thick White or Velouté Sauce. With blades revolving pour in 1 cup heavy cream.

NEWBURG SAUCE

Makes about 3 cups

Make Thick White Sauce. With blades revolving, add 2 egg yolks, 1½ cups heavy cream, and ¼ cup dry sherry.

MOCK HOLLANDAISE SAUCE

Makes 3 cups

Make just 1 cup Medium White Sauce (use only half the ingredients in basic recipe). With blades revolving, add 2 cups mayonnaise, 1 tablespoon lemon juice, and Tabasco sauce to taste.

GOOD CURRY SAUCE FOR LAMB
OR CHICKEN

Makes 2½ cups

1	medium onion, coarsely chopped	4	tablespoons flour
1	clove garlic	3	tablespoons butter
1	medium apple, peeled, cored, and sliced	1	cup hot chicken broth or beef consommé
1	tablespoon curry powder	1	cup hot milk or water
		½	cup cream

1. Into container put the onion, garlic, apple, curry powder, flour, butter, and broth or consommé. Cover and turn motor on LOW speed. As soon as blades reach full motion, switch to HIGH.

2. Without stopping blender, remove cover and gradually pour in the hot milk or water and the cream. Blend for 3 seconds longer.

3. Empty into a saucepan, correct seasoning to taste, and cook over low heat for 10 minutes, stirring frequently.

HERE IS ANOTHER basic curry sauce for chicken, lamb, beef, or fish. Add to it any additional spices to make it more fragrant, such as poppy seeds, ground cumin, turmeric, or coriander; add red pepper or ginger to make it hotter and more typical of the East. And a wonderfully good last minute touch to any curry is the addition of diced papaya or melon just before serving. Let the fruit heat in the sauce, but do not cook it.

Should fresh coconuts be available, you might like to substitute coconut milk for the milk and coconut cream for the heavy cream. It's so easy to make with an electric blender (below).

BLENDER CURRY SAUCE

Makes about 5 cups, for 4 cups cooked meat, fish or poultry.

½ cup butter (1 stick)
1 medium onion, coarsely
   chopped
1 small tart apple, quartered
   and cored
1 tablespoon curry powder
2 large pieces preserved ginger

½ cup flour
2 cups hot chicken stock
1 cup milk or coconut milk
   Salt to taste
1 cup heavy cream or coconut
   cream

1. Melt butter in a saucepan and in it sauté onion over moderate heat for 8 minutes, or until onion is tender but not browned.

2. Empty onion and butter into container. Add apple, curry powder, ginger, flour, and chicken stock. Cover and blend on HIGH speed for 10 seconds, or until ingredients are well blended.

3. Return blended mixture to saucepan and cook over moderate heat, stirring constantly, for 4 minutes. Stir in milk.

4. Add the meat, fish, or poultry and keep hot over simmering water until just ready to serve. Add salt to taste and just before serving stir in the cream or coconut cream. Heat for a few minutes longer, but do not boil.

COCONUT MILK AND CREAM

Remove coconut meat from shell and dice coarsely (no need to peel). Put 1 cup of the diced coconut into container and add 2 cups boiling water. Cover and blend on HIGH speed for 30 seconds.

Pour into a sieve which is set into a bowl and press coconut with back of a spoon to extract as much coconut milk as possible. Let the milk stand so that the cream rises to the top. There will be about ½ cup coconut cream and 1 cup coconut milk.

Condensed-Soup Sauces

MANY canned, condensed soups—mushroom, celery, and cream of chicken— make quick and interesting sauces when combined with each other, with sour cream, or with diced cheese and spices. Here are just a few samples— you take it from there.

GOLDEN CREAM SAUCE

Makes 1¾ cups.   For fish, chicken or vegetables.

Put into container a 10½-ounce can condensed cream of chicken soup, ½ cup mayonnaise, ¼ teaspoon curry, a few clusters of parsley, and 1 table-spoon lemon juice. Cover and blend on HIGH speed for 6 seconds. Serve hot or cold.

MUSHROOM ONION SAUCE

Makes 2½ cups.   For lamb, chicken, fish or casserole dishes.

Put into container a 10½-ounce can condensed cream of mushroom soup, a 10½-ounce can cream of onion soup, and ⅛ teaspoon nutmeg. Cover and blend on HIGH speed for 10 seconds. Pour into a saucepan and heat to serving temperature.

CELERY CUCUMBER SAUCE

Makes 1¾ cups.   For fish.

Put into container a 10½-ounce can condensed cream of celery soup, 1 slim cucumber, peeled and coarsely cut, 1 small onion, quartered, and a few clusters of parsley. Cover and blend on HIGH speed for 10 seconds. Cor-rect seasoning and fold in ½ cup sour cream. Serve hot or cold.

ZESTY CREAM SAUCE

Makes 1½ cups. For fish or vegetables.

One	10½-ounce can condensed cream of chicken, celery, or mushroom soup	1	tablespoon lemon juice or vinegar
¼	cup milk	1	hard-cooked egg
½	teaspoon dry mustard	2	tablespoons sweet pickle relish

1. Put into container the soup, milk, mustard, and lemon juice or vinegar. Cover and blend on HIGH speed for 10 seconds.

2. With blades revolving, add the egg and push it down into the blades with a rubber spatula.

3. Turn off motor immediately and fold in the pickle relish.

Barbecue Sauces & Basting Sauces

HERB SAUCE FOR BROILED STEAK

Makes enough for 1 large or 4 individual steaks

¼	cup brandy or bourbon	½	teaspoon tarragon
½	clove garlic	½	teaspoon thyme
½	small onion	¼	teaspoon rosemary
¼	cup parsley clusters	1	tablespoon oil
½	teaspoon salt		
½	teaspoon coarsely ground pepper		

1. Put all ingredients into container. Cover and blend on HIGH speed for 15 seconds.

2. Brush over steak frequently during the broiling period.

BARBECUE SAUCE FOR STEAK OR CHOPS

Makes about 2 cups

1   small onion, chopped
1   large clove garlic
1   cup catsup
½   cup water
2   tablespoons brown sugar
½   teaspoon salt
    Good dash of cayenne pepper

¼   cup vinegar
¼   cup lemon juice
3   tablespoons Worcestershire
    sauce
1   tablespoon prepared mustard

1. Put all ingredients into container. Cover and blend on HIGH speed for 15 seconds.

2. Empty into saucepan, bring to a boil, and simmer for 30 minutes, stirring occasionally.

BARBECUE SAUCE FOR BROILED CHICKEN

Makes 1½ cups

1   cup chicken stock
½   clove garlic
1   tablespoon salad oil
1   stalk celery with leaves,
        coarsely cut
1   carrot, coarsely cut

1   teaspoon salt
¼   teaspoon pepper
1   teaspoon curry powder
½   teaspoon dry mustard
¼   cup parsley clusters

1. Put all ingredients into container. Cover and blend on HIGH speed for 10 seconds.

2. Pour into small saucepan and simmer for 20 minutes, stirring occasionally.

3. Brush chicken frequently with the sauce while broiling.

BARBECUE SAUCE FOR SPARERIBS, PORK CHOPS, OR CHICKEN

Makes 3 cups

1   cup catsup
½   cup chili sauce
¼   cup vinegar
⅓   cup brown sugar
½   large onion, coarsely cut
1   large stalk celery, coarsely cut

2   teaspoons Worcestershire
      sauce
1   teaspoon dry mustard
½   teaspoon salt
Dash of cayenne pepper

1. Put all ingredients into container. Cover and blend on HIGH speed for 20 seconds.

2. Empty into saucepan, bring to a boil, and simmer for 15 minutes.

BASTING SAUCE FOR ROAST OR BARBECUED DUCK

Makes 1 cup

1   small unpeeled orange, coarsely cut and seeded
½   cup vinegar
¼   teaspoon tarragon
¼   cup light brown sugar
1   tablespoon prepared mustard

1. Put all ingredients into container. Cover and blend on HIGH speed for 30 seconds, or until orange is finely cut.

2. Empty into a saucepan, bring to a boil, and simmer for 5 minutes.

3. Use to baste duck every half hour after the first 30 minutes of roasting.

BARBECUE SAUCE FOR ROAST PORK OR DUCKLING

Makes 1½ cups

¼ cup lemon juice
¼ cup salad oil
½ teaspoon salt
¼ teaspoon pepper
1 piece preserved or candied ginger
1 cup seeded orange or tangerine segments

Put all ingredients into container. Cover and blend on HIGH speed for 30 seconds. Heat until bubbling.

Miscellaneous Sauces for Meats, Seafood, & Vegetables

AND FINALLY, a small collection of good savory sauces quickly combined in your blender. Throughout the book you will find many other sauces, so if you don't find what you are looking for in this chapter, consult the Index.

MINT SAUCE

Makes 1½ cups. Good with cold meats.

1 cup fresh mint leaves
1 tablespoon sugar
2 tablespoons vinegar
½ teaspoon salt
1 cup warm water

Put all ingredients into container. Cover and blend on HIGH speed until mint is finely chopped.

GOOD STRONG HORSERADISH

Makes about 1 cup.   If you know anyone who has fresh horseradish growing in his backyard, beg or steal a root. Once you've tasted it freshly grated, you'll never be satisfied with the commercial brands. And if you've ever hand-grated horseradish, you'll bless your blender! No tears!

1   large fresh horseradish root
1   cup white vinegar
2   teaspoons sugar

1. Wash and peel the horseradish, and cut into coarse chunks.

2. Pour the vinegar into container and turn motor on HIGH speed. Remove cover, and with blades spinning, drop in the chunks of horseradish. Add sugar.

3. Pour into jar with tight-fitting lid and store in refrigerator. If the sauce is too strong for you, leave the jar uncapped for a couple of hours before refrigerating.

CHINESE MUSTARD SAUCE

Makes ¾ cup

¾   cup beer
2   teaspoons cornstarch
1   tablespoon soft butter
1   tablespoon dry mustard

½   teaspoon salt
Dash of pepper
1   teaspoon vinegar

1. Pour beer into a saucepan and heat to simmering. Empty into container and add remaining ingredients. Cover and blend on MEDIUM speed for 20 seconds.

2. Return to saucepan and cook over low heat for 3 minutes, stirring constantly.

ORIENTAL PLUM SAUCE
FOR ROAST DUCKLING OR PORK

Makes 1¼ cups

1   cup plum jam
4   tablespoons vinegar
¼   teaspoon allspice
1   teaspoon dry mustard

Put all ingredients into container, cover, and blend on HIGH speed for 15 seconds, or until smooth.

RED CURRANT SAUCE FOR
GOOSE OR DUCK

Makes 2 cups

Thin rind of ½ orange,   ½   cup orange juice
   coarsely cut   2   tablespoons lemon juice
1   cup currant jelly   1   teaspoon dry mustard
½   cup sherry or port wine   2   teaspoons cornstarch

1. Put all ingredients into container. Cover and blend on HIGH speed for 10 seconds, or until rind is finely cut.

2. Empty into saucepan and simmer for 5 minutes, stirring constantly.

SWEET-AND-SOUR SAUCE FOR
BATTER-FRIED SHRIMP

Makes 1 cup

1   cup canned crushed pineapple with juice
2   tablespoons soy sauce
2   teaspoons curry powder
½   teaspoon powdered ginger
1   teaspoon tomato paste

1. Put all ingredients into container. Cover and blend on MEDIUM speed for 20 seconds.

2. Empty sauce into a saucepan and heat to bubbling, stirring occasionally.

CRANBERRY GLAZE FOR HAM

Makes 1 cup

2	tablespoons vinegar	¼	teaspoon pepper
¼	cup brown sugar	½	teaspoon dry mustard
One	½-inch slice of lemon with rind	1	teaspoon salt
		One	7-ounce can cranberry sauce

1. Put all ingredients into container. Cover and blend on HIGH speed for 15 seconds, or until smooth.

2. Brush on ham steaks while sautéeing or broiling or over ham during baking.

CREOLE SAUCE FOR SEAFOOD, MEAT, OR VEGETABLES

Makes 2 cups

1	medium onion, coarsely cut	1	clove garlic
½	green pepper, seeded and cut in strips	½	teaspoon salt
2	tablespoons butter	3	good dashes of Tabasco sauce or to taste
One	1-pound can stewed tomatoes		

1. In a small saucepan, sauté the onion and green pepper in the butter for 6 minutes, or until vegetables are soft.

2. Empty vegetables into container and add remaining ingredients. Cover and blend on HIGH speed for 3 seconds, or until vegetables are coarsely chopped.

3. Empty into saucepan, bring to a boil, and simmer for 10 minutes, stirring occasionally.

GIBLET GRAVY

Makes 2½ cups

4 tablespoons flour	The cooked turkey gizzard
1 cup boiling water or turkey	and heart, coarsely cut
broth	The cooked turkey liver,
½ teaspoon salt or to taste	finely diced
Dash of pepper	4 tablespoons drippings from
1 cup milk	roasting pan

1. Into container put the flour, water or broth, salt, and pepper. Cover and turn motor on HIGH. With blades spinning, remove cover and add the milk, gizzard, and heart. Turn off motor immediately. Add diced liver.

2. Stir blended mixture gradually into hot pan drippings and cook, stirring in all the brown bits from the bottom and sides of pan, until gravy is thickened.

QUICK MUSHROOM SAUCE #1

Makes 2 cups

3 tablespoons soft butter	⅛ teaspoon pepper
½ medium onion, coarsely cut	One 3-ounce can broiled sliced
3 tablespoons flour	mushrooms
1½ cups hot chicken broth	1 tablespoon lemon juice
Pinch of thyme	

1. Put all ingredients into container. Cover and blend on MEDIUM speed for 10 seconds.

2. Empty into saucepan and bring to a boil, stirring constantly, until sauce is thickened. Cook over low heat for 2 minutes before serving.

QUICK MUSHROOM SAUCE #2

Makes 1½ cups

Put into container a 3-ounce can mushroom bits and pieces, ½ cup sour cream, ½ cup hot chicken broth, 2 tablespoons butter, and 2 tablespoons flour. Cover and blend on HIGH speed for 15 seconds. Empty into saucepan and cook over low heat for 15 minutes, stirring occasionally.

SALADS &
SALAD DRESSINGS

Salad & Salad Dressings

A BASIC French or Italian salad dressing is very simple to make, yet your electric blender can mix it faster than you can and can blend and homogenize the ingredients so that the oil and liquid will stay in suspension for several hours. It can finely chop such additions as capers, garlic, green onions, dill pickles, olives, parsley, or other herbs to give you infinite variations and can extend the flavor of these additions more positively than if they were hand chopped. Indeed, it's wise to remember to add these flavor ingredients in small quantities, lest they overpower rather than contribute to the salad dressing.

Good green salads can be made with any variety of greens, such as tender Bibb lettuce, escarole, curly endive, romaine, watercress, young leaves of spinach and dandelions, or field salad, plus vegetables if you wish, tossed with a blender oil-and-vinegar dressing (lemon juice, if you prefer). Or you can just use crisp, firm-headed iceberg lettuce, cut into wedges and bathed with one of the many excellent mayonnaise salad dressings in this chapter.

The foolproof method for making mayonnaise and for shredding cabbage for cole slaw can be found in Mini-Course in Blender Cooking, page 26 and page 27. In this chapter you will find a selection of cold vegetable dishes, molded gelatin salads, some frosty freezer salads for those particularly scorching summer days, and a large variety of French-type and mayonnaise-base dressings.

Vegetable Salads

ITALIAN SALAD

Serves 4. Crumbled blue cheese makes a nice addition to this mixed salad.

1	small head curly endive (chicory) or romaine
¼	green pepper
½	cucumber
4 to 8	radishes
½	medium onion

cut for blender-chopping *

1. Tear half the head of curly endive or romaine into container. Add half the other vegetables and water-chop with motor on HIGH. Turn off immediately or the moment the last piece of vegetable at top of container takes a nose dive to bottom.

2. Drain in sieve and repeat until all vegetables are finely shredded.

3. Empty chopped vegetables into a towel and refrigerate until ready to use. Empty chilled greens into salad bowl and toss with favorite salad dressing.

TABBOULEH

Serves 4. An unusual and exceptionally good salad from the Near East. It makes a nutritious luncheon dish during the warm months when fresh tomatoes are in season and parsley and mint are abundant.

½	cup cracked wheat (bulgur)	3	tablespoons lemon juice
1	cup water	4	tablespoons olive oil
½	small onion	¼	teaspoon black pepper
1	large bunch fresh parsley, stemmed	½	clove garlic
		8–10	fresh mint leaves
1	medium tomato, coarsely cut		Tomato sections for garnish
¾	teaspoon salt		

1. Soak wheat in the water for 1 hour. Drain and press out excess liquid. Empty into a salad bowl.

2. Put onion and parsley clusters into container. Add water just to cover. Cover and blend on HIGH speed for just 4 seconds. Drain and add to wheat.

3. Put all remaining ingredients, except tomato sections, into container. Cover and blend on HIGH speed for 2 seconds. Pour over salad and toss lightly.

4. Garnish top of salad with tomato sections.

CUCUMBERS IN SOUR CREAM

Serves 4

¾ cup sour cream
2 tablespoons vinegar
1 teaspoon sugar
½ teaspoon salt
2 green onions, coarsely cut

¼ teaspoon coarsely cracked
    pepper
½ teaspoon dill weed, or
    1 tablespoon fresh dill
2 firm cucumbers, peeled and
    thinly sliced

1. Put sour cream into container. Add vinegar, sugar, salt, green onions, pepper, and dill. Cover and blend on HIGH speed for 10 seconds.

2. Pour dressing over cucumbers and chill for 1 to 2 hours before serving.

SOUR CREAM POTATO SALAD

Serves 6

5 cups diced cooked potatoes
1 cup peeled, seeded, and diced
    cucumber
½ cup sliced radishes
1 cup Blender Mayonnaise
    (page 27)
2 tablespoons lemon juice
1 teaspoon dry mustard
3 green onions, coarsely cut

1 teaspoon salt
¼ teaspoon pepper
1 cup sour cream
½ cup coarsely cut celery
    Salad greens
4 hard-cooked eggs, quartered
2 ripe tomatoes, cut into
    sections

1. In a mixing bowl, combine potatoes, cucumber, and radishes.

2. Put mayonnaise into blender container. Add lemon juice, mustard, onions, salt, pepper, sour cream, and celery. Cover and blend on HIGH speed for 15 seconds, or until celery is coarsely cut.

3. Pour dressing over potatoes and mix well. Empty into salad bowl lined with salad greens and garnish with hard-cooked eggs and tomatoes.

ASPARAGUS VINAIGRETTE

Serves 6

½ cup oil
2   tablespoons vinegar
    Small bunch of parsley,
      stemmed
½ clove garlic
1   teaspoon salt

¼ teaspoon pepper
1   green onion, cut up
¼ teaspoon dill weed
1   teaspoon capers
2   pounds fresh asparagus,
      cooked and drained

1. Put into container the oil, vinegar, parsley, garlic, pepper, green onion, dill, and capers. Cover and blend on HIGH speed for 15 seconds, or until vegetables are finely chopped.

2. Arrange asparagus on serving dish and top with sauce. Chill.

CHICKEN-STUFFED TOMATOES

Serves 4

4   ripe tomatoes, peeled
1   tablespoon capers
¼ cup parsley clusters
1   teaspoon salt

¼ teaspoon pepper
1   cup diced cooked chicken
3   hard-cooked eggs
    Lettuce

1. Cut a half-inch slice from tops of tomatoes and reserve slices. Scoop out pulp and set aside. Place tomato shells upside down to drain.

2. Put into container the tomato pulp, capers, parsley, salt, and pepper. Cover and blend on HIGH speed for 5 seconds. With blades spinning, remove cover, and gradually add the chicken. Continue blending until smooth, stopping to stir down if necessary.

3. Drop eggs into blending mixture, one at a time, and blend only until last egg is drawn down into the blades.

4. Arrange tomato shells on crisp lettuce. Fill shells with the chicken mixture. Top each with a reserved slice of tomato and chill.

Molded Salads

MOLDED COLE SLAW

Serves 8

*	Small head of green cabbage, blender-shredded with next 3 vegetables	½	cup cider vinegar
		1	cup cold water
		1	cup mayonnaise
2	carrots, coarsely cut	1	tablespoon prepared mustard
1	green pepper, seeded and cut in strips		Salt and pepper to taste
			Salad greens
8	radishes		Tomatoes for garnish
1	cup boiling water		
One	6-ounce package lemon-flavored gelatin		

1. Blender-shred enough cabbage to measure 4 cups along with the carrots, green pepper, and radishes. Drain thoroughly and empty into mixing bowl.

2. Into container put boiling water and lemon gelatin. Cover and blend on HIGH speed for 3 seconds. With blades spinning, remove cover and add vinegar, cold water, mayonnaise, and mustard. Turn off motor when mixture is smooth, season to taste with salt and pepper, and chill until mixture just begins to thicken.

3. Fold in vegetables and empty mixture into a 9-inch loaf pan and chill until firm.

4. Unmold onto cold serving dish and garnish with salad greens and sliced tomatoes.

PERFECTION SALAD

Serves 6

1	cup boiling water
One	3-ounce package lemon-flavored gelatin
1	cup pineapple juice
1	tablespoon lemon juice
1	cup coarsely cut cabbage
2	carrots, coarsely cut

1. Put water and gelatin into container. Cover and blend on HIGH speed for 20 seconds.

2. Add remaining ingredients. Cover and blend on HIGH speed for just 5 seconds, or until last piece of carrot is pulled down into the blades.

3. Pour into six 4-ounce individual molds and chill until firm.

4. Unmold on salad greens.

MOLDED POTATO SALAD

Serves 6

½ cup boiling water
2 tablespoons lemon juice
1 slice medium onion
1 envelope plain gelatin
1 cup Blender Mayonnaise
  (page 27)
1 teaspoon salt
½ cup parsley clusters
½ teaspoon pepper

1 canned pimiento
1 cup coarsely cut celery
4 cups diced, cooked potatoes
1 cup peeled, seeded, and
  chopped cucumber
Salad greens, radishes, rolls of
  thinly sliced ham, and
  cucumber spears for garnish

1. Put boiling water, lemon juice, onion slice, and gelatin into container. Cover and blend on HIGH speed for 50 seconds.

2. Add mayonnaise, salt, parsley, pepper, pimiento, and celery. Cover and blend on HIGH speed for 20 seconds, or until celery is coarsely cut.

3. Pour mixture over diced potatoes, add chopped cucumber, and mix well.

4. Pack mixture into a 6-cup mold and chill until firm.

5. Turn out onto cold serving platter and garnish with salad greens, radishes, rolled ham slices, and cucumber spears.

MUSHROOM CREAM MOLD

Serves 6.   Excellent served with sliced ham or cold cuts.

½ pound mushrooms, washed and sliced	1 cup water
¼ teaspoon salt	1 envelope unflavored gelatin
½ small onion, sliced	1 cup sour cream
	Salad greens

1. In a saucepan, combine mushrooms, salt, onion, and water. Cover and simmer for 10 minutes, or until mushrooms are tender.

2. Into container put gelatin and ½ cup hot liquid from the mushrooms. Cover and blend on HIGH speed for 50 seconds. Leave motor on, remove lid, and pour in remaining liquid and mushroom mixture. Continue blending until smooth.

3. Add sour cream. Cover and blend on HIGH speed for 2 to 3 seconds, or until mixed.

4. Turn into lightly oiled 1-quart mold. Chill until set. Unmold and garnish with salad greens.

MOLDED CUCUMBER MOUSSE

Serves 6.   Lovely to serve with cold poached salmon.

2 tablespoons lemon juice	2 cups peeled, seeded, and diced cucumbers
2 envelopes plain gelatin	1 drop green food coloring
1 thin slice onion	1 cup heavy cream, whipped
½ cup boiling water	Salad greens and cucumber slices for garnish
½ teaspoon salt	
Few dashes of Tabasco sauce	
½ cup parsley clusters	

1. Put lemon juice, gelatin, onion, boiling water, salt, and Tabasco into container. Cover and blend on HIGH speed for 50 seconds.

2. With blades spinning, remove cover and add parsley and cucumbers. Blend for just 3 seconds.

3. Chill mixture until it just begins to thicken, then fold in the whipped cream.

4. Pour into a lightly oiled 4-cup mold and chill until firm. Unmold onto salad greens and garnish with sliced cucumbers.

AVOCADO RING

Serves 4. Here is a lovely salad for the buffet table. Unmold the Avacado Ring on a bed of salad greens and fill center with shrimp, crabmeat, or chicken salad.

1 tablespoon lemon juice	½ teaspoon salt
1 envelope plain gelatin	Few grains of cayenne pepper
½ cup boiling water	¼ cup mayonnaise
1 avocado, peeled and coarsely sliced	Shrimp, crab meat, or chicken salad and crisp lettuce for garnish
1 cup sour cream	

1. Into container put lemon juice, gelatin, and boiling water. Cover and blend on HIGH speed for 60 seconds.

2. Add avocado, sour cream, salt, cayenne pepper, and mayonnaise. Cover and blend on HIGH speed for 30 seconds, or until smooth, stopping to stir down if necessary.

3. Empty into 3-cup ring mold. Cover with aluminum foil and chill until set.

4. Unmold onto a serving platter garnished with salad greens, and fill center of ring with shrimp, crab meat, or chicken salad.

HAM RING FOR POTATO SALAD

Serves 6

2 tablespoons vinegar	½ teaspoon celery salt
1 envelope plain gelatin	1 teaspoon prepared mustard
Thin slice of onion	2 cups diced, cooked lean ham
⅓ cup boiling water	3 cups potato salad
1½ cups sour cream	Salad greens for garnish
½ teaspoon salt	

1. Put vinegar into container. Add gelatin, onion slice, and boiling water. Cover and blend on HIGH speed for 50 seconds.

2. Add sour cream, seasonings, and ham. Cover and blend on HIGH speed for about 2 minutes, or until smooth, stopping to stir down once or twice if necessary.

3. Empty into a lightly oiled 1-quart ring mold and chill until firm.

4. When ready to serve, unmold onto chilled serving platter and fill center with potato salad. Garnish with salad greens.

MOLDED HAM AND RICE SALAD

Serves 6 to 8

* 3 cups diced, cooked ham, blender-shredded	½ cup sour cream
2 cups cooked rice	¼ cup parsley clusters
One 10½-ounce can beef consommé	2 canned pimientos
	1 teaspoon dry mustard
2 tablespoons vinegar	¼ teaspoon Tabasco sauce
1 envelope plain gelatin	1½ teaspoons salt
½ small onion, halved	¼ teaspoon pepper
⅓ cup boiling water	1 cucumber, peeled and coarsely cut
1 small clove garlic	Cucumbers for garnish

1. Blender-shred the ham, ½ cup at a time, and combine in a mixing bowl with rice and consommé. Set aside.

2. Put into container the vinegar, gelatin, onion, and boiling water. Cover and blend on HIGH speed for 50 seconds.

3. Add garlic, sour cream, parsley, pimientos, mustard, Tabasco, salt, pepper, and coarsely cut cucumber. Cover and blend on HIGH speed for 15 seconds, or until cucumber is chopped.

4. Pour over rice and ham in mixing bowl and mix well. Turn into an oiled 2-quart mold and chill until set.

5. Unmold and garnish with thin slices of cucumber.

MOLDED CHICKEN SALAD

Serves 4 to 6

½	cup hot chicken broth	½	green pepper, seeded and cut in strips
2	tablespoons lemon juice		
1	envelope plain gelatin	2	stalks celery, coarsely cut
½	cup mayonnaise	4	green onions, coarsely cut
½	teaspoon dry mustard	2	cups diced, cooked chicken
3–4	parsley clusters		

1. Pour hot chicken broth into container. Add lemon juice and gelatin. Cover and blend on HIGH speed for 60 seconds.

2. Add mayonnaise, mustard, parsley, green pepper, celery, and onions. Cover and blend on MEDIUM speed just until vegetables are coarsely cut.

3. Add chicken, cover, and blend on HIGH speed, stopping to stir down if necessary.

4. Pour into a 1-quart loaf pan or ring mold and chill until set.

SMORGASBORD SALAD

Serves 6

2	tablespoons lemon juice	½	teaspoon dry mustard
1	envelope plain gelatin	1½	cups tomato juice
½	cup hot water	6	stuffed olives
1	thin slice onion	¼	cup diced green pepper
½	pound liverwurst, coarsely cut		Salad greens for garnish
½	teaspoon salt		

1. Put lemon juice, gelatin, hot water, and onion into container. Cover and blend on HIGH speed for 50 seconds.

2. Add liverwurst, salt, mustard, tomato juice, olives, and green pepper. Cover and turn motor on LOW speed. As soon as blades reach full speed, switch to HIGH and blend for 20 seconds, or until mixture is smooth.

3. Turn into lightly oiled 1-quart mold and chill until firm.

4. Unmold on chilled serving plate and surround with salad greens.

MOLDED SALMON SALAD

Serves 4 to 6

One 1-pound can salmon, with
    liquid
1 envelope plain gelatin
¼ cup boiling water
2 tablespoons white wine
    vinegar
½ teaspoon salt
½ cup mayonnaise

1 teaspoon dill weed
½ teaspoon paprika
1 cup light cream
2 green onions, coarsely cut
½ cup pitted ripe olives
    Lettuce
    Hard-cooked eggs

1. Drain salmon liquid into container. Add gelatin and boiling water, cover and blend on HIGH speed for 50 seconds.

2. Add vinegar, salt, mayonnaise, dill and paprika. Cover and turn motor on HIGH. With blades spinning, remove cover and gradually pour in cream. Add green onions and olives and turn off motor the second that the last olive is drawn down into the blades.

3. Flake salmon in a mixing bowl. Pour blended mixture over the salmon and mix well. Turn into a 1-quart loaf pan or mold and chill for several hours, or until firm.

4. Unmold onto chilled platter and garnish with crisp lettuce leaves and sliced, hard-cooked eggs.

CRAB SALAD MOLD

Serves 4

1 package lime-flavored gelatin
1 cup boiling water
1 cup hot water
1 cup coarsely cut cabbage

½ cup sliced carrots
½ cup coarsely cut celery
One 6-ounce box frozen king crab
    meat, partially defrosted

1. Put lime-flavored gelatin and boiling water into container. Cover and blend on MEDIUM speed for about 50 seconds.

2. Add remaining ingredients. Cover and blend on HIGH speed just until vegetables and crab meat are coarsely cut, about 3 seconds.

3. Pour into oiled 1-quart mold and chill until firm.

4. Unmold onto a bed of crisp salad greens.

CRAB MEAT, SHRIMP, OR LOBSTER SALAD

Serves 4

½ cup hot chicken broth
3 tablespoons vinegar
1 envelope plain gelatin
1 cup sour cream
1 teaspoon salt
1 cup cooked crab meat, shrimp, or lobster

1 slim cucumber, peeled and coarsely cut
6–8 parsley clusters
3 green onions, coarsely cut

1. Pour chicken broth into container. Add vinegar and gelatin. Cover and blend on HIGH speed for 60 seconds.

2. Add sour cream, salt, crab meat, cucumber, parsley, and onions. Cover and blend on MEDIUM speed just until vegetables are chopped, stopping to stir down if necessary.

3. Pour into a 1-quart mold and chill until firm.

4. Unmold and garnish with cucumber slices and tomato wedges.

COTTAGE CHEESE RING

Serves 6. Before serving, fill center of this ring with fruit or vegetable salad or Cucumbers in Sour Cream.

1 tablespoon lemon juice
½ teaspoon salt
1 thin slice onion
2 envelopes plain gelatin
½ cup boiling water
2 cups cream-style cottage cheese

1 cup Blender Mayonnaise (page 27)
½ cup heavy cream
¼ cup parsley clusters
Lettuce, or romaine or watercress

1. Put lemon juice, salt, onion, gelatin, and boiling water into container. Cover and blend on HIGH speed for 50 seconds.

2. Add remaining ingredients except lettuce leaves, cover, and blend on HIGH speed for 15 seconds.

3. Empty into 5-cup ring mold and chill until firm. Unmold onto bed of salad greens.

COTTAGE CHEESE AND TOMATO SALAD

Serves 8

½	cup hot beet juice	½	cup sliced, cooked beets
1	envelope plain gelatin	½	teaspoon sugar
1¼	cups tomato juice	1	teaspoon salt
1	thin slice onion	⅛	teaspoon pepper
½	cup celery	¼	teaspoon Worcestershire sauce
½	cup diced green pepper	1	cup cottage cheese (8 ounces)

1. Put beet juice and gelatin into container. Cover and blend on HIGH speed for 50 seconds.

2. Add tomato juice and remaining ingredients in the order listed. Cover container and blend on HIGH speed for about 30 seconds, or until vegetables are finely chopped.

3. Pour into lightly oiled shallow pan, about 10 x 6 inches. Chill.

4. Serve cut in squares.

BEET, COTTAGE CHEESE, AND HORSERADISH MOLD

Serves 6

1	cup boiling beet juice	1	tablespoon drained horseradish
One	3-ounce package lemon-flavored gelatin	1	cup diced cooked beets
1	teaspoon salt	1	cup cottage cheese (8 ounces)
1	thin slice medium onion		

1. Put beet juice, gelatin, salt, and onion into container. Cover and blend on HIGH speed for 20 seconds.

2. Add remaining ingredients, cover and blend on HIGH speed for 30 seconds.

3. Put into 1-quart mold and chill until firm.

4. Unmold, garnish with salad greens, and serve with mayonnaise.

TOMATO-CHEESE ASPIC

Serves 6 to 8

TOMATO MOLD

2	envelopes unflavored gelatin	1	teaspoon salt
⅓	cup boiling water	¼	teaspoon pepper
½	small onion	½	cucumber, diced
One	1-pound can tomatoes, or 3 medium tomatoes, quartered	1	carrot, coarsely cut
		2	cups coarsely cut cabbage

1. Put gelatin and water into container. Cover and blend on HIGH speed for 40 seconds.

2. Turn off motor and add onion, tomatoes, salt, and pepper. Cover and blend on HIGH speed for 15 seconds.

3. With blades spinning, remove cover and gradually add vegetables. Blend only until last piece of cabbage is drawn down into the blades.

4. Pour into round 8-inch, 2-inch-deep cake pan. Chill until set.

CHEESE MOLD

1	envelope unflavored gelatin	¼	teaspoon salt
½	cup boiling water	1	tablespoon lemon juice
1	strip lemon rind	1	cup cottage cheese (8 ounces)
¼	small onion		

1. Put the gelatin and water into container. Cover and blend on HIGH speed for 40 seconds.

2. Turn off motor and add remaining ingredients. Cover and blend on HIGH speed for 15 seconds, or until smooth.

3. Pour into 2-cup mold. Chill until set.

4. Unmold tomato mold onto serving plate. Unmold cheese mold on top of tomato mold. Garnish with crisp chicory and tomato wedges.

Molded & Frozen Fruit Salads

CRANBERRY-ORANGE MOLD

Serves 6

1   cup boiling water
One 3-ounce package orange-flavored gelatin
1   tablespoon lemon juice
    Thin rind of 1 orange
1   orange, with all white pith and seeds removed
One 1-pound can whole cranberry sauce

1. Put boiling water, gelatin, and lemon juice into container. Cover and blend on HIGH speed for 20 seconds.

2. Add remaining ingredients. Cover and blend on HIGH speed for 20 seconds or until orange rind is finely grated.

3. Pour into 6-cup mold and chill until set.

MOLDED CRANBERRY RELISH

Serves 6. A colorful accompaniment to holiday dinners.

One 3-ounce package orange-flavored gelatin
1   cup boiling water
½   unpeeled lemon, sliced
3   cups raw cranberries
1   cup pineapple juice
    Salad greens

1. Put gelatin in container. Add boiling water and lemon. Cover and blend on HIGH speed for 30 seconds, or until lemon is finely chopped.

2. Add cranberries and blend on HIGH for 3 seconds, or until cranberries are coarsely chopped.

3. Combine with pineapple juice and chill until mixture begins to thicken. Mix well. Pour into lightly oiled individual molds. Chill until firm. Unmold onto crisp salad greens.

GINGER ORANGE SALAD

Serves 6

1 medium orange, peeled, diced, and seeded	1/4 cup lemon juice
	1/2 cup chopped celery
1 envelope unflavored gelatin	1 cup ginger ale
1/2 cup hot water	2 medium bananas, diced
2 tablespoons sugar	Salad greens
1/4 teaspoon salt	

1. Put orange in container.

2. Add gelatin and hot water. Cover and blend on HIGH speed for 50 seconds.

3. Add sugar, salt, lemon juice, and celery and blend for 3 seconds.

4. Stir in ginger ale and chill until mixture begins to thicken.

5. Fold in diced bananas and pour into lightly oiled flat dish, about 10 x 6 inches, or 6 individual salad molds. Chill until firm. Cut in squares, or unmold, and serve on crisp salad greens with a cream dressing.

FROZEN PINEAPPLE AND NUT SALAD

Serves 8

One 1-pound can jellied cranberry sauce	One 8-ounce can crushed pineapple, drained
1 cup cream-style cottage cheese (8 ounces)	1 cup miniature marshmallows
1/2 cup mayonnaise	* 1 cup heavy cream, blender-whipped
1/2 cup walnut meats	Lettuce leaves
1/2 cup maraschino cherries, drained	

1. Put cranberry sauce, cottage cheese, and mayonnaise into container. Cover and blend on HIGH speed until smooth.

2. Add walnuts and cherries and blend on MEDIUM speed just until fruit and nuts are coarsely chopped.

3. Empty into a mixing bowl and fold in pineapple, marshmallows, and whipped cream.

4. Pour into refrigerator trays and freeze until firm.

5. Slice and serve on a bed of lettuce leaves.

FROZEN FRUIT AND NUT SALAD

Serves 8

2 tablespoons lemon juice	One 1-pound, 13-ounce can fruit
1 envelope plain gelatin	cocktail, drained
⅓ cup boiling water	½ cup walnut or pecan meats
½ cup mayonnaise	1 cup heavy cream, whipped
	Lettuce leaves

1. Put lemon juice, gelatin, and water into container. Cover and blend on HIGH speed for 50 seconds.

2. Add mayonnaise and fruit cocktail, cover and blend on HIGH speed for 30 seconds.

3. Add nut meats and flick motor on and off HIGH several times until nut meats are coarsely chopped.

4. Pour into freezer tray and freeze until mushy.

5. Empty into bowl and beat until smooth. Fold in the whipped cream and freeze until firm.

6. Cut into bars or squares and serve on a bed of lettuce leaves.

French Dressing & Variations

BASIC FRENCH DRESSING

Makes 1¼ cups

¼ cup cider, malt, or wine vinegar, or lemon juice
1 cup fresh salad oil (part olive, please)
1 teaspoon salt
¼ teaspoon pepper
1 teaspoon dry mustard

1. Put all ingredients into container. Cover and turn blender on LOW speed. Rest hand lightly on cover and switch to HIGH. Blend for 20 seconds.

2. Pour into jar, cover, and store in refrigerator.

BLUE-CHEESE DRESSING

Add ½ cup crumbled blue cheese or Roquefort to basic recipe.

CURRY DRESSING

Add 1 teaspoon curry powder to basic recipe.

HERB DRESSING

Add ½ cup parsley clusters and 1 teaspoon favorite dried herb or 1 tablespoon fresh to basic recipe.

ANCHOVY DRESSING

Use lemon juice in basic recipe, and add 1 small can drained anchovy fillets.

SAUCE LORENZO

Makes 1½ cups

Blend 1¼ cups Basic French Dressing with 3 tablespoons chili sauce, 2 green onions, coarsely cut, 1 canned pimiento, and a few sprigs watercress, until onions are finely chopped.

BLUE-CHEESE FRENCH DRESSING

Makes 1½ cups

Blend 1¼ cups Basic French Dressing with 2 tablespoons mayonnaise, 1 small clove garlic, and 2 ounces crumbled blue cheese for about 6 seconds.

CREAMY FRENCH DRESSING

Makes about 1½ cups

Blend 1¼ cups Basic French Dressing with ½ small clove garlic, 1 teaspoon tomato paste, 2 tablespoons mayonnaise, and ½ teaspoon dried tarragon, dill, or sweet basil.

SOUR-CREAM FRENCH DRESSING

Makes 1½ cups

Blend 1¼ cups Basic French Dressing with ½ small clove garlic, 3 or 4 parsley clusters, 1 teaspoon tomato paste, and ¼ cup sour cream.

VINAIGRETTE DRESSING

Makes about 1½ cups.   Marvelous for cooked, chilled artichokes.

Blend 1¼ cups Basic French Dressing with 6 stuffed olives, 1 tablespoon drained capers, 2 green onions, coarsely cut, and ¼ cup parsley clusters for 6 seconds.

Mayonnaise Dressings

IF YOU'VE NEVER made your own mayonnaise, TRY it! You'll be a blender-mayonnaise disciple forever. The basic recipe is on page 27. Here, we begin with a few variations of the basic recipe, followed by a selection of classic mayonnaise sauces and salad dressings that have been converted to blender use. But do not be bound by the recipes found here. Experiment. Substitute one ingredient for another, add a different flavor combination, create your own special salad dressings that are yours alone.

Try using lemon juice instead of vinegar or add an extra dash of coarsely ground pepper. Make your dressing more tart, or sweeter if you wish. And when fresh tarragon, dill, and other herbs are in season, add them (and to Basic French Dressing, too), for no dried herb can surpass the flavor of fresh-grown garden herbs.

CELERY SEED MAYONNAISE

Makes 1½ cups. For fruit salads.

⅓ cup honey
1 teaspoon celery seed
1 egg
½ teaspoon salt
2 tablespoons lemon juice
1 cup salad oil

1. Put honey, celery seed, egg, salt, lemon juice, and ¼ cup of the salad oil into container. Cover container and turn motor on LOW speed.

2. Immediately remove cover and add the remaining oil in a steady stream (should take 15 seconds). Turn off motor when the last drop of oil has been added.

GREEN MAYONNAISE

Makes 1¼ cups. For sliced tomatoes or iceberg lettuce.

½ small clove garlic
1 tablespoon fresh dill
1 tablespoon coarsely cut chives
     or green onion
1 egg
½ teaspoon salt
1 teaspoon dry mustard
2 tablespoons wine vinegar
1 cup salad oil

1. Put garlic, dill, chives or green onion, egg, salt, mustard, vinegar, and ¼ cup salad oil into container. Cover and turn motor on LOW speed.

2. Immediately remove cover and pour in remaining oil in a steady stream (should take 15 seconds). Turn off motor when last drop of oil has been added.

SAUCE VERTE

Makes 1½ cups.   For cold poached fish or for seafood molds or mousses.

Make Blender Mayonnaise and leave in container. Add 1½ tablespoons chopped chives, 1 teaspoon dry tarragon (or 1 tablespoon chopped fresh), ¼ cup parsley clusters, 1 teaspoon dry dill weed (or 1 tablespoon fresh). Stir to combine, cover, and blend on HIGH speed for 6 seconds.

SAUCE AÏOLI

Make Blender Mayonnaise and leave in container. Add 4 peeled cloves garlic, stir to combine, cover, and blend on HIGH speed for 10 seconds.

CURRY MAYONNAISE

Makes 1⅓ cups.   For fruit salads and fish or seafood molds.

1	teaspoon curry powder	½ small clove garlic
¼	teaspoon ginger	¼ very small onion
2	tablespoons lime or lemon juice	2 tablespoons honey
1	egg	1 cup salad oil

1. Put curry powder, ginger, lime or lemon juice, egg, garlic, onion, honey, and ¼ cup of the salad oil into container. Cover and turn motor on LOW speed.

2. Immediately remove cover and add remaining oil in a steady stream. Turn off motor when last drop of oil has been added.

EGGLESS MAYONNAISE

Makes about 1 cup

½   teaspoon salt
½   teaspoon mustard
½   cup cold evaporated milk
½   cup chilled salad oil
1   tablespoon vinegar or lemon juice

1. Put salt, mustard, and evaporated milk into container. Cover and turn motor on LOW speed.

2. Remove cover and add oil in a steady stream.

3. Turn off motor when the last drop of oil has been added.

4. Add vinegar and flick motor on and off HIGH speed until blended.

SAUCE MICHELE

Makes 1½ cups. For chicken salads.

Make Blender Mayonnaise and leave in container. Add 1 tablespoon capers, 1 stalk celery, coarsely cut, 1 thin slice medium onion, 6 or 8 parsley clusters, and ½ small clove garlic. Stir to combine, cover, and blend on HIGH speed for 6 seconds.

SAUCE NIÇOISE

Makes 1¾ cups. For salad greens, seafood molds, or hard-cooked eggs.

Make Blender Mayonnaise and leave in container. Add ½ cup coarsely cut green pepper, ¼ teaspoon tomato paste, 1 teaspoon tarragon, 1 tablespoon chopped chives. Stir to combine, cover, and blend on HIGH speed for 6 seconds.

SAUCE À LA RITZ

Makes 1½ cups. For salad greens or mixed-vegetable mold.

Make Blender Mayonnaise and leave in container. Add 1 ripe tomato, peeled and quartered, 1 tablespoon chili sauce, 1 clove garlic, and 6 or 8 parsley clusters. Stir to combine, cover, and blend on HIGH speed for 6 seconds.

SAUCE RÉMOULADE

Makes 1½ cups. For seafood or hard-cooked eggs.

Make Blender Mayonnaise and leave in container. Add 1 tablespoon capers, ¼ cup coarsely cut sour pickles, ½ teaspoon mustard, 3 or 4 parsley clusters, and 1 teaspoon tarragon. Stir to combine, cover, and blend on HIGH speed for 6 seconds.

THOUSAND ISLAND DRESSING

Makes 2 cups.   For iceberg lettuce.

Make Blender Mayonnaise and leave in container. Add ¼ cup chili sauce, 1 slice medium onion, 1 stalk celery with leaves, coarsely cut, ¼ cup stuffed olives, 4 gherkins, ½-inch strip green pepper, 6 or 8 parsley clusters, 1 teaspoon paprika. Stir to combine, cover, and blend on HIGH speed for 10 seconds. With blades spinning, remove cover and drop in 1 hard-cooked egg. Turn off motor as soon as egg is pulled down into the blades.

SAUCE CAPPON MAGRO

Makes 1½ cups.   For fish salads or molds.

Make Blender Mayonnaise and leave in container. Add 1 cup parsley clusters, 1 clove garlic, 1 tablespoon drained capers, 6 green olives, pitted, and ½ teaspoon fennel seeds. Stir to combine. Cover and blend on HIGH speed for 6 seconds.

GREEN GODDESS DRESSING

Makes 1½ cups.   For seafood or salad greens.

Make Blender Mayonnaise and leave in container. Add 1 clove garlic, 2 anchovy fillets, 4 green onions, coarsely cut, ¼ cup parsley clusters, 1 tablespoon lemon juice, 1 tablespoon tarragon vinegar, and ½ teaspoon coarsely ground pepper. Cover and blend on HIGH speed for 10 seconds.

VARIATION: Fold in ½ cup sour cream.

SAUCE GRIBICHE

Makes about 3 cups.   For iceberg lettuce.

Make Blender Mayonnaise and leave in container. Add 6 or 8 parsley clusters, 1 teaspoon dill weed, 1 small sour pickle, coarsely cut, 1 tablespoon coarsely cut onion, 1 tablespoon lemon juice, 3 drops Tabasco sauce. Stir to combine. Cover and blend on HIGH speed for 6 seconds. With blades spinning, remove cover and push 3 hard-cooked eggs, one at a time, down into the blades with a rubber spatula. Turn off motor immediately.

LAMAISE DRESSING

Makes 3 cups. For seafood or salad greens.

Make Blender Mayonnaise and leave in container. Add 1 cup chili sauce, 1/4 cup pickle relish, 1 canned pimiento, 1 stalk celery, coarsely cut, 2 green onions, coarsely cut, 1/2-inch strip of green pepper, and 1 teaspoon dry mustard. Cover and blend on HIGH speed for 10 seconds. Fold in 1/2 cup sour cream, if desired.

CUCUMBER DRESSING

Makes 1 1/2 cups. For seafood salads, mousses, or molds.

1   cup peeled, seeded and coarsely cut cucumber
2   tablespoons lemon juice
1   teaspoon onion salt
1/4   teaspoon celery salt
1/3   cup sour cream
1/3   cup Blender Mayonnaise (page 27)

Blend cucumber on HIGH speed until smooth, or for about 30 seconds. Add remaining ingredients, cover, and blend on HIGH speed for 5 seconds longer.

SAUCE GUSTAV

Makes about 3 cups. For wedges of iceberg lettuce.

1   cup parsley clusters
1   cup shredded fresh spinach
1/2   bunch watercress, leaves only
5   peeled shallots or green onions, coarsely cut
1   clove garlic
2   teaspoons dry mustard
1   egg yolk
1 1/2   tablespoons vinegar
      Juice of 1 lemon
1/4   teaspoon pepper
1/2   teaspoon salt
1 1/4   cups Blender Mayonnaise (page 27)
1/2   cup sour cream

1. Put parsley into container. Cover and blend on HIGH speed for 6 seconds.

2. Add spinach, cover, and blend on HIGH speed for another 6 seconds.

3. Add watercress leaves, cover, and blend on HIGH speed for 6 seconds longer. Turn motor off and press greens down into the blades with a rubber spatula.

4. Add shallots or onions, garlic, mustard, egg yolk, vinegar, lemon juice, pepper, and salt. Cover and blend on HIGH speed for 30 seconds.

5. Add mayonnaise and sour cream. Cover and blend on HIGH speed for 30 seconds.

Miscellaneous Dressings

CELERY SEED DRESSING

Makes 1½ cups.   For fruit salads.

⅓ cup sugar	½ cup wine or malt vinegar
1 teaspoon salt	1 cup salad oil
1 tablespoon paprika	1 thin slice medium onion
½ teaspoon dry mustard	1 tablespoon celery seed

Put all ingredients into container. Cover and blend on HIGH speed for 30 seconds, or until thick and smooth.

CREAM-CHEESE DRESSING

Makes 2 cups.   For fruit salads.

½   cup currant jelly
One   3-ounce package cream cheese, quartered
2   tablespoons lemon juice
¼   teaspoon salt
1   cup heavy cream, whipped

Put jelly, cream cheese, lemon juice, and salt into container. Cover and blend on HIGH speed for 20 seconds, or until smooth. Fold into whipped cream.

AVOCADO DRESSING

Makes about 2 cups. For fruit salads.

2 tablespoons lemon juice
1 cup heavy cream
1/4 teaspoon salt
2 tablespoons confectioners' sugar
1 small ripe avocado, peeled, seeded, and coarsely cut

1. Put lemon juice, half the cream, salt, sugar, and avocado into container. Cover and blend on HIGH speed for 30 seconds, or until smooth and fluffy.

2. Whip remaining 1/2 cup cream and fold into dressing. Chill until ready to serve.

SWEET FRENCH DRESSING

Makes 1 1/2 cups. For fruit salads.

1/3 cup lemon juice
1 thin strip lime or lemon peel
1/2 teaspoon dry mustard
1/2 teaspoon salt
1 teaspoon paprika
2 tablespoons sugar
1 cup salad oil
1 thin slice garlic (optional)

Put all ingredients into container. Cover and blend on HIGH speed for 15 seconds.

STRAWBERRY SAUCE

Makes 2 cups. For fruit salads.

2 tablespoons lemon juice
3 tablespoons confectioners' sugar
1/4 cup Blender Mayonnaise (page 27)
1 cup fresh strawberries
1/2 cup heavy cream, whipped

1. Put lemon juice, sugar, mayonnaise, and strawberries into container. Cover and blend on HIGH speed for 10 seconds, or until smooth.

2. Pour into mixing bowl and fold in whipped cream. Chill until ready to serve.

COTTAGE-CHEESE CHIVE DRESSING

Makes 1¼ cups.   For fruit or mixed vegetable salads.

2   tablespoons lemon juice
2   tablespoons salad oil
½   teaspoon salt
2   tablespoons chopped chives
1   cup cream-style cottage cheese (8 ounces)

Put all ingredients into container. Cover and blend on HIGH speed for 10 seconds, or until smooth.

LOW-CALORIE SOUR CREAM

Makes 1¼ cups

1   cup cottage cheese
¼   cup non-fat milk or buttermilk
1   tablespoon lemon juice

Put ingredients into container. Cover and blend on HIGH speed for 10 seconds, or until smooth.

SOUR-CREAM DILL SAUCE

Makes 1 cup

Add to 1 cup Low-Calorie or dairy sour cream, 1 teaspoon dried dill weed or 1 tablespoon fresh dill. Blend on HIGH speed for 20 seconds.

DOUBLE CHEESE DRESSING

Makes about 2 cups.   For hearts of lettuce.

¾	cup milk or buttermilk	1	sliver garlic
¼	cup vinegar	¼	cup parsley clusters
2	tablespoons salad oil	4	ounces cream cheese,
½	teaspoon salt		quartered
⅛	teaspoon pepper	4	ounces blue cheese, crumbled

Put all ingredients into container. Cover and blend on HIGH speed for 30 seconds, or until smooth, stopping to stir down if necessary. Chill until ready to serve.

YOGURT DRESSING

Makes about 1⅓ cups.   For crisp salad greens.

¼	cup coarsely diced onion	1	teaspoon salt
½	clove garlic (optional)	1	teaspoon sugar
¼	cup celery leaves	1	tablespoon tomato paste
¼	cup parsley clusters	1	cup yogurt (8-ounces)

Put all ingredients into container in order listed. Cover and blend on HIGH speed for about 1 minute. Pour over crisp salad greens and toss lightly.

LOW-CALORIE SALAD DRESSING

Makes 1½ cups

½	cup cottage cheese	1	sliver garlic
½	cup low-fat milk	½	green pepper, cut in strips
1	teaspoon salt	4	radishes
1	teaspoon paprika	2	green onions, coarsely cut
2	tablespoons lemon juice		

Put all ingredients into container. Cover and blend on HIGH speed for 10 seconds, or until vegetables are finely chopped.

BLUE-CHEESE PIMIENTO DRESSING

Makes 1¼ cups

One 4-ounce can pimientos with juice
2 tablespoons crumbled blue cheese
⅓ cup salad oil

¼ cup vinegar or lemon juice
½ teaspoon salt
½ teaspoon dry mustard
Dash of pepper

Put all ingredients into container. Cover and blend on HIGH speed for 10 seconds, or until smooth.

GUACAMOLE DRESSING

Makes 2 cups. This is a marvelous salad dressing, best simply served over a wedge of chilled iceberg lettuce.

1½ cups peeled ripe tomatoes, coarsely cut
½ cup diced green pepper
½ cup diced sweet onion
2 tablespoons lemon juice

¼ teaspoon dry mustard
Dash of Tabasco sauce
1 ripe avocado, peeled, seeded, and cut into sections

Put all ingredients into container in order given. Cover and blend on HIGH speed for about 10 seconds, or just until avocado is smooth and mixture is thick.

PASSOVER SALAD DRESSING

Makes 1½ cups

½ cup lemon juice
1 cup peanut oil (special for Passover use)
1 teaspoon salt
¼ cup sugar

1 teaspoon paprika (special for Passover use)
Thin slice medium onion
6–8 parsley clusters
2 tablespoons celery leaves

Put all ingredients into container. Cover and blend on HIGH speed for 6 seconds.

VEGETABLES

Vegetables

Your ELECTRIC BLENDER can help you in many ways to prepare new and interesting vegetable dishes. It can blend herb and vinaigrette sauces for hot or cold, steamed or simmered vegetables. It can make, as you know from the Mini-Course, velvety smooth cream sauces for creamed or scalloped vegetables and quickly crumb bread, crackers and cheese for au gratin toppings.

It can water-chop large quantities of crisp raw vegetables, as for making cole slaw (page 26), and this same technique is applied in this chapter for cooked red cabbage dishes. It can shred vegetables in raw egg for fritters and pancakes and can purée vegetables with liquids for soufflés and puddings.

One of my favorite uses for the blender in the vegetable department is for baking shredded raw vegetables, with just butter and salt and pepper, in a tightly-covered baking dish. The baking time is short, so that the vegetable remains tooth-crisp and retains most of its vitamins and minerals.

One such recipe is the one on page 217 for Vitamin Carrots, but, as in all the following recipes, do substitute one vegetable for another. In the Vitamin Carrots recipe, you can substitute raw beets, turnips, parsnips, Jerusalem artichokes, or other root vegetables. Winter squash or pumpkin may also be substituted for sweet potatoes and vice versa. Most leafy vegetables are also interchangeable in a given recipe.

STRING BEANS WITH CREAM HAM SAUCE

Serves 4

* 1   slice buttered bread,
      blender-crumbed
1   cup sour cream
½   cup diced, cooked ham
½   small onion

2   teaspoons paprika
¼   teaspoon salt
⅛   teaspoon pepper
2   cups cooked string beans

1. Make buttered crumbs, empty out onto waxed paper, and set aside.

2. Into container put sour cream, ham, onion, paprika, salt, and pep-

per. Cover and blend on HIGH speed for 10 seconds, or until smooth, stopping to stir down if necessary.

3. Mix sauce lightly with beans and place in buttered 1-quart casserole.

4. Sprinkle with crumbs. Bake in preheated 350° F. oven for 15 minutes.

DEVILED BEETS

Serves 6

3	cups sliced, cooked beets	3	tablespoons vinegar
2	tablespoons prepared mustard	½	teaspoon salt
1	tablespoon honey	2	tablespoons butter
1	teaspoon Worcestershire sauce		

1. Put 1 cup of the beets into container. Add mustard, honey, Worcestershire, vinegar, and salt. Cover and blend on HIGH speed for 10 seconds, or until smooth.

2. Put remaining beets into a saucepan and add blended mixture and the butter. Bring to a boil and simmer for 10 minutes, stirring frequently.

GINGERED BEETS

Serves 3 to 4

One	1-pound can whole beets	⅓	cup vinegar
⅔	cup sugar	½	teaspoon salt
3	tablespoons cornstarch		Dash of pepper
1	teaspoon ginger	1	tablespoon butter

1. Drain liquid from beets into container and add remaining ingredients except butter. Cover and blend on HIGH speed for 5 seconds.

2. Empty beets into a saucepan and pour blended mixture over. Add butter and bring to a boil, stirring constantly, until sauce is thickened and transparent.

DANISH RED CABBAGE

Serves 6

1   small head red cabbage
1   small onion   } water-chopped in blender *
1   large apple, peeled, quartered
    and cored
2   tablespoons butter or
    margarine
1   beef bouillon cube
1   cup hot water
2   teaspoons salt
¼   teaspoon pepper
1   tablespoon vinegar
1   tablespoon brown sugar

1. Loosely fill container with coarsely cut cabbage, onion, and apple and water-chop. Drain and repeat until all cabbage, onion, and apple are shredded.

2. In a large saucepan, melt the butter or margarine. Add vegetables, cover, and let steam over low heat.

3. Meanwhile put bouillon cube, hot water, salt, and pepper into container. Cover and blend on HIGH speed until bouillon cube is dissolved. Add to cabbage mixture, cover, and simmer for 10 minutes.

4. Stir in vinegar and sugar and simmer for 20 minutes longer, or until cabbage is tender.

SWEET AND SOUR SPICED RED CABBAGE

Serves 6

1   small head red cabbage
2   tart apples, peeled, quartered   } water-chopped in blender *
    and cored
2   tablespoons shortening or butter
1   teaspoon salt or to taste
½   teaspoon pepper
4   cloves
½   teaspoon allspice
½   cup sugar
½   cup vinegar

1. Loosely fill container with coarsely cut cabbage and apples and water-chop.

2. Drain vegetables lightly as they are chopped, and empty into a saucepan containing the shortening or butter. Repeat until all vegetables and apples are chopped.

3. Sprinkle cabbage with salt and pepper and add cloves, allspice, and sugar. Cover and simmer for 1 hour, stirring occasionally.

4. Add vinegar and simmer for 1 hour longer.

VITAMIN CARROTS

These are so easy that a recipe is hardly needed. Scrape a bunch of carrots. Blender-shred them * in your blender by dropping one at a time into the revolving blades, and empty into a buttered baking dish until the dish is almost full. Then sprinkle with salt (and white pepper, if you like—it gives the carrots an undefinable extra flavor), and dot with 1 to 2 tablespoons butter. Cover tightly and bake in a preheated 350° F. oven for 30 minutes. That's it!

CARROT SOUFFLÉ

Serves 4

1½	cups diced, cooked carrots	3	eggs, separated
1	cup milk	¼	cup cream of rice or other
2	tablespoons butter		quick cooking rice cereal
½	teaspoon salt	½	cup diced American cheese
⅛	teaspoon pepper		(optional)

1. Put drained carrots in container. Add milk, butter, salt, pepper, and the egg yolks.

2. Cover container and blend on HIGH speed until carrots are finely cut, or about 5 seconds.

3. Pour blended mixture into saucepan. Add cream of rice and bring to a boil, stirring constantly. Cook until thickened, about 30 seconds.

4. Add cheese, if desired, stirring until melted, then remove from heat.

5. Beat egg whites until stiff but not dry and gently fold carrot mixture into beaten whites.

6. Pile lightly in ungreased 1-quart baking dish. Bake in moderate oven, 350° F, until center is set and firm to the touch, or about 45 minutes.

CAULIFLOWER-CHEESE CASSEROLE

Serves 4

4 eggs	½ teaspoon dry mustard
1 cup cubed Cheddar cheese	⅛ teaspoon cayenne pepper
(4 ounces)	3 parsley clusters
1 cup milk	2 slices whole wheat bread
1 teaspoon Worcestershire sauce	2 cups cooked cauliflowerets

1. Preheat oven to 350° F.

2. Break eggs into container. Add cheese, milk, Worcestershire, mustard, cayenne, and parsley. Tear in bread. Cover and blend on HIGH speed for 45 seconds.

3. Place cauliflowerets in a shallow baking dish and pour the cheese sauce over them.

4. Bake in preheated oven for 45 minutes. Serve hot.

BAKED STUFFED CAULIFLOWER

Serves 4 to 5

1 large head cauliflower	1 cup hot milk
* ¼ cup blender-buttered bread	½ teaspoon salt
crumbs	¼ teaspoon pepper
* 2 tablespoons blender-grated	2 hard-cooked eggs
Parmesan cheese	1 canned pimiento
2 tablespoons soft butter	6 green onions, coarsely cut
2 tablespoons flour	

1. Trim cauliflower, but leave whole. Cook, covered, in boiling salted water, for 20 minutes, or until just fork tender. Drain and let cool.

2. Make and set aside the buttered bread crumbs.

3. Make and set aside grated cheese.

4. Into container put butter, flour, milk, salt, and pepper. Cover and blend on HIGH speed for 6 seconds, or until mixture is smooth.

5. With blades spinning, remove cover and drop in eggs, one by one, then pimiento, and finally, green onions. Turn motor off the second that the last piece of green onion is pulled down into blades.

6. Put cauliflower in baking dish. Cut a deep round wedge from top. Fill center with sauce. Replace top and pour remaining sauce over the top.

7. Sprinkle with crumbs and cheese, and bake in a preheated 375° F. oven for 20 minutes.

CAULIFLOWER TIMBALES

Serves 6

*	¼ cup diced cheese, blender-shredded		Dash of pepper
	1 medium head cauliflower	2	tablespoons soft butter
	2 eggs	1	cup hot milk
	½ teaspoon salt	¼	cup diced cheese, unshredded
			Paprika

1. Make blender-shredded cheese and set aside.

2. Trim cauliflower, separate into flowerets, and parboil in simmering, salted water for 10 minutes. Drain and empty into container.

3. Add to container the eggs, salt, pepper, butter, hot milk, and remaining cheese. Cover and blend on HIGH speed for 6 seconds. Do not over-blend. Cauliflower and cheese should just be coarsely grated.

4. Divide blended mixture into 6 buttered custard cups. Set cups in shallow pan containing about 1 inch hot water. Bake in preheated 325° F. oven for 30 to 40 minutes, or until knife inserted in center comes out clean.

5. Loosen edges with sharp knife and invert the timbales on serving dish. Sprinkle with shredded cheese and top each timbale with a dash of paprika.

VARIATION: 3 cups any other suitable cooked vegetable may be used in place of the cauliflower.

CELERY AMANDINE

Serves 8

4 cups sliced celery	1 thin slice medium onion
¼ cup boiling water	1½ tablespoons flour
½ teaspoon salt	1 cup hot light cream or
Dash of pepper	half-and-half
4 tablespoons soft butter	½ cup chicken broth
(½ stick)	½ cup slivered almonds
1 tablespoon coarsely cut chives	
or green onion tops	

1. Put celery and boiling water into saucepan. Cover tightly and simmer for 20 minutes, shaking pan occasionally to make sure celery is not scorching.

2. Meanwhile, put into container the salt, pepper, butter, chives, onion, flour, and hot cream. Cover and blend on HIGH speed for 6 seconds. Remove cover and pour in chicken broth.

3. Pour blended mixture over celery and cook, stirring, for 2 minutes, or until sauce is thickened. Add almonds and simmer for 1 minute longer.

GOLDEN CELERY LOAF

Serves 6.   This is an unusually good vegetable loaf to serve with roast chicken or turkey with gravy.

1½ cups coarsely cut celery	2 eggs
¼ cup parsley clusters	3 tablespoons soft butter
1 medium onion	1½ cups warm milk
½ green pepper	1 teaspoon salt
¾ cup walnut meats	2 slices whole wheat bread, torn

1. Put all ingredients into container. Cover and blend on HIGH speed just until last piece of bread is pulled down into blades.

2. Empty into 1½-quart baking dish and let stand at room temperature for 20 minutes.

3. Preheat oven to 350° F.

4. Bake the "loaf" in the preheated oven for 1 hour, or until set. Serve with chicken or turkey gravy.

SOUTHERN CORN CUSTARD

Serves 4 to 6

2 cups fresh or canned corn kernels	2 tablespoons flour
6 tablespoons soft butter or margarine (¾ stick)	1 teaspoon salt
	4 eggs
1 tablespoon sugar	1¾ cups warm milk

1. Preheat oven to 325° F. Grease a 1½-quart casserole.

2. Put all ingredients into blender container. Cover and blend on MEDIUM speed for 8 seconds.

3. Empty into casserole and bake in preheated oven for 30 minutes.

4. Stir mixture lightly with a large spoon and continue to bake for 15 minutes longer, or until lightly browned and set.

CORN FRITTERS

Makes 12, serves 4 or 6

1 cup fresh, canned, or defrosted corn kernels	1½ teaspoons baking powder
1 egg, separated	½ teaspoon salt
5 tablespoons flour	¼ cup milk
	Fat for frying

1. Put corn, egg yolk, flour, baking powder, salt, and milk into container. Cover and blend on HIGH speed for 15 seconds.

2. In a mixing bowl, beat egg white until stiff but not dry. Add blended mixture and fold together.

3. Drop batter by teaspoons into skillet containing 1 inch hot shortening. Fry for 2 to 3 minutes, or until golden brown on all sides.

VARIATION: 1 cup diced water chestnuts may be substituted for the corn.

EGGPLANT CAKES

Serves 4

1 medium eggplant, peeled and diced
1 egg
½ teaspoon baking powder
1 tablespoon soft butter
   About ½ cup flour
   Fat for frying

1. Put eggplant into saucepan with boiling salted water to half cover. Cover saucepan and simmer for 15 minutes.

2. Drain eggplant and empty into container. Add egg, baking powder, and soft butter. Cover and blend on HIGH speed for 10 seconds, or until eggplant is mashed, stopping to stir down if necessary.

3. Stir in enough flour to make a thick batter.

4. Drop by tablespoonfuls into about 1 inch hot oil in skillet and fry for 4 minutes, or until golden, turning once.

5. Drain on absorbent paper and sprinkle lightly with salt.

EGGPLANT SICILIENNE

Serves 6

* 2 slices bread, blender-crumbed
* ½ cup cubed Cheddar cheese,
     blender-shredded
One 1-pound, 4-ounce can tomatoes
1 medium onion, quartered
2 large cloves garlic
1 teaspoon salt
1 teaspoon oregano
¼ teaspoon pepper
2 stalks celery, coarsely cut
2 carrots, coarsely cut
1 medium eggplant, peeled and
     cut in 1 inch cubes

1. Crumb bread and shred cheese. Empty onto piece of waxed paper.

2. Into container put tomatoes, onion, garlic, salt, oregano, and pepper. Cover and blend on HIGH speed for 5 seconds.

3. With blades spinning, remove cover and add celery and carrots. Turn off motor as soon as celery and carrots have been finely chopped.

4. Turn ingredients in container into a saucepan and add eggplant. Cover and cook over low heat for 30 minutes. Transfer to a buttered casserole.

5. Top with crumbs and cheese. Bake in preheated 375° F. oven for 20 minutes, or until browned and bubbly.

HOMINY CASSEROLE

Serves 4. This is a delicious casserole to serve with a tossed salad.

One	1-pound, 12-ounce can whole hominy	¼	cup coarsely diced onion
1½	cups milk	3	tablespoons butter or bacon drippings
2	eggs	4	ounces Cheddar cheese, diced
1	teaspoon salt	½	cup corn meal.
½	cup coarsely diced green pepper		

1. Drain hominy and empty into a 1½-quart casserole.

2. Put remaining ingredients into glass container. Cover and blend on MEDIUM speed for about 15 seconds.

3. Pour blended mixture over hominy and bake in a preheated 325° F. oven for about 1 hour, or until custard is set.

4. Serve hot.

BAKED STUFFED ONIONS

Serves 6

6	large onions	¼	teaspoon pepper
* ½	cup blender buttered crumbs	1	teaspoon dry mustard
1	cup diced Cheddar cheese	1	tablespoon soft butter
One	4-ounce can mushrooms, drained	1½	tablespoons flour
½	teaspoon salt	½	cup hot milk

1. Peel onions. Put into a saucepan with boiling salted water to cover. Simmer with pan covered for about 15 minutes, or until barely tender.

2. Drain onions and scoop out onion centers, leaving several layers as shell. Arrange shells in a buttered 9-inch square baking dish.

3. Make bread crumbs and set aside.

4. Put scooped-out onion into container. Add cheese, mushrooms, salt, pepper, mustard, butter, flour, and hot milk. Cover and blend on HIGH speed for 10 seconds.

5. Fill onion shells with the cheese mixture and sprinkle with buttered crumbs.

6. Pour about ½ inch hot water into bottom of baking pan. Bake in preheated 375° F. oven for 35 minutes, or until crumbs are golden.

POTATO LATKES

Makes 8 or 10, or 4 servings

3	medium potatoes, peeled and quartered	1	teaspoon salt
		¼	teaspoon pepper
1	medium onion, coarsely cut	2	tablespoons flour
1	egg	½	teaspoon baking powder

1. Into container put half the potatoes, the onion, egg, salt, and pepper. Cover and blend on HIGH speed for 6 seconds, or until potatoes are chopped.

2. Add remaining potatoes, flour, and baking powder. Blend on HIGH speed for 6 to 10 minutes longer, stopping to stir down once or twice.

3. Drop by tablespoonfuls into frying pan containing a little very hot oil and fry until brown and puffy on both sides.

4. Drain on absorbent paper and serve hot with applesauce or sour cream.

LITHUANIAN POTATO PUDDING

Serves 6

3	eggs	1	teaspoon salt
½	cup milk	4–5	large potatoes, peeled and coarsely diced
½	teaspoon baking powder		
2	tablespoons flour	½	pound bacon slices

1. Break eggs into container. Add milk, baking powder, flour, salt, and half the potatoes. Cover and turn motor on HIGH.

2. Uncover and with blades spinning, add remaining potatoes to fill container. Turn off motor as soon as last potato cube has been added.

3. Grease a 10 x 6-inch baking pan. Arrange half the bacon slices in the pan. Pour in potato mixture. Top with remaining bacon slices.

4. Bake in preheated 350° F. oven for 50 minutes.

5. Serve with applesauce.

MASHED POTATO SOUFFLÉ

Serves 6

1	cup hot mashed potatoes	6	egg yolks
1	tablespoon butter	½	teaspoon salt
1	tablespoon milk	6	egg whites
1	green onion, coarsely cut		

1. Preheat oven to 325° F. Butter six 10-ounce individual casseroles and arrange them in a shallow pan.

2. Put all ingredients except egg whites into container. Cover and blend on HIGH speed for 30 seconds, stopping to stir down if necessary.

3. In a mixing bowl, beat egg whites with a rotary beater until stiff, but not dry. Pour potato mixture over and fold together gently but thoroughly.

4. Divide soufflé mixture into prepared casseroles. Add boiling water to the pan to come halfway up sides of casseroles and bake in preheated oven for 45 minutes.

TIPSY SWEET POTATO CASSEROLE

Serves 4

* ½	cup blender-chopped pecans	½	teaspoon salt
½	cup milk or orange juice	½	teaspoon nutmeg
3	eggs	¼	cup brown sugar
2	tablespoons rum or bourbon	4–5	cooked, small sweet potatoes

1. Coarsely chop pecans on LOW speed, empty onto waxed paper, and set aside.

2. Put milk, eggs, rum or bourbon, salt, nutmeg, and brown sugar into container. Cover and turn motor on HIGH.

3. Remove cover and push potatoes, one at a time, down into the blades with a rubber spatula, until mixture reaches top of container.

4. Pour blended mixture into a buttered baking dish. Sprinkle with the chopped pecans and bake in preheated 350° F. oven for 30 minutes.

SWEET POTATO CASSEROLE

Serves 4

1	orange, skin and white pith removed	½ cup brown sugar
		2 eggs
4	tablespoons melted butter (½ stick)	½ cup milk
		One 1-pound, 1-ounce can sweet potatoes, drained
½	teaspoon salt	
½	teaspoon cinnamon	

1. Put orange, butter, salt, cinnamon, sugar, eggs, and milk into container. Cover and blend on HIGH speed for 10 seconds.

2. With blades spinning, remove cover and add sweet potatoes, one at a time.

3. Pour into buttered 1-quart casserole and bake in preheated 350° F. oven for 40 minutes. Serve hot.

SWEET POTATO SOUFFLÉ

Serves 4

½ cup light cream	1 teaspoon cinnamon
⅓ cup brown sugar	3 cooked, medium sweet potatoes
½ teaspoon salt	
2 tablespoons melted butter	Marshmallows
2 eggs, separated	

1. Put into container the cream, brown sugar, salt, butter, egg yolks, and cinnamon. Cover and turn motor on HIGH. Remove cover and push potatoes, one by one, down into blades with rubber spatula.

2. In a mixing bowl, beat egg whites until stiff but not dry. Add blended mixture and fold together.

3. Turn mixture into a buttered 1-quart casserole or soufflé dish. Top with marshmallows.

4. Bake in preheated 350° F. oven for 30 minutes.

VARIATION: Cooked, buttered squash may be substituted for the sweet potatoes.

BAKED SHREDDED SWEET POTATOES OR YAMS

Serves 6

4 medium sweet potatoes, peeled and coarsely diced	½ cup light corn syrup
½ cup salt	1 cup water
2 cups sugar	1 long strip orange rind
	Juice of ½ orange

1. Sprinkle sweet potatoes with salt, cover with 2 quarts water, and soak for 1½ hours. Drain and rinse.

2. In a saucepan, combine the sugar, light corn syrup, and water. Bring to a boil and boil for 5 minutes.

3. Empty syrup into container. Add orange rind, juice, and half the potatoes. Cover and turn motor on HIGH. Remove cover and, with blades spinning, gradually add remaining potatoes.

4. Pour into a buttered baking pan and bake in preheated 350° F. oven for 35 minutes. Do not stir. When edges of the potatoes are transparent, remove from oven and serve.

SPINACH PURÉE

Serves 2

One 10-ounce package frozen chopped spinach
½   small clove garlic
1   teaspoon lemon juice
     Pinch each nutmeg, salt, and pepper
½   stick butter, melted and hot

1. Defrost spinach. Do not drain. Empty spinach and liquid into container and add garlic, lemon juice, and seasonings. Cover and blend on HIGH for 10 seconds.

2. Turn off blender. Add hot butter, cover, and blend again to a smooth purée, stopping to stir down once or twice if necessary.

3. Empty purée into a small saucepan and stir over moderate heat until most of the excess liquid is evaporated. Correct seasoning with salt and pepper to taste.

SPINACH OR BROCCOLI SOUFFLÉ

Serves 4

One 10-ounce package frozen   1   teaspoon cornstarch
     chopped spinach or broccoli   1   teaspoon salt
4   egg yolks   ⅛   teaspoon pepper
4   tablespoons soft butter   ⅛   teaspoon nutmeg
     (½ stick)   1   cup hot light cream or milk
4   tablespoons flour

1. Cook frozen vegetable according to package directions. Drain well and empty into container.

2. Add remaining ingredients, except egg whites. Cover and blend on HIGH speed for 15 seconds.

3. Pour into saucepan and cook over low heat, stirring constantly, until sauce is thick. Cool slightly.

4. Beat the egg whites in large mixing bowl until stiff but not dry. Pour blended mixture over and fold together lightly but thoroughly.

5. Empty into a 1½-quart casserole or soufflé dish.

6. Bake in preheated 375° F. oven for 35 to 40 minutes, or until set. Serve immediately.

BAKED SQUASH

Serves 6

* 1 cup blender-crumbed crackers
½ cup hot milk or light cream
4 tablespoons soft butter (½ stick)
1 slice medium onion

½ cup coarsely diced celery
2 cups cooked diced winter squash
1 egg
½ teaspoon salt
⅛ teaspoon pepper

1. Make cracker crumbs and set aside.

2. Into container put milk, half the butter, and remaining ingredients. Cover and blend on HIGH speed until squash is well mashed, stopping to stir down if necessary.

3. Stir in half the cracker crumbs, then scrape mixture into a 1½-quart casserole. Sprinkle with remaining cracker crumbs and dot with remaining butter.

4. Bake in preheated 350° F. oven for 25 minutes.

VARIATION: Chopped walnuts may be substituted for half the cracker crumbs stirred into blended mixture. Black walnuts are especially good.

TOMATOES PROVENÇALE

Serves 4 or 8

4 ripe tomatoes
1 slice bread
1 clove garlic
½ cup parsley clusters

3 tablespoons melted butter
½ teaspoon salt
⅛ teaspoon pepper

1. Trim a thin slice from both top and bottom of tomatoes. Cut tomatoes in half and set cut side down to drain.

2. Tear bread into container. Add remaining ingredients. Cover and blend on HIGH speed for 6 to 8 seconds.

3. Arrange tomatoes cut side up in shallow baking pan. With sharp knife, make criss-cross shallow cuts over surface of tomatoes and spread with the blended mixture.

4. Broil 4 to 5 inches from source of heat for 8 minutes, or until crumbs are golden.

SPECIAL-OCCASION VEGETABLE CASSEROLE

Serves 6 to 8

3–4	cups cooked carrots, oyster plant, kohlrabi, or other root vegetable, and cauliflower, cut into bite-size pieces	¼	cup coarsely cut green pepper
		½	pound mushrooms, quartered
		¼	cup flour
		1	teaspoon salt
* 2	cups blender-shredded Cheddar cheese	2	cups hot milk
		1	can pimientos, drained and sliced
5	tablespoons butter		Paprika

1. Spread half the cooked vegetable in a buttered 1½-quart baking dish. Reserve remaining vegetable.

2. Blender-shred the cheese and set aside.

3. In a saucepan, melt butter and in it sauté green pepper and mushrooms for 8 minutes, or until fork tender. Empty into container. Add flour, salt, and half the hot milk. Cover and blend on HIGH speed for 6 minutes. Remove cover and, with blades spinning, pour in remaining hot milk.

4. Sprinkle half the cheese over the vegetable in the baking dish. Cover with half the pimiento slices and half the sauce. Repeat layers, starting with remaining vegetable and finishing with sauce.

5. Sprinkle generously with paprika and bake in a preheated 400° F. oven for 15 minutes or until brown and bubbling.

DESSERTS

Desserts

BECAUSE of the blender's ability to disperse solids evenly throughout a mixture, it can save many precious moments in the making of desserts, both plain and fancy, and produce in one easy-to-clean container a great variety of luscious pie fillings, creamy puddings, sherbets, frozen creams, and delectable sweet sauces.

It can make in just minutes many of the classic French desserts that otherwise require lengthy and tedious sieving, beating, and hand-blending.

Once you get into the habit of letting your blender work for you, you will wonder how you ever managed without it!

Crumb-Crust Pies

CRUMB CRUST FOR SWEET PIES

Makes one 8- or 9-inch pie crust

* 16 graham cracker squares, blender-crumbed
  2 tablespoons sugar
  ½ teaspoon cinnamon
  ¼ cup melted butter

1. Crumb crackers five at a time. Empty crumbs into a mixing bowl and repeat until all crackers have been crumbed.

2. Stir in sugar and cinnamon. Add melted butter and mix until all crumbs are moistened.

3. Butter sides of pie plate and press crumbs firmly against sides and bottom of pan to make an even coating.

VARIATIONS:

Use 12 zwieback or 16 vanilla, chocolate, or ginger wafers in place of the graham crackers.

Use bran flakes or corn flakes (1 cup) in place of the graham crackers.

NUT CRUST

Makes one 8-inch pie crust

* 6   ounces walnut or pecan meats, blender-ground
  3   tablespoons sugar
  ⅓   cup melted butter

Follow instructions for Crumb Crust.

VARIATION: Use 1½ cups shredded coconut (plain or toasted) instead of nuts.

FRESH COCONUT CHIFFON PIE

Makes one 11-inch pie

Ingredients for crumb crust— increase recipe by half (page 232)	3 egg yolks
	⅔ cup sugar
	2 teaspoons vanilla
* 1 cup blender-shredded fresh coconut	Dash of salt
	3 egg whites
1½ cups milk	1½ cups whipping cream
1 envelope plain gelatin	

1. Prepare crumb crust for an 11-inch pie plate.

2. Blender-shred the coconut and set aside.

3. Heat 1 cup milk to steaming hot.

4. While milk is heating, pour remaining ½ cup milk into container. Add gelatin and let soak until other milk is hot.

5. Add egg yolks, sugar, vanilla, and salt to softened gelatin in container. Cover and turn motor on HIGH. Remove cover, and with blades spinning, pour in the hot milk, and continue to blend for 30 seconds.

6. Pour into a bowl and chill until custard begins to set.

7. In a large mixing bowl, beat egg whites until stiff. Fold into partially set custard. Then whip cream until stiff and fold into custard mixture. Turn into crumb-lined plate and sprinkle the top heavily with shredded coconut.

8. Chill until cold and set.

GRASSHOPPER PIE

Makes one 9-inch pie

Ingredients for crumb crust (page 232)
- ¼ cup boiling water
- 1 envelope plain gelatin
- 2 tablespoons cold coffee or milk
- 2 egg yolks
- 2 drops green food coloring
- ½ cup confectioners' sugar
- ¼ cup crème de menthe
- ¼ cup crème de cacao
- 2 egg whites, stiffly beaten
- 1 cup heavy cream, whipped

1. Prepare crumb crust.

2. Put boiling water, gelatin, and cold coffee or milk into container. Cover and blend on HIGH speed for 40 seconds.

3. Add egg yolks, food coloring, sugar, crème de menthe, and crème de cacao. Cover and blend on HIGH speed for 5 seconds, or until mixture is smooth.

4. In a mixing bowl, combine egg whites and whipped cream. Add blended mixture and fold together gently but thoroughly.

5. Spoon into prepared crust and chill until set.

PUMPKIN CHIFFON PIE

Makes one 8-inch pie or four 3-inch tarts

Ingredients for crumb crust (page 232)
- 2 egg whites
- ½ cup hot orange juice
- 2 envelopes plain gelatin
- 1 tablespoon lemon juice
- 4 pieces preserved or crystallized ginger
- Dash of salt
- 1 teaspoon cinnamon
- ⅓ cup brown sugar
- 2 egg yolks
- 1 cup mashed cooked pumpkin
- 1 cup heavy cream
- Milk

1. Beat egg whites until stiff but not dry. Set aside.

2. Into container pour hot orange juice. Add gelatin and lemon juice. Cover and blend on HIGH speed for 40 seconds.

3. Add ginger, salt, cinnamon, sugar, egg yolks, and pumpkin. Cover and blend on HIGH speed for 10 seconds or until smooth.

4. Remove cover and, with blades spinning, pour in cream and enough milk so that the blending mixture reaches almost to top of container.

5. Pour over egg whites and fold together gently but thoroughly.

6. Spoon into crust and chill until ready to serve.

APRICOT CHIFFON PIE

Substitute 1 cup cooked apricots for the pumpkin.

SOUR-CREAM PRUNE PIE

Makes one 9-inch pie

Ingredients for crumb crust (page 232)	¼ teaspoon cinnamon
2 eggs	¼ teaspoon salt
1 cup sour cream	⅓ cup blanched almonds
1 cup pitted cooked prunes	Additional sour cream for topping
⅓ cup brown sugar	

1. Prepare crumb crust.

2. Break eggs into container. Add sour cream, prunes, brown sugar, cinnamon, and salt. Cover and blend on HIGH speed for 15 seconds, or until smooth.

3. Remove cover and, with blades spinning, pour in almonds. Turn off blender the moment the last almond has been drawn down into the blades.

4. Empty into prepared crust and bake in a preheated 375° F. oven for 35 minutes.

5. Serve warm with a topping of sour cream.

NUT PIE

Serves 6

* 12 graham cracker squares, blender-crumbed
* 1 cup brazil nuts or walnuts, blender-ground
¼ cup melted butter or margarine

4 eggs
1 cup sugar
Dash of salt
1 teaspoon vanilla
1 cup heavy cream, whipped

1. Crumb 4 graham crackers at a time and empty into a mixing bowl.

2. Grind nuts and empty into mixing bowl with crumbs. Mix in butter or margarine.

3. Press crumb mixture on bottom and sides of 9-inch pie plate.

4. Put eggs, sugar, salt and vanilla into container. Cover and blend on HIGH speed for 5 seconds, or until smooth. Pour into prepared shell.

5. Bake in preheated 300° F. oven for 35 minutes.

6. Cool and top with whipped cream before serving.

Puddings, Fritters & Crépes

STEAMED PUDDING

Serves 8

* 6 slices bread, blender-crumbed
1 cup currants
1 cup seedless raisins
1 cup seedless white raisins
3 eggs
⅔ cup melted shortening
½ teaspoon salt
1 carrot, coarsely cut

¼ teaspoon nutmeg
¼ teaspoon allspice
1 cup brown sugar
½ medium orange, halved and seeded
1 cup flour
½ cup walnuts

1. Crumb 2 slices bread at a time and empty into a mixing bowl.

2. Mix currants and both kinds of raisins with crumbs.

3. Into container put eggs, shortening, salt, carrot, nutmeg, allspice, sugar, orange, flour, and walnuts. Cover and blend on HIGH speed for 40 seconds, stopping to stir down if necessary. Pour over crumbs and fruit and mix well.

4. Empty into greased 2-quart mold. Cover and steam for 4 hours.

5. Unmold and serve with custard sauce.

WARSAW BREAD PUDDING

Serves 6

* 3	slices dark pumpernickel bread, blender-crumbed	¼	teaspoon cloves
		½	teaspoon cinnamon
4	eggs, separated	2	tablespoons soft butter
⅓	cup sugar		Dash of salt
1	cup sour cream		

1. Crumb 1 slice bread at a time and empty onto a piece of waxed paper. When all is done, you should have 1¼ cups crumbs.

2. Put egg yolks, sugar, sour cream, cloves, cinnamon, butter, and salt in container. Cover and blend on HIGH speed for 5 seconds, or until smooth.

3. In a mixing bowl, beat egg whites until stiff but not dry. Fold egg yolk mixture and crumbs into beaten egg whites.

4. Empty into a greased 2½-quart casserole. Bake in 350° F. oven for 40 minutes.

5. Serve hot with whipped cream or custard sauce.

WISCONSIN APPLE CRISP

Serves 6

4	cups peeled, sliced apples	* 1	cup diced aged Wisconsin cheese, blender-shredded
1	teaspoon cinnamon		
½	teaspoon nutmeg	2	tablespoons butter
1	cup brown sugar		Whipped cream
* 6	thin slices bread, blender-crumbed		

1. In a mixing bowl, combine apples, cinnamon, nutmeg, and sugar.

2. Crumb 2 slices bread at a time and empty onto piece of waxed paper.

3. Shred cheese ½ cup at a time and empty onto waxed paper with bread crumbs.

4. In an 8-inch square, buttered baking dish, put alternate layers of apple mixture and crumb-cheese mixture, ending with a layer of crumbs. Dot with butter. Bake in preheated 350° F. oven for 40 minutes or until crisp and tender.

5. Serve with whipped cream.

FRUIT FRITTERS

Makes enough batter to coat fruit for 6 servings

1 egg	1 teaspoon salt
½ cup milk	¼ cup sugar
1 teaspoon soft butter	Fresh fruit (bananas, oranges,
1 cup flour	apples, pineapple, peaches)
2 teaspoons baking powder	Confectioners' sugar

1. Put egg and milk into container. Add butter, flour, baking powder, salt, and sugar. Cover and blend on HIGH speed for 15 seconds, stopping to stir down once or twice.

2. Pour batter into a measuring cup and let stand while preparing fruit.

3. Peel bananas and cut into sections; peel and core apples, cut into quarters, and sprinkle with lemon juice; peel and section oranges; slice fresh, peeled pineapple and cut slices in half; peel and halve peaches, discarding stones.

4. Dry fruit well on paper towels. Dip into fritter batter a few pieces at a time and fry in 1-inch hot fat in skillet until brown on all sides. Drain on absorbent paper and serve hot with a sprinkling of confectioners' sugar.

HAZELNUT CRÊPES FROM BRITTANY

Makes 24 crêpes

½	cup soft butter	¾	cup cold milk
1	cup confectioners' sugar	3	egg yolks
4	tablespoons Cognac	1	tablespoon sugar
½	cup hazelnuts	½	teaspoon salt
2	thin strips of lemon rind	3	tablespoons Cognac
	Juice of 1 lemon	1¼	cups presifted flour
¾	cup cold water	5	tablespoons melted butter

1   Put soft butter into container. Add sugar, the 4 tablespoons Cognac, the hazelnuts, lemon rind, and lemon juice. Cover and blend on HIGH speed until mixture is smooth, stopping to stir down when necessary. Empty into a mixing bowl and set aside.

2.   Put water and milk into container (without washing it). Add remaining ingredients. Cover and blend on HIGH speed for 10 seconds. Empty into a pitcher or large measuring cup and set aside for at least 2 hours.

3.   When the batter is ready, make crêpes by the method on page 282. As each crêpe is baked, spread with the hazelnut butter and roll up. Place on a shallow dish set over a saucepan of simmering water.

4.   When all are baked and rolled, serve hot on hot plates.

Fruit Desserts

FRESH APPLESAUCE

Makes 1 pint

4	large, juicy apples
3	tablespoons lemon juice
½	cup apple or orange juice
¼–½	cup sugar to taste
	Whipped cream or sour cream

1.   Wash, core, and cube apples, but do not peel. As cut, drop them into a bowl of water containing 2 tablespoons of the lemon juice to prevent discoloration.

2. Into container put the remaining tablespoon lemon juice, the fruit juice and ½ cup cubed apples. Cover and turn motor on HIGH. Remove cover and, with motor on, gradually drop in the additional apple cubes. Stop to scrape down the sides of the container with a rubber spatula, if necessary.

3. Serve the raw sauce as soon as possible. If necessary to let stand, cover with a blanket of whipped cream or sour cream.

PACIFIC PEARS

Serves 4

* ⅓ cup blanched almonds, blender-chopped
2 strips lemon rind
2 tablespoons lemon juice
1 tablespoon rum

⅓ cup honey
One 1-pound, 13-ounces can pear halves, drained, or 4 pears, peeled, cored, cut in half, and poached

1. Blender-chop almonds and empty onto a piece of waxed paper. Set aside.

2. Into container put lemon rind, lemon juice, rum, and honey. Cover and blend on HIGH speed for 10 seconds, or until rind is finely chopped.

3. Arrange pear halves in shallow baking dish. Pour honey mixture over pears and sprinkle with almonds. Broil 4 or 5 inches from heat for 5 minutes, or until nuts are golden.

4. Serve at once with sour cream.

PEACH SNOW

Serves 6

One 6-ounce package orange-flavored gelatin
¾ cup hot water
1 cup confectioners' sugar

3 fresh peaches, peeled, stoned, and quartered
1 tablespoon lemon juice
Dash of salt
2 egg whites

1. Put gelatin and hot water into container. Cover and blend on HIGH speed for 20 seconds.

2. Add sugar, peaches, lemon juice, and salt. Cover and blend on HIGH speed for 30 seconds, or until mixture is smooth.

3. In a mixing bowl, beat egg whites until stiff but not dry. Fold in blended peach mixture.

4. Pour into 1-quart mold and chill until set.

STRAWBERRY CREAM

Serves 4 to 6

½ cup water	1 pint fresh strawberries
½ cup sugar	1 cup heavy cream, whipped
2 envelopes unflavored gelatin	Strawberries for garnish
2 tablespoons lemon juice or brandy	

1. In a small saucepan, combine water and sugar. Bring to a boil and boil for 3 minutes.

2. Into container put the hot syrup, gelatin, and lemon juice or brandy, cover, and blend on HIGH speed for 40 seconds.

3. Add strawberries. Cover and blend on HIGH speed for 10 seconds, or until smooth.

4. Fold into the whipped cream and turn into lightly oiled 1-quart mold. Chill until set.

5. Unmold and decorate with whole strawberries.

PRUNE WHIP

Serves 4 to 6

1 cup pitted, cooked prunes	1 strip yellow lemon rind
3 tablespoons prune juice	½ cup sugar
Dash of salt	3 egg whites
2 tablespoons lemon juice	

1. Put prunes, prune juice, salt, lemon juice and rind, and sugar into container. Cover and blend on HIGH speed for 20 seconds, or until smooth.

2. Beat egg whites until stiff but not dry. Fold in prune purée.

3. Spoon into serving dish and chill.

4. Serve with heavy cream.

PRUNE-PINEAPPLE WHIP

Serves 6

2   cups pitted, cooked prunes
½   cup crushed pineapple with juice
1   slice orange with rind, seeded
2   tablespoons honey
1   whole egg
¼   cup walnuts

1. Put all ingredients except walnuts into container. Cover and blend on HIGH speed for 20 seconds, or until smooth.

2. Remove lid and with blades spinning, add walnuts. Stop motor as soon as last piece of walnut is drawn down into blades.

3. Empty into serving dish and chill.

Classic Desserts

COEUR À LA CRÈME

Serves 6

* 2   cups heavy cream, 1½ cups blender-whipped
One   8-ounce package soft cream cheese, quartered
½   cup confectioners' sugar
     Pinch of salt
1   teaspoon vanilla
     Strawberries or Raspberry Sauce (page 255)

1. Line *coeur à la crème* basket or mold with a double thickness of wet cheesecloth large enough to come 1½ inches above the mold.

2. Pour 1½ cups of the heavy cream into container and whip until stiff. Scrape out into mixing bowl.

3. Add remaining cream to container (no need to wash). Add soft cream cheese, confectioners' sugar, salt, and vanilla. Cover and blend on HIGH speed for 30 seconds, or until smooth.

4. Pour cheese mixture into bowl and fold whipped cream and cheese mixture together.

5. Fill prepared mold with the cheese mixture, piling it up as high as possible. Cover with ends of the cheesecloth and place basket or mold into a shallow pan to catch the drippings.

6. Chill for 6 hours or overnight.

7. Unmold and serve with sliced fresh strawberries or Raspberry Sauce.

MOUSSE AU CHOCOLAT BASQUE

Serves 6 to 8

6 ounces semi-sweet chocolate pieces	4 egg yolks
Pinch of salt	4 egg whites
¼ cup boiling water or hot coffee	* 1 cup heavy cream, blender-whipped with 1 tablespoon confectioners' sugar
3 tablespoons rum or orange Curaçao	

1. Empty chocolate pieces into container, add salt and boiling water or coffee. Cover and blend on HIGH speed for 20 seconds.

2. Add rum or Curaçao and egg yolks. Cover and blend on HIGH speed for 10 seconds, or until smooth.

3. In a mixing bowl, beat egg whites until stiff but not dry. Fold in chocolate mixture.

4. Spoon mixture into individual serving dishes and refrigerate for 6 to 7 hours, or overnight. Or set into the freezer for 2 hours.

5. Blender-whip the cream with the confectioners' sugar. Serve the dessert with a large rosette of whipped cream on top of each portion.

CHARLOTTE NESSELRODE

Serves 6

12   ladyfingers, split
⅓   cup boiling water
1   envelope plain gelatin
2   tablespoons rum
½   cup milk
⅓   cup sugar
   Pinch of salt

1½   teaspoons vanilla
¾   cup bottled Nesselrode mix
1   cup heavy cream
   Additional cream for garnish

1. Butter a 1-quart mold and line bottom and sides with ladyfingers.

2. Put boiling water, gelatin, and rum into container. Cover and blend on HIGH speed for 40 seconds.

3. Add milk, sugar, salt, vanilla, and Nesselrode mix. Cover and blend on HIGH for 20 seconds.

4. In a mixing bowl, beat cream until stiff. Fold in blended Nesselrode mixture.

5. Pour into prepared mold and chill until firm. Unmold and garnish with additional whipped cream.

CHOCOLATE CHARLOTTE MARQUISE

Serves 8

12   ladyfingers, split
2   tablespoons brandy mixed
   with ¼ cup water
6   ounces semi-sweet chocolate
   pieces
⅓   cup boiling water or very hot
   coffee

¼   cup confectioners' sugar
4   egg yolks
¼   pound soft butter (1 stick)
2   tablespoons rum
4   egg whites
*   Blender-whipped cream for
   garnish

1. Dip ladyfingers into the brandy-water mixture and line the bottom and sides of a 6-inch spring form pan with them.

2. Put chocolate pieces and water or coffee into container. Blend on HIGH speed for 15 seconds.

3. Add sugar, egg yolks, butter, and rum and blend on HIGH speed until mixture is smooth, stopping to stir down if necessary.

4. In a mixing bowl, beat egg whites until stiff. Fold the chocolate mixture into egg whites and spoon into the prepared mold. Chill overnight.

5. To serve, unmold and garnish with whipped cream.

PRALINE SOUFFLÉ

Serves 6. The speciality of many French restaurants.

* ¼	cup blender-chopped toasted almonds	2	egg yolks
		1	cup praline powder (page 246)
⅓	cup hot water	1½	cups heavy cream
1	envelope plain gelatin	2	egg whites
1	tablespoon dark rum		Additional cream for garnish

1. Blender-chop toasted almonds and and set aside.

2. Prepare a 1-quart soufflé dish by tying a double strip of waxed paper around outside of dish, allowing paper to come about 2 inches above edge of the dish. Set aside.

3. Into container put hot water, gelatin, and rum. Cover and blend on HIGH speed for 40 seconds.

4. Add egg yolks and praline powder. Cover and blend on HIGH for 20 seconds, or until smooth.

5. Set container and praline mixture into refrigerator until it begins to set.

6. Beat egg whites until stiff but not dry. In a mixing bowl, whip cream until stiff. Fold praline mixture into whipped cream; then fold in egg whites.

7. Spoon into prepared dish and chill until set.

8. When ready to serve, remove band of waxed paper and press the toasted almonds all around the exposed edge of the soufflé. Decorate with rosettes of additional whipped cream.

PRALINE POWDER

Makes 1 cup.   Praline is simply sugar and nuts cooked to the taffy stage and blended to a powder after it is cold and set. It is used in most fine restaurants for soufflés and other fine desserts.

¾   cup sugar
¼   cup water
     Dash of cream of tartar
½   cup blanched almonds

1. Put ingredients into a small saucepan and bring to a boil, stirring once or twice until sugar is dissolved.

2. Boil over high heat without stirring, until syrup and almonds turn the color of dark molasses. Watch carefully that it does not burn.

3. Immediately pour onto an oiled cookie sheet and cool.

4. When cold, remove from sheet and break about half the praline into container. Cover and blend on HIGH speed for 5 seconds, or until praline is powdered.

5. Empty into glass container with tight-fitting lid. Repeat with remaining praline.

6. Store in refrigerator, tightly capped, where it will keep a long time.

HOT LEMON SOUFFLÉ

Serves 4

½   cup lemon juice
     Thinly shaved lemon rind from ½ lemon
¼   cup sugar
4   egg yolks
4   egg whites

1. Preheat oven to 375° F.

2. Put lemon juice, rind, and sugar into container. Cover and blend on HIGH speed for 15 seconds.

3. Add egg yolks, cover, and blend on HIGH for 6 seconds longer.

4. In a 1-quart soufflé dish, beat egg whites until stiff but not dry. Gradually fold in blended lemon mixture.

5. Bake in preheated oven for 20 to 30 minutes, or until set.

COFFEE SOUFFLÉ

Serves 3

¼ cup water	1 teaspoon instant coffee
1 envelope unflavored gelatin	3 egg yolks
6 tablespoons sugar	3 egg whites
¾ cup hot skim milk or coffee	¼ teaspoon cream of tartar
1 teaspoon vanilla	

1. Measure water into container. Add gelatin and half the sugar. Pour in hot milk or coffee, cover, and blend on HIGH speed for 40 seconds.

2. With motor on, remove cover and add vanilla, instant coffee, and egg yolks. Empty into a bowl and chill until mixture just begins to thicken.

3. Beat egg whites and cream of tartar until foamy. Gradually add remaining sugar, beating well after each addition until egg whites stand in stiff, glossy peaks.

4. Fold egg whites into coffee mixture. Pour into a 1-quart soufflé dish (which has been collared with waxed paper to extend 1 inch above edge of dish).

5. Chill for at least 2 hours, or until set.

STRAWBERRIES IMPÉRATRICE

Serves 6 to 8. Here is another classic dessert, the darling of French restaurants.

½ cup raw rice	1 tablespoon lemon juice
1 cup boiling water	2 envelopes plain gelatin
2 cups milk	½ cup sugar
¾ cup mixed candied fruits	3 egg yolks
¼ cup kirsch or rum	1 pint fresh strawberries
⅓ cup boiling water	1 cup heavy cream

1. In a saucepan, cook rice in the 1 cup boiling water for 2 minutes. Drain and cover rice in the saucepan with the milk. Bring to a boil and simmer for 25 minutes, or until rice is tender, stirring occasionally. Cool.

2. Meanwhile, soak the candied fruits in the rum or kirsch.

3. Put ⅓ cup boiling water, lemon juice, and gelatin into container. Cover and blend on HIGH speed for 40 seconds.

4. Add sugar and egg yolks. Cover and blend on HIGH for 5 seconds longer.

5. Remove cover and with blades spinning, add the candied fruit and liquid and half the strawberries. Blend until mixture is well mixed.

6. In a mixing bowl, beat cream until stiff. Fold in the cooked rice and the blended strawberry mixture.

7. Spoon into an oiled 1½-quart mold and chill until set.

8. To serve, unmold and decorate with remaining whole strawberries.

STRAWBERRY BAVARIAN CREAM

Makes 1-quart mold

½	cup hot milk	1	pint fresh strawberries
	Dash of salt	1	cup heavy cream
1	envelope plain gelatin	*	Blender-whipped cream for
½	cup sugar		garnish
3	egg yolks		

1. Put milk, salt, and gelatin into container. Cover and blend on HIGH speed for 40 seconds.

2. Add sugar, egg yolks, and strawberries. Cover and blend on HIGH speed for 15 seconds, or until smooth.

3. Set container into refrigerator until cream just starts to set.

4. In a mixing bowl, whip the heavy cream until stiff. Fold in blended strawberry cream.

5. Spoon into 1-quart mold and chill until set.

6. To serve, unmold and decorate with rosettes of blender-whipped cream.

Sherbets & Ice Creams

CRANBERRY-ORANGE SHERBET

Makes about 3 cups

¼ cup water
One 1-pound can cranberry sauce
One 6-ounce can frozen orange juice concentrate

Into container put all the ingredients. Cover and blend on HIGH speed for 10 seconds, or until smooth. Turn into refrigerator tray and freeze until frozen.

RASPBERRY MILK SHERBET

Makes about 1 pint

1 cup milk
One 6-ounce can frozen raspberry-lemon punch concentrate
1½ cups crushed ice

1. Put all ingredients into container. Cover and blend on HIGH speed for 15 seconds, or until smooth.

2. Turn into refrigerator tray. Freeze until firm.

PINEAPPLE SHERBET

Makes about 1 pint. This is a quick and attractive party dessert when served in a hollowed-out pineapple shell.

1 egg white
2 tablespoons orange juice
Rind of ½ orange
One 13½-ounce can frozen pineapple chunks cut into pieces

1. Put into the container the egg white, orange juice, and rind. Cover and blend on HIGH speed for 10 seconds.

2. Add pineapple, cover, and blend on HIGH speed for 20 seconds, or until smooth.

3. Spoon into refrigerator tray and freeze for 30 minutes.

BUTTERMILK PINEAPPLE SHERBET

Makes about 1 quart

2 cups buttermilk	2 teaspoons vanilla
⅔ cup sugar	1 egg yolk
Dash of salt	1 egg white, stiffly beaten
1 cup crushed pineapple with juice	

1. Put buttermilk, sugar, salt, pineapple, vanilla, and egg yolk into container. Cover and blend on MEDIUM speed for 20 seconds.

2. Empty into refrigerator tray and freeze to a mush.

3. Fold in egg white and return to freezer until firm.

FRUIT ICE CREAM

Makes about 1 quart

1   cup apricot, peach, prune, or raspberry purée
1½ cups heavy cream
2   egg yolks
2   egg whites
4   tablespoons sugar

1. Make fruit purée in blender. Measure, return 1 cup to container, and add egg yolks. Cover and blend on HIGH speed for 6 seconds.

2. Remove cover and with blades spinning, gradually pour in the heavy cream.

3. In a mixing bowl, beat egg whites until stiff but not dry. Beat in sugar, then fold in the blended mixture.

4. Pour into refrigerator tray and freeze until firm.

STRAWBERRY ICE CREAM

Makes 1 quart

1 pint fresh strawberries, hulled
⅔ cup sweetened condensed milk
1 cup heavy cream, whipped

1. Put strawberries and milk into container. Cover and blend on HIGH speed for 10 seconds, or until smooth.

2. Fold strawberry purée into whipped cream. Spoon into refrigerator tray and freeze for 2 to 3 hours or longer before serving.

FROZEN BISCUIT SIGURD

Serves 18

* 1 cup pistachio nuts, blender-
        grated
¾ cup sugar
2 tablespoons water
⅛ teaspoon cream of tartar

2 egg whites
    Dash of salt
3 egg yolks
1 pint fresh strawberries, hulled
1 cup heavy cream, whipped

1. Blender-grate pistachio nuts, empty onto piece of waxed paper, and set aside.

2. In a small saucepan, dissolve sugar in water over low heat. Add cream of tartar and bring to a boil. Cook rapidly until syrup spins a long thread (240° F.).

3. Meanwhile, in a mixing bowl, beat egg whites until stiff. Gradually beat half the syrup into the egg whites and continue to beat until meringue is smooth and glossy.

4. Into container put salt, egg yolks, and strawberries. Cover and blend on HIGH speed for 10 seconds, or until smooth.

5. Remove lid and with blades spinning, pour in remaining hot syrup. Turn off motor as soon as all syrup has been added.

6. Fold strawberry purée into the beaten egg whites. Then beat in whipped cream. Spoon mixture into 18 paper soufflé cups and sprinkle with pistachios.

7. Freeze for 2 hours or longer before serving.

COFFEE ICE CREAM

Makes about 1 quart

⅓ cup sugar	1 tablespoon rum or vanilla
3 tablespoons water	Dash of salt
3 egg yolks	1½ cups heavy cream, whipped
4 tablespoons powdered instant coffee	

1. In a small saucepan, combine sugar and water. Bring to a boil and boil rapidly for 3 minutes.

2. Put egg yolks, coffee, rum or vanilla, and salt into container. Cover and turn motor on HIGH. Remove cover and with blades spinning, gradually pour in the hot syrup.

3. Fold the blended mixture into the whipped cream, spoon into refrigerator tray, cover with waxed paper, and freeze for about 3 hours, or until firm.

FROZEN EGGNOG

Enough for a 6-cup mold or 18 small soufflé cups

1 cup sugar	1½ ounces rum, Cognac, or
⅓ cup water	bourbon
Pinch of cream of tartar	3 cups heavy cream, whipped
4 egg yolks	Nutmeg
⅛ teaspoon salt	

1. In a saucepan, combine sugar, water, and cream of tartar. Bring to a boil and boil rapidly for 5 minutes.

2. Put egg yolks, salt, and liquor into container. Cover and turn motor on HIGH. Remove cover and with blades spinning, pour in the hot syrup.

3. Chill blended mixture until thick, then fold into the whipped cream.

4. Spoon mixture into a 6-cup mold or 18 small paper soufflé cups, sprinkle top with a little nutmeg, and freeze.

Dessert Sauces

BRANDY OR RUM HARD SAUCE

Makes 1 cup

2	tablespoons rum or brandy
2	tablespoons cream or milk
2	cups confectioners' sugar
¼	pound soft butter (1 stick)

1. Into container put the rum or brandy, cream, and 1 cup confectioners' sugar. Cover and blend on HIGH speed for 5 seconds.

2. Add butter and remaining 1 cup confectioners' sugar. Cover and blend on HIGH speed for 30 seconds, stopping to stir down if necessary.

3. Turn into serving dish and chill until firm.

VANILLA CUSTARD SAUCE

Makes 2 cups sauce

3	egg yolks
	Dash of salt
2	tablespoons sugar
One	1-inch piece of vanilla bean
1	cup scalded milk
½	cup heavy cream, whipped

1. Into container put egg yolks, salt, sugar, and vanilla. Turn motor on HIGH speed. Remove cover and with blades spinning, pour in milk. Turn off motor as soon as all the milk has been added.

2. Empty egg mixture into top of double saucepan and cook over hot water, stirring constantly, until thickened and smooth. Strain to remove vanilla bean and cool over cracked ice, stirring occasionally.

3. Fold whipped cream into custard. Serve with Coffee Soufflé (page 247) or other desserts.

CHEESE SAUCE FOR FRUIT

Makes 1½ cups

1	strip yellow rind of a lemon	2	tablespoons sugar
3	strips orange rind from an orange	One	8-ounce package cream cheese, quartered
2	tablespoons orange juice	⅓	cup walnuts
⅓	cup milk		

1. Into container put rinds, orange juice, milk, and sugar. Cover and blend on HIGH speed for 10 seconds.

2. Add cream cheese, cover, and blend on HIGH speed for 15 seconds. Remove lid and with blades spinning, add walnuts. Turn off motor as soon as walnuts are drawn down into blades.

FRENCH CREAM SAUCE

Makes 2½ cups.   Here is a dessert sauce that closely approximates the famous *crème fraîche* served in France. It's marvelous over fresh raspberries, strawberries, or peaches.

1	egg yolk
One	3-ounce package soft cream cheese
1	cup sour cream
1	teaspoon sugar
1	cup heavy cream

1. Put all ingredients into container. Cover and blend on MEDIUM speed for 10 seconds.

2. Chill before serving.

FUDGE SAUCE

Makes about 1 cup

1   tablespoon soft butter
One 1-ounce square bitter chocolate, quartered
⅓   cup boiling water
1   cup sugar
2   tablespoons corn syrup
     Pinch of salt

1. Into container put soft butter, chocolate, and boiling water. Cover and blend on HIGH speed for 10 seconds.

2. Remove cover and with blades spinning, add remaining ingredients.

3. Serve hot or cold. Store in refrigerator.

PINEAPPLE SAUCE

Makes 3 cups sauce

1   tablespoon lemon juice
One 9-ounce can crushed pineapple with juice
1½   cups sour cream
¼   teaspoon powdered ginger

1. Put all ingredients into container. Cover and blend on HIGH speed for 10 seconds, or until smooth.

2. Chill and serve on fruit, ice cream, or cake.

RASPBERRY SAUCE

Makes 1 cup

One 10-ounce package raspberries, defrosted
1   teaspoon cornstarch
1   tablespoon water

1. Put raspberries into container. Cover and blend on HIGH speed for 15 seconds.

2. Pour through a sieve into a saucepan to remove seeds.

3. Combine cornstarch and water. Stir into raspberry sauce and bring to a simmer, stirring constantly.

4. Serve hot or cold.

STRAWBERRY SAUCE

Makes 2 cups

½   cup water
    Rind of ½ orange
1   pint fresh strawberries
1   tablespoon cornstarch
⅓   cup sugar

1. Into container put all ingredients. Cover and blend on HIGH speed for 10 seconds, or until smooth.

2. Empty into a small saucepan and cook over low heat, stirring occasionally, until thickened.

3. Serve hot or cold over ice cream.

FRESH STRAWBERRY SAUCE FOR ICE CREAM

Makes 1½ cups

1   pint fresh strawberries
½   cup confectioners' sugar
1   teaspoon lemon juice
1   strip lemon rind

1. Put all ingredients in container. Cover and blend on HIGH speed for 10 seconds or until smooth, and rind is finely chopped.

2. Chill. Serve with vanilla ice cream.

COOKING WITH ICE

Cooking with Ice

"COOKING WITH ICE" is one of the more recent blender techniques, enabling one to blend gelatin mixtures, both sweet and savory, with cracked ice to the setting point in about one minute. The dish will be ready to unmold and serve in as little as 10 minutes.

Originally this technique was worked out, after many weeks of testing, with finely crushed ice. However, few homemakers today own ice crushers, and it's a great bore to have to crack ice with a mallet, so now all "instant-set" recipes have been retested using cracked ice cubes. Ice cubes are easily cracked into small pieces by holding a cube in the palm of your hand and giving it a sharp whack with the back of a teaspoon or one of those inexpensive ice-cracking discs about the size of a quarter attached to the end of a flexible handle.

Cooking gelatin mixtures with ice is a little tricky until you understand the chemistry of how and why it works. The size of the container plays a role. Today most containers are of 5-cup capacity, and the contents of 2 envelopes of plain gelatin have the ability to "quick set" an amount of liquid that this size of container can hold WHILE THE BLENDER IS BLENDING AT HIGH SPEED— not a full 5 cups but about a full quart.

The high-speed revolutions of the blender liquefy the gelatin in a small quantity of quite hot liquid. Then it is simply a question of lowering the temperature of the blending mixture rapidly with cold liquids and ice to the point at which it jells and sets.

The temperature of ice cubes can vary greatly depending on whether they are stored in the freezer compartment of a refrigerator or in a deep freeze. So sometimes it is necessary to add a couple of additional ice cubes or to let the mixture stand for a few minutes before serving it.

With this knowledge under your bonnet, you can improvise on the recipes in this chapter ad infinitum. Good luck. I think you'll find blender ice-cooking a lot of fun.

Savory Instant-Set Molds

BLUE CHEESE MOLD

Serves 4

1	envelope unflavored gelatin	½	cup crumbled blue cheese
½	cup boiling water	1	cup cottage cheese
One	½-inch slice of onion	1	heaping cup cracked ice
½	teaspoon salt	¼	cup parsley clusters
	Dash of cayenne pepper	1	canned pimiento
1	teaspoon Worcestershire sauce		Salad greens for garnish

1. Put into container the gelatin, boiling water, onion, salt, cayenne pepper, and Worcestershire sauce. Cover and blend on HIGH speed for 50 seconds.

2. Add crumbled blue cheese, cottage cheese, and cracked ice. Cover and blend on HIGH speed for 30 seconds, or until smooth. With blades spinning, remove lid and add parsley clusters and pimiento. Continue blending only until vegetables are chopped.

3. Turn into a 3-cup mold. Chill until set. Unmold and garnish with salad greens.

AVOCADO RING-MOLD SALAD

Serves 6

One	9-ounce can crushed pineapple	½	cup mayonnaise
One	3-ounce package lemon gelatin	½	cup heavy cream
2	tablespoons lemon juice	1	cup cracked ice
1	ripe avocado, peeled, seeded and coarsely cut	2	cups diced fresh or canned fruit

1. Drain juice from pineapple into measuring cup and add water to make a total of ½ cup liquid. Empty into a small saucepan and heat to simmering.

2.   Empty hot juice into container and add lemon gelatin and lemon juice. Cover and blend on HIGH speed for 20 seconds.

3.   With blades spinning, remove cover and add avocado, mayonnaise, and heavy cream. When mixture is smooth, add ice and continue to blend until all particles of ice have disappeared.

4.   Pour into a 5-cup ring mold and chill for 10 minutes, or until set. Unmold onto cold serving dish and fill center with diced fruit.

CRAB MEAT MOUSSE

Serves 4

1	tablespoon lemon juice	¼	cup parsley clusters
1	envelope plain gelatin	½	cup sour cream
⅓	cup boiling water	1	cup cracked ice
	Thin slice of a medium onion		Lettuce and tomatoes for
½	teaspoon salt		garnish
One	7½-ounce can crab meat, drained and cartilege removed		

1.   Put lemon juice, gelatin, boiling water, onion, and salt into container. Cover and blend on HIGH speed for 40 seconds.

2.   With blades spinning, remove cover and add crab meat, sour cream, and ice. Blend until all ice particles have disappeared, stirring surface of blending mixture, if necessary, to introduce air.

3.   Pour into a 3-cup mold and chill for 10 minutes.

4.   Unmold and garnish with lettuce leaves and tomato wedges.

QUICK-SET CREAMY SALMON SALAD

Serves 6

	Juice of ½ lemon	½	cup blender mayonnaise
2	envelopes plain gelatin		(page 27)
½	cup boiling clam or chicken broth	1	cup heavy cream
1	thin slice onion	1	heaping cup cracked ice
One	1-pound can salmon with liquid		Salad greens and sliced cucumbers for garnish

1. Put lemon juice, gelatin, broth, and onion into container. Cover and blend on HIGH speed for 50 seconds.

2. Add salmon, cover, and blend on HIGH speed for 5 seconds.

3. With blades spinning, remove cover or inner cap and add mayonnaise, cream, and ice. Continue blending until smooth, stopping to stir down, if necessary.

4. Pour into 4-cup mold and chill for 20 to 30 minutes, or until set.

5. Unmold onto cold platter and garnish with salad greens and sliced cucumbers.

Molded Fruit Salads

BLACK CHERRY SALAD

Serves 6

One	1-pound can sweet black cherries	½	cup boiling water
		1	heaping cup cracked ice
One	13½-ounce can crushed pineapple	½	cup chopped celery
		½	cup chopped pecans
One	3-ounce package black cherry gelatin		Whipped cream for garnish

1. Drain liquid from cherries and pineapple into a measuring cup and reserve ½ cup.

2. Put gelatin and boiling water into container. Cover and blend on HIGH speed for 20 seconds.

3. With blades spinning, remove cover and add drained pineapple, the ½ cup reserved juices, and the ice. Continue to blend until every particle of ice disappears.

4. Turn blender off and fold in cherries, celery, and pecans.

5. Pour into a 6-cup mold and chill for 20 minutes, or until firm.

6. Unmold onto cold serving dish and decorate with whipped cream.

MOLDED WALDORF SALAD

Serves 4

⅓ cup boiling water
One 3-ounce package lemon-
      flavored gelatin
One ½-inch slice onion
  1 teaspoon salt
  1 tablespoon vinegar or lemon
      juice

½ cup mayonnaise
1 teaspoon prepared mustard
1 cup crushed ice cubes
½ cup finely chopped celery
½ cup finely diced apple
⅓ cup chopped walnuts
    Salad greens for garnish

1. Put boiling water, gelatin, onion, and salt into container. Cover and blend on HIGH speed for 20 seconds.

2. Add vinegar or lemon juice, mustard, mayonnaise, and ice. Cover and blend on HIGH speed for 30 seconds, or until smooth.

3. Fold in celery, apple, and walnuts. Turn into 3-cup mold. Chill for 20 to 30 minutes, or until set.

4. Unmold and garnish with salad greens.

SUMMER SALAD

Serves 4

One 11-ounce can mandarin oranges with juice
One 3-ounce package orange gelatin
One 8-ounce can crushed pineapple, with juice
  1 cup orange sherbet
  1 heaping cup cracked ice

1. Drain juice from mandarin oranges into measuring cup and add water to make a total of ½ cup liquid. Empty into a saucepan and heat to simmering.

2. Meanwhile, line bottom of a 4-cup mold with orange segments.

3. Empty hot liquid into container and add orange gelatin. Cover and blend on HIGH speed for 20 seconds.

4. With blades spinning, remove cover and add the can of pineapple, orange sherbet, and enough cracked ice to bring blending mixture to top of container.

5. Pour over orange segments and chill for 10 minutes.

VARIATION: Fold orange segments into the blended mixture before pouring into mold.

PINK PARTY SALAD

Serves 4

One 8-ounce can fruit cocktail
One 3-ounce package raspberry gelatin
One 5-ounce package minature marshmallows
One 3-ounce package cream cheese, quartered
  1 cup heavy cream, whipped
  2 cups cracked ice

1. Drain juice from fruit cocktail into measuring cup and add water to make a total of ½ cup liquid. Pour into a small saucepan and heat until simmering.

2. Pour hot liquid into container and add raspberry gelatin. Cover and blend on HIGH speed for 20 seconds.

3. Add marshmallows and cream cheese and blend until smooth.

4. With blades spinning, remove cover and pour in heavy cream and ice. When mixture begins to set, turn blender off and fold in the fruit cocktail.

5. Pour into a 1-quart mold and chill for 10 minutes, or until set.

PEACHES-AND-CREAM SALAD

Serves 8

  2 cups sliced peaches, fresh or
       canned
One 3-ounce package lemon gelatin
  ½ cup hot orange juice

  ⅔ cup cream-style cottage cheese
  2 cups heavy cream
  ½ cup pecans
  1 heaping cup cracked ice

1. Line the bottom of a 6-cup mold with peach slices.

2. Put lemon gelatin and hot orange juice into container. Cover and blend on HIGH speed for 20 seconds.

3. With blades spinning, remove cover and add cottage cheese. Gradually pour in the heavy cream and add the cracked ice. Continue to blend until mixture is smooth and on the verge of setting. Add pecans and turn blender off the second that the last pecan is drawn down into the blades.

4. Pour over peaches in mold and chill for 20 minutes, or until set.

NOTE: Keep cream in refrigerator until just before using it in recipe.

Bavarian Creams & Fruit Desserts

MOCHA BAVARIAN CREAM

Serves 6

¼ cup cold milk	2	egg yolks
2 envelopes plain gelatin	1	cup heavy cream
½ cup hot double-strength coffee	1	or more cups cracked ice
6 ounces semi-sweet chocolate pieces		Whipped cream for garnish

1. Pour milk into container. Add gelatin and coffee. Cover and blend on HIGH speed for 40 seconds.

2. Add chocolate. Cover and blend on HIGH speed for 10 seconds.

3. With blades spinning, remove cover and add egg yolks, cream, and 1 cup cracked ice. If necessary, add additional cracked ice to bring blending mixture to top of container.

4. Pour into 4-cup mold and let set for 10 minutes. Unmold and garnish with whipped cream.

PEACH OR STRAWBERRY BAVARIAN CREAM

Serves 6

One 10-ounce package frozen
      peaches or strawberries
2   envelopes plain gelatin
2   tablespoons milk

¼   cup sugar
2   egg yolks
1   cup heavy cream
1   or more cups cracked ice

1. Defrost fruit and drain ½ cup of the juice into a saucepan. Heat juice to simmering.

2. Pour hot juice into container and add gelatin and milk. Cover and blend on HIGH speed for 40 seconds.

3. With blades spinning, remove cover and add sugar, the fruit, and egg yolks. Pour in cream and some of cracked ice, and continue adding cracked ice until the blending mixture reaches top of container. Blend until no particles of ice remain.

4. Pour into 4-cup mold, and chill for 10 minutes before serving.

RASPBERRY RUFFLE

Serves 6

2   tablespoons lemon juice
1   envelope plain gelatin
⅓   cup boiling water
⅔   cup raspberry syrup
½   cup milk or cream
2   cups cracked ice

1. Put lemon juice, gelatin, and boiling water into container. Cover and blend on HIGH speed for 40 seconds. Remove cover and, with blades spinning, pour in raspberry syrup and milk or cream.

2. Turn blender off and add ice. Cover and blend on HIGH speed for 15 seconds. If mixture sets too quickly, stir rapidly with a rubber spatula, taking care to avoid hitting blender blades.

3. Spoon into serving dishes, or pour into a mold. This dessert may be unmolded in about 10 minutes.

ORANGE CREAM

Serves 6

½ cup hot orange juice
2 envelopes plain gelatin
  Thin orange rind of ½ orange
⅓ cup sugar
1 cup sour cream
2 cups cracked ice

1. Pour orange juice into container. Add gelatin and orange rind. Cover and blend on HIGH speed for 40 seconds.

2. Remove cover and add sugar. Turn blender off and add sour cream and crushed ice. Cover and blend on HIGH speed for 15 seconds.

3. Remove cover and add more cracked ice if needed to bring blending mixture to top of container. If mixture sets too quickly, stir rapidly with rubber spatula being careful not to hit blender blades.

4. Spoon into serving dishes, or pour into a mold. This may be unmolded in about 10 minutes.

STRAWBERRY GELATO

Serves 6

½ cup orange juice
¼ cup lemon juice (juice of 1 lemon)
2 envelopes plain gelatin
One 10-ounce package sliced strawberries, partially defrosted
½ cup heavy cream
  Cracked ice cubes

1. In a small saucepan, heat orange juice until just steaming.

2. Empty the hot orange juice into container, add gelatin and lemon juice and blend on HIGH speed for 40 seconds. Add strawberries, cover, and blend on HIGH speed for 6 seconds.

3. Remove cover and, with blades spinning, pour in cream, then add enough ice to bring liquid to top of container. Continue to blend until all bits of ice are blended with the strawberry mixture.

4. Spoon into sherbet glasses and serve immediately.

FRUIT FLING

Serves 6

½   cup juice drained from can of fruit cocktail
2   envelopes plain gelatin
One   20-ounce can fruit cocktail
½   cup tiny marshmallows
1   heaping cup cracked ice

1. Heat fruit juice to simmering and empty into container. Add gelatin, cover, and blend on HIGH speed for 40 seconds.

2. Add fruit cocktail, marshmallows, and ice. Cover and blend on HIGH speed for 12 seconds. Remove cover and add more cracked ice to bring blending liquid to top of container. If mixture sets too quickly, stir rapidly with rubber spatula, being careful not to hit the spinning blades.

3. Spoon into serving dishes and serve.

FROZEN FRUIT FLUFF

Serves 4.   This "ice" recipe can be made with any frozen fruit except raspberries (use them, too, if you don't object to the raspberry seeds). The frozen fruit takes the place of cracked ice. Simply cut the frozen fruit into about 16 pieces.

One   10-ounce package frozen fruit or berries
2   tablespoons lemon juice
1   envelope plain gelatin
½   cup hot milk or water
1   egg

1. Cut the fruit into about 16 pieces with a heavy knife. Set aside.

2. Put lemon juice, gelatin, and hot milk or water into container. Cover and blend on HIGH speed for 40 seconds.

3. Add egg, cover, and blend on HIGH speed for 20 seconds.

4. Remove cover and, with blades spinning, drop in the pieces of frozen fruit, a few at a time. Blend until mixture is smooth.

5. Spoon into serving glasses and serve immediately.

PINEAPPLE MOLD

Serves 4

⅓ cup boiling water	½ teaspoon ground ginger
1 envelope unflavored gelatin	⅓ cup heavy cream
One 9-ounce can crushed pineapple with juice	1 heaping cup cracked ice
	Pineapple sticks for garnish

1. Put water and gelatin into container. Cover and blend on HIGH speed for 50 seconds.

2. Add remaining ingredients except pineapple sticks. Cover and blend on HIGH speed for 30 seconds, or until smooth.

3. Turn into 3-cup mold and chill for 10 to 20 minutes, or until set.

4. Unmold and decorate with pineapple sticks.

FRUIT FOAM

Serves 4. You can use any fruit flavored gelatin and any complementary fruit juice in this refreshing instant dessert.

One 3-ounce package lemon- or lime-flavored gelatin
½ cup hot pineapple, orange, apricot, prune juice
2 cups cracked ice

1. Put gelatin and hot juice into container. Cover and blend on HIGH speed for 20 seconds.

2. Add cracked ice, cover, and blend on HIGH speed for 30 seconds.

3. Pour into a 2-cup mold and chill for 30 minutes, or until firm.

Instant-Set Crumb-Crust Pies

SOUR-CREAM CHEESE PIE

Makes one 8-inch pie

Ingredients for a crumb crust (page 232)	⅓ cup sugar
2 tablespoons lemon juice	One 8-ounce package soft cream cheese, quartered
Thin strip of lemon rind	1 heaping cup cracked ice
2 envelopes plain gelatin	1 cup sour cream
½ cup hot milk	Heavy cream
2 eggs	

1. Prepare crumb crust.

2. Put lemon juice, rind, gelatin, and hot milk into container. Cover and blend on HIGH speed for 40 seconds.

3. Add eggs and sugar. Cover and blend on HIGH for 10 seconds.

4. Remove cover and, with blades spinning, pour in ice cubes. Gradually add sour cream. Then add sufficient heavy cream to bring blending mixture to top of container.

5. Turn off motor and immediately pour filling into prepared crust. It will be ready to serve in 5 minutes.

VARIATION: Garnish top of pie with halved strawberries, or with fresh, frozen, or canned peaches or apricots.

INSTANT-SET PEACH CHEESE CAKE

Serves 8

* 22 graham crackers, blender-crumbed	2 envelopes plain gelatin
¼ cup sugar	2 strips of orange rind
¼ teaspoon cinnamon	One 8-ounce package soft cream cheese, quartered
⅛ teaspoon cloves	1 cup heavy cream
⅓ cup melted butter	One 12-ounce package frozen sliced peaches, quartered
½ cup orange juice	

1. Mix graham cracker crumbs with sugar, cinnamon, cloves and melted butter. Line an 8-inch spring-form cake pan with the crumbs.

2.   Heat orange juice to simmering. Pour into container and add gelatin and orange rind. Cover and blend on HIGH speed for 40 seconds. Remove cover and, with blades spinning, add cream cheese, heavy cream, and peach slices. Continue to blend for 10 seconds, or until smooth.

3.   Pour into crumb-lined pan and chill until set. (This sets almost before you can pour it into the pan.) Remove spring-form rim and decorate cheese cake with additional peach slices, fresh or frozen, if desired.

COCONUT MERINGUE CREAM PIE OR TARTS

Makes one 8-inch pie or four 3-inch tarts

	Ingredients for crumb crust (page 232)	2	egg yolks
One	3½-ounce can moist coconut	1	heaping cup cracked ice
1	cup hot milk	1	cup heavy cream
2	envelopes plain gelatin		Additional milk or
3	tablespoons light rum		half-and-half
⅓	cup sugar	2	egg whites
		½	cup sugar

1.   Prepare crumb crust or tart shells.

2.   Empty coconut into container. Add hot milk, cover, and blend on HIGH speed for 30 seconds.

3.   Strain liquid through a sieve into a bowl, pressing through as much of the liquid as possible.

4.   Return hot liquid to container and reserve the ground coconut.

5.   Add the gelatin to container, cover, and blend on HIGH speed for 40 seconds.

6.   Add rum, the ⅓ cup sugar, and egg yolks. Cover and blend on HIGH speed for 5 seconds.

7.   Remove cover and, with blades spinning, add ice, and gradually pour in heavy cream. Add enough more milk or half-and-half to bring blending mixture to top of the container.

8.   Pour blended mixture into prepared pie or tart shells.

9.   Beat egg whites until stiff. Beat in the ¼ cup sugar and fold in the reserved coconut. Spread the coconut meringue over the cream filling.

10.   Brown meringue in a 425° F. oven for 5 minutes.

11.   Chill pie until ready to serve.

EGGNOG CHIFFON PIE

Makes one 8-inch pie

	Ingredients for a crumb crust (page 232)	2	egg yolks
½	cup rum	¼	cup plus 2 tablespoons sugar
2	envelopes plain gelatin	1	heaping cup cracked ice
½	cup hot milk	1	cup heavy cream
		2	egg whites

1. Prepare crumb crust.

2. Put rum, gelatin, and hot milk into container. Cover and blend on HIGH speed for 40 seconds.

3. Add egg yolks and the ¼ cup sugar, cover, and blend on HIGH for 5 seconds.

4. Remove cover and, with blades spinning, add ice, and gradually pour in heavy cream.

5. In a mixing bowl, beat egg whites until stiff and beat in the 2 tablespoons sugar.

6. Pour the already partially set blended mixture over egg whites and fold together gently but thoroughly.

7. Pour into prepared pie shell and refrigerate until ready to serve.

NOTE: If blended mixture is too set, blend again on HIGH speed briefly before pouring over egg whites.

CHOCOLATE CHIFFON PIE

Makes one 8-inch pie

	Ingredients for crumb crust (page 232)	3	tablespoons sugar
½	cup hot strong coffee	2	egg yolks
2	envelopes plain gelatin	1	cup heavy cream
6	ounces semi-sweet chocolate pieces	1	heaping cup cracked ice
		2	egg whites

1. Prepare crumb crust.

2. Put hot coffee and gelatin into container. Cover and blend on HIGH speed for 40 seconds.

3. Add chocolate pieces and 1 tablespoon sugar, cover, and blend on HIGH speed for 20 seconds.

4. Add egg yolks, cover, and blend for 5 seconds.

5. Remove cover and, with blades spinning, add ice, and gradually pour in heavy cream. Continue to blend for 15 seconds.

6. In a mixing bowl, beat egg whites until stiff and beat in sugar. Empty chocolate mixture over egg whites and fold together gently but thoroughly.

7. Spoon into prepared crust and refrigerate until ready to serve.

PINEAPPLE LIME PIE

Makes one 9-inch pie

	Ingredients for crumb crust (page 232)	Juice of 1 large lime
		¼ cup sugar
One	1-pound can crushed pineapple	2 egg yolks
		1 heaping cup cracked ice
2	envelopes plain gelatin	1 cup heavy cream
	Wide strip of green lime rind	

1. Prepare crumb crust.

2. Drain juice from pineapple into a small saucepan and heat to simmering.

3. Empty hot pineapple juice into container and add gelatin, strip of lime rind, and half the lime juice. Cover and blend on HIGH speed for 40 seconds.

4. Add remaining lime juice, sugar, and egg yolks, cover, and blend on HIGH for 10 seconds.

5. Remove cover and, with blades spinning, add ice, and gradually pour in cream.

6. Fold blended mixture into the reserved crushed pineapple and spoon into prepared crust. Chill until ready to serve.

HOT BREADS
& YEAST LOAVES

Hot Breads & Yeast Loaves

MORE and more homemakers are making their own breads today. Children seem to be anxious to try their hand at kneading a yeast dough and shaping it into a loaf. This is great, because even the simplest form of bread—homemade pancakes, waffles, and popovers—are a big step forward nutritionally from those commercially available.

Stone-ground flours, easily found in most communities, combined with dry milk solids, eggs, and cheese, enable the homemaker to put high protein, "gutsy" breads on her table at any meal from morning to night—breads that contribute rather than detract from the overall diet of her family.

No bread is really difficult or time-consuming to make. Still, your electric blender can shorten the time, save on pots and pans, and can give new lightness and texture to waffles and pancakes. It aerates popover batter to give you the poppingest popovers ever. It blends eggs, sugar, butter, and milk to a creamy mixture in which nuts, fruit rind, or candied fruits may be chopped or in which soft fruit or berries may be puréed. It distributes yeast spores so completely in liquid that yeast breads need only one rising and virtually no kneading.

Once the basic technique of making yeast bread in your blender is mastered the method can be translated to any of your favorite one-loaf recipes. Whole-wheat, rye, and other flours, wheat germ, bran, or rolled oats may take the place of all or part of the all-purpose flour called for in a recipe. And when using all-purpose flour, do by all means use the unbleached now available in all supermarkets.

Popovers & Pancakes

NO-TRICK POPOVERS

Makes 4 large popovers. There's no trick to making popovers when you have an electric blender. You can even blend the batter and fill the custard cups the night before, set the cups onto a baking sheet, and put them into a cold oven. Next morning, all you have to do is set the oven to 450° F. By the time the orange juice is squeezed and the eggs are ready, so are the popovers.

If you don't believe me, try them!

2   eggs
½   teaspoon salt
1   cup milk
1   level measuring cup all-purpose flour

1. Butter 4 heat-resistant custard cups generously—use about 1 teaspoon soft butter per cup.

2. Put ingredients into container in order listed. Cover and blend on HIGH speed for 30 to 60 seconds, stopping to stir down if necessary.

3. Pour batter into prepared cups set wide apart on a baking sheet, filling the cups ¾ full.

4. Set baking sheet in a cold oven until ready to bake. Turn oven to 450° F., and bake popovers for 30 minutes. Toward end of baking time, but not before, check popovers and if they are becoming too brown, reduce temperature to 400° F. Bake until popovers are well browned and crisp.

POPOVER PIZZA

Serves 2 or 4.   Try this one for Sunday breakfast. It's fun to make and great to eat with honey, jam, or lingonberries.

2   eggs
½   cup milk
½   cup all-purpose flour
4   tablespoons butter (½ stick)
2   tablespoons sugar
     Juice of ½ lemon

1. Preheat oven to 425° F.

2. Put eggs, milk, and flour into container. Cover and blend on HIGH speed for 30 seconds, stopping to stir down if necessary.

3. Melt butter in a 12 x 8-inch oval fireproof dish or a 12-inch skillet with an oven-proof handle. If you don't have one, wrap wooden handle of skillet with aluminum foil. When butter is very hot, but before it begins to brown, pour in batter.

4. Bake in preheated oven for 20 minutes, or until pancake is puffed

all around sides of dish and is golden brown on top. Remove from oven and sprinkle with the sugar and lemon juice. Return to oven for 2 to 3 minutes, or until sugar turns to a glaze. Serve immediately.

YORKSHIRE PUDDING

Serves 4

2 eggs
1 cup flour
½ teaspoon salt
1 cup milk

1. Put all ingredients into container. Cover and blend on HIGH speed for 20 seconds, stopping to stir down if necessary.

2. Drain ¼ cup beef drippings from roast beef into a 10 x 6 x 2-inch baking pan. Place in middle of oven and turn oven to 425° F.

3. When drippings are smoking hot, pour the batter into the pan, and bake in the hot oven for about 25 minutes, or until pudding is puffed and well browned.

4. Cut into serving portions and serve with the roast.

PANCAKE, waffle, crêpe, and fritter batters are also made in seconds in an electric blender. If you prefer to use packaged mixes (they're more expensive), go ahead. Just remember always to put liquid ingredients into container before adding the dry ingredients.

BASIC FLUFFY PANCAKES

Makes eight 4-inch pancakes

1 cup milk	1 teaspoon baking powder
1 egg	½ teaspoon salt
1 tablespoon sugar	2 tablespoons soft butter or
1 cup all-purpose flour	cooking oil

1. Put all ingredients into container. Cover. Blend on MEDIUM speed for 15 seconds, stopping to stir down once.

2. Pour batter from container, ¼ cup at a time, onto hot greased griddle and bake until cakes are brown on both sides.

BUTTERMILK PANCAKES

Follow recipe above, but use buttermilk for the sweet milk, and substitute baking soda for the baking powder.

BLUEBERRY PANCAKES

Before pouring batter onto griddle, fold in ½ cup fresh blueberries.

WHOLE-WHEAT PANCAKES

Makes 16 to 18 pancakes

2	eggs	¾	cup all-purpose flour
1	cup milk	1	cup whole wheat flour
3	tablespoons molasses	1	teaspoon salt
4	tablespoons soft butter	2	tablespoons sugar
	(1 stick) or cooking oil	1	teaspoon baking powder

1. Put all ingredients into container. Cover and blend on MEDIUM speed for 15 seconds, stopping to stir down once.

2. Pour batter from container, ¼ cup at a time, onto hot greased griddle to make 3-inch pancakes. When surface of cakes becomes bubbly and underside is nicely browned, turn cakes and cook on other side until brown.

CORN-MEAL BUTTERMILK PANCAKES

Makes about twenty 2-inch pancakes

2	eggs	1⅓	cups white or yellow
2	cups buttermilk		stone-ground corn meal
4	tablespoons soft or melted	¼	cup all-purpose flour
	butter or cooking oil	1	teaspoon salt
		½	teaspoon baking powder

1. Put all ingredients into container in order listed. Cover and blend on MEDIUM speed for 15 seconds, stopping to stir down once.

2. Pour batter onto hot greased griddle, making pancakes about 2 inches in diameter. When surface of the cakes becomes bubbly and lightly browned on underside, turn and brown lightly on the other side.

Muffins & Corn Breads

BRAN MUFFINS

Makes 12

1	cup presifted all-purpose flour	2	tablespoons soft butter
2½	teaspoons baking powder	¼	cup sugar
½	teaspoon salt	¾	cup milk
1	egg	1	cup bran

1. Preheat oven to 400° F. Grease 12 medium muffin cups.

2. In a mixing bowl, combine flour, baking powder, and salt.

3. Put into container remaining ingredients. Cover and blend on LOW speed for 15 seconds. Pour over dry ingredients and stir just until all the flour is moistened.

4. Fill prepared muffin cups ⅔ full and bake in preheated oven for 10 to 15 minutes.

DATE-NUT BRAN MUFFINS

Follow recipe above, but add to ingredients in container, ¾ cup pitted dates and ¼ cup walnut meats.

RAISIN BRAN MUFFINS

Follow recipe above, but add to ingredients in container 1 cup seedless or light raisins.

CORN-MEAL MUFFINS

Follow recipe above, but use 1 cup stone-ground yellow corn meal in place of the bran.

WHEAT-GERM MUFFINS

Makes 1 dozen 2½-inch muffins

1 cup presifted all-purpose flour	1 cup milk
3 teaspoons baking powder	1 egg
1 teaspoon salt	1 cup wheat germ
2 tablespoons sugar	

1. Preheat oven to 400° F. Grease 12 muffin cups.

2. Combine in a mixing bowl the flour, baking powder, salt, and sugar.

3. Put remaining ingredients into container. Cover and blend on LOW speed for 15 seconds. Pour over dry ingredients and stir just until all the flour is moistened.

4. Fill prepared muffin cups ⅔ full and bake in preheated oven for 10 to 15 minutes.

FOR SWEETER MUFFINS:

Follow recipe above, but increase sugar to ¼ or ½ cup.

FOR BUTTERMILK MUFFINS:

Follow recipe above, but use only 2 teaspoons baking powder, add ½ teaspoon baking soda, and substitute buttermilk for the sweet milk.

BERRY MUFFINS

Follow recipe above for Sweeter Muffins, and fold into batter in container 1 cup washed and drained blueberries or raspberries, before dividing into muffin cups.

APPLE-PECAN MUFFINS

Make Sweeter Muffins adding ½ teaspoon cinnamon or nutmeg to the dry ingredients. Add to ingredients in container 1 apple, peeled, cored, and coarsely cut, and ½ cup pecans.

BUTTERMILK SPOON BREAD

Serves 6

½ cup water	2 eggs
2 cups white corn meal	1 teaspoon salt
1½ tablespoons soft butter	1 teaspoon baking soda
2 cups boiling water	1½ cups buttermilk

1. Measure water, corn meal, and butter into blender container. Turn blender on LOW speed and gradually pour in the boiling water. Turn off blender and let mixture stand in container for 15 minutes, or until ready to bake the bread.

2. Preheat oven to 425° F. Butter a 1½-quart baking dish.

3. Add eggs, salt, and baking soda. Cover and turn blender on LOW speed. With blades spinning, remove cover and gradually fill to top with buttermilk. Reserve any remaining buttermilk.

4. Pour batter into prepared pan, stir in any remaining buttermilk, and bake in the preheated oven for about 45 minutes, or until well browned on top.

CHEESE SPOON BREAD

Serves 6

2 cups steaming hot milk	1½ cups diced Cheddar cheese
2 tablespoons soft butter	½ teaspoon salt
1⅓ cups yellow corn meal	2 egg whites
2 egg yolks	

1. Preheat oven to 375° F. Butter a 1½-quart casserole.

2. Pour hot milk into container. Add butter and corn meal. Cover and turn blender on LOW speed. As soon as blades reach full speed, switch to HIGH speed and blend for 45 seconds.

3. Remove cover and add egg yolks, cheese, and salt and continue to blend for 20 seconds longer.

4. In a mixing bowl, beat egg whites until stiff, but not dry. Pour corn-meal mixture over egg whites and fold together gently but thoroughly.

5. Empty into casserole and bake in preheated oven for 35 minutes.

CRISP CORN DOLLARS

Makes about 36

1¾ cups boiling water
1   teaspoon salt
¼   teaspoon sugar
1   cup white or yellow stone-ground corn meal

1. Preheat oven to 450° F. Butter a baking sheet generously.

2. Put all ingredients into container. Cover and blend on MEDIUM speed for 15 seconds, stopping to stir down once.

3. Put baking sheet into hot oven until the butter begins to sizzle. Remove from oven (careful! use pot holder) and pour batter onto the hot pan in little cakes about the size of a silver dollar.

4. Return pan to hot oven and bake for 15 minutes, or until corn dollars are lightly browned. Serve hot.

HUSH PUPPIES

Makes 30 to 40

2   cups fine corn meal
1   tablespoon flour
½   teaspoon soda
1   teaspoon salt

1   egg
1   cup buttermilk
½   cup coarsely diced onion

1. Combine corn meal, flour, soda, and salt in a mixing bowl.

2. Put egg, buttermilk and onion into container. Cover and blend on MEDIUM speed until onion is finely cut, about 10 seconds.

3. Pour blended mixture over sifted corn meal mixture. Stir until completely moistened. Let stand 5 minutes.

4. Drop by rounded teaspoons, or tablespoons, into 1½ inches of moderately hot fat or oil (370° F.). Fry about 1 minute, turning when brown on one side if necessary. Drain on absorbent paper and serve hot.

Fritters, Crêpes & Blintzes

APPLE FRITTERS

Makes about 30

1½	cups presifted all-purpose flour	½	cup milk
¼	cup sugar	2	eggs
	Dash of salt	2	tart apples, washed, cored, and quartered
2	teaspoons baking powder		

1. In a mixing bowl, combine flour, sugar, salt, and baking powder.

2. Put remaining ingredients into container. Cover and blend on HIGH speed for 6 seconds only. DO NOT OVERBLEND.

3. Stir apple mixture into dry ingredients until dry ingredients are moistened.

4. Drop batter by teaspoonfuls into deep fat heated to 370° F. and fry for about 6 minutes, or until fritters are golden brown.

5. Remove fritters with a slotted spoon to absorbent paper to drain. Sprinkle with confectioners' sugar and serve hot.

THIN PANCAKES OR CRÊPES

Makes 12 crêpes

1½	cups milk
3	eggs
1	cup presifted all-purpose flour
½	teaspoon salt
1	tablespoon melted butter or cooking oil

1. Put all ingredients into container. Cover and blend on MEDIUM speed for 15 seconds, stopping to stir down once. Set batter aside for 30 minutes before baking.

2. To bake, heat a small frying pan (6-inches in diameter). Brush generously with butter, using about ½ teaspoon for each crêpe. When butter

is foaming and just about to brown, pour in about 2 tablespoons batter and tip and swirl the pan to cover bottom with a thin layer. When under side is brown (about 1 minute), turn with a spatula and brown on the other side.

3. Sprinkle each thin cake with confectioners' sugar and serve with a wedge of lemon, OR COOL AND REFRIGERATE OR FREEZE for use in various recipes.

NOTE: To use later, turn the cooked cakes out onto absorbent paper to cool. When cool, stack with a double thickness of waxed paper in between each. Wrap in waxed paper or foil and store in refrigerator where they will stay fresh for several days, or freeze.

BLINTZES

Makes 16 blintzes

1 cup milk	2 tablespoons lemon juice
2 eggs	1 egg yolk
1 tablespoon soft butter	⅓ cup sugar
½ cup all-purpose flour	1 cup cream-style cottage cheese
Dash of salt	(8 ounces)
Thin yellow rind of ½ lemon	

1. Put into container the milk, whole eggs, butter, flour, and salt. Cover and blend on HIGH speed for 10 seconds, or until smooth.

2. Melt a small amount of butter in a 6-inch skillet. Pour in sufficient blintz batter to thinly cover bottom of pan (about 2 tablespoons). Raise skillet over heat and cook until the batter is set but not brown. Shake out onto waxed paper and repeat until all blintzes have been made.

3. Clean container and put in lemon rind, juice, egg yolk, and sugar. Cover and blend on HIGH speed for 10 seconds, or until rind is finely chopped.

4. Stir egg mixture into cottage cheese.

5. Place 1 tablespoon filling in center of each blintz. Fold sides of blintz toward center and roll, enclosing the filling. Chill until ready to cook.

6. To cook, melt about ¼ cup butter in skillet and in it sauté the blintzes for about 5 minutes on each side over low heat, or until golden.

7. Serve with sour cream and jelly.

Tea Cakes & Breads

SCOTTISH OAT CAKES

Makes 8

4   tablespoons soft butter or shortening (½ stick)
¾   teaspoon salt
¼   teaspoon baking soda (regular or instant)
⅓   cup boiling water
2½   cups rolled oats

1. Put into container the butter or shortening, salt, soda, and boiling water. Cover and blend on HIGH speed for 5 seconds.

2. With blades spinning, remove cover and add 1 cup of the oats. Blend for 5 seconds longer, or until mixture is smooth.

3. Preheat oven to 350° F. Grease a baking sheet and set aside.

4. Spread remaining 1½ cups oats on a work surface. Empty mixture from container into the center of the oats. Knead the dry oats into the moist mixture, then roll dough out into a 10-inch circle. If the edges crack, pinch together with fingers. Cut into 8 pie-shaped wedges and bake on a hot greased griddle for 10 minutes, or until corners begin to curl. Brush off any excess oats, as these burn on the griddle and become bitter.

5. Transfer the cakes to a greased baking sheet and bake in the preheated oven for 15 minutes.

6. Cool on a cake rack and serve with sweet butter and honey.

PINEAPPLE-PECAN BREAD

Makes one 8 x 4-inch loaf

1¾	cups all-purpose flour	3	tablespoons soft butter
2	teaspoons baking powder	¾	cup light brown sugar
¼	teaspoon soda	One	8-ounce can crushed pineapple
¼	teaspoon salt		with juice
2	eggs	One	4-ounce can pecans

1. Preheat oven to 350° F. Grease loaf pan.

2. Combine in mixing bowl the flour, baking powder, soda, and salt.

3. Put into container the eggs, butter, brown sugar, and pineapple with juice. Cover and blend on HIGH speed for 12 seconds or until well blended.

4. With blades spinning, remove cover and pour in the pecans. Stop motor as soon as pecans are drawn down into blades.

5. Empty batter into prepared pan and bake in preheated oven for about 50 minutes, or until cake tests done. Cool in pan for 5 minutes, then turn out on cake rack to cool completely.

DATE-NUT BREAD

Makes one 8½ x 4½-inch loaf

2	cups all-purpose flour	5	tablespoons soft butter
1	teaspoon baking powder	5	tablespoons cold water
½	teaspoon salt	1	teaspoon soda
1	pound pitted dates	¾	cup brown sugar
1	cup boiling water	One	8-ounce can walnuts

1. Preheat oven to 350° F. Grease loaf pan.

2. Combine in mixing bowl the flour, baking powder, and salt.

3. Put dates, boiling water, and butter into container. Cover and blend on HIGH speed for 12 seconds.

4. With blades spinning, remove cover and add the cold water, soda, and brown sugar. Blend for 6 seconds, then add the walnuts. Turn off motor as soon as walnuts are drawn down into the blades.

5. Pour date mixture over dry ingredients and mix until all ingredients are well blended.

6. Empty batter into prepared pan and bake in the preheated oven for about 1 hour, or until loaf tests done. Remove loaf from pan to cake rack to cool.

BANANA BRAN TEA BREAD

Makes 1 loaf

1	cup all-purpose flour	2	small ripe bananas, peeled and
1	cup bran flakes		quartered
2	teaspoons baking powder	½	cup milk
1	teaspoon salt	⅔	cup light brown sugar
2	eggs	1	teaspoon vanilla
5	tablespoons soft butter	½	cup nuts

1. Preheat oven to 350° F. Grease a 9 x 5 x 3-inch loaf pan.

2. Combine in mixing bowl the flour, bran flakes, baking powder, and salt.

3. Put into container the eggs, butter, bananas, milk, brown sugar, and vanilla. Cover and blend on HIGH speed for 20 seconds.

4. With blades spinning, remove cover and pour in nuts. Turn off motor as soon as nuts are pulled down into the blades.

5. Pour mixture over dry ingredients and mix just until all dry ingredients are moistened.

6. Pour batter into prepared loaf pan and bake in preheated oven for about 1 hour, or until loaf tests done. Remove from baking pan to cake rack to cool.

APPLE SPICE LOAF

Makes 1 loaf

2	cups all-purpose flour	4	tablespoons soft butter or
2	teaspoons baking powder		margarine (½ stick)
½	teaspoon baking soda	2	eggs
½	teaspoon salt	¼	teaspoon cinnamon
½	cup currants	⅛	teaspoon cloves
2	strips lemon rind	⅛	teaspoon nutmeg
2	cups applesauce (1-pound can)	¼	cup walnuts
¼	cup sugar		

1. Preheat oven to 375° F.

2. In a mixing bowl, combine flour, baking powder, baking soda, salt, and currants.

3. Into container put lemon rind and 1 cup applesauce. Cover and blend on HIGH speed for 10 seconds, or until rind is grated.

4. Add remaining cup applesauce, sugar, butter or margarine, eggs, cinnamon, cloves, and nutmeg. Cover and blend on HIGH speed for 10 seconds, or until smooth.

5. With blades spinning, remove lid and add the nuts. Continue blending only until last walnut has been drawn down into the blades.

6. Pour applesauce mixture over dry ingredients in bowl and mix with spoon until dry ingredients are moistened.

7. Turn into greased loaf pan (9½ x 5¼ x 2¾ inches) and bake in preheated oven for 45 minutes.

Yeast Breads & Rolls

BASIC YEAST BREAD AND ROLLS

Makes 1 loaf or 2 dozen rolls

1	cup lukewarm water	1	egg
1	envelope active dry yeast	1	teaspoon salt
¾	cup dry milk solids	3	cups all-purpose flour
¼	cup cooking oil		

1. Put lukewarm water and yeast into container. Let stand for 5 minutes, then cover, and blend on HIGH speed for 20 seconds.

2. Add dry milk solids, oil, egg, and salt. Cover and blend on HIGH speed for 6 seconds.

3. Pour into mixing bowl and add flour. Stir until flour and liquid are thoroughly mixed, then cover lightly with a towel, and let rise for 1½ hours, or until double in bulk.

4. Punch dough down, then shape into loaf or rolls, and bake as directed in a preheated 350° F. oven. Remove bread or rolls from pan to a cake rack to cool.

TO MAKE A LOAF

Oil a 9 x 5 x 3-inch loaf pan. Flatten dough with palms of hands into a rectangle about ½ inch thick and as long as the pan. Roll lengthwise and tuck under ends to make a neat oval of dough. Place seam side down in pan. Cover with towel and let rise until dough is nicely rounded above edges of pan. Bake for 45 to 50 minutes.

TO MAKE ONION PARSLEY BREAD

Oil a 9 x 5 x 3-inch loaf pan. Blender-chop 1 medium onion, peeled and quartered, and empty out onto waxed paper. Blender-chop ½ cup parsley clusters (be sure they are dry), and mix with onion. Roll dough out on lightly floured surface into a large circle about ¼ inch thick. Spread surface with soft butter and sprinkle with the onion-parsley mixture. Roll lengthwise, tuck ends under, and place seam side down in loaf pan. Cover with towel and let rise until dough is nicely rounded above edges of pan. Bake for 45 to 50 minutes.

TO MAKE DINNER ROLLS

Butter 24 muffin cups generously. Divide dough into 24 pieces. Form each piece into a ball and place in a cup. Let rise until almost double in bulk, brush tops of rolls with melted butter, and if desired, sprinkle with sesame or poppy seeds. Bake for 25 minutes.

TO MAKE CLOVER LEAF ROLLS

Butter 24 muffin cups generously. Divide dough into 24 pieces. Divide each of these pieces into 3 parts and form into balls. Place 3 balls in each cup and let rise until almost double in bulk. Brush with melted butter and bake for 25 minutes.

TO MAKE PARKER HOUSE ROLLS

Butter a baking sheet. Divide dough into 24 pieces. Roll each piece out on a floured surface into a round about ¼ inch thick. Crease each round with back of a knife, just a little off center. Brush rounds with melted butter and fold in half, pinching ends together. Arrange on baking sheet and let rise until almost double in bulk. Brush with melted butter and bake for 25 minutes.

HUNGARIAN POPPY SEED ROLLS

Makes 3 dozen

* ½ cup walnuts, blender-chopped
  ½ cup brown sugar
  3 tablespoons poppy seeds
  1 envelope dry yeast
  ½ cup lukewarm water
  ⅓ cup granulated sugar
  4 tablespoons soft butter
    (½ stick)

⅓ cup milk
.2 egg yolks
1 teaspoon vanilla
½ teaspoon salt
2½ cups all-purpose flour
½ cup melted butter (1 stick)

1. Blender-chop the walnuts and empty into a mixing bowl.

2. Put into container brown sugar and poppy seeds. Cover and blend on HIGH speed for 10 seconds, or until sugar is powdered and poppy seeds are ground. Empty onto a piece of waxed paper and reserve.

3. Put into container lukewarm water and yeast. Let stand for 5 minutes, then cover, and blend on HIGH speed for 20 seconds. Add granulated sugar, butter, milk, egg yolks, vanilla, and salt. Cover and blend on HIGH speed for 10 seconds, or until smooth.

4. Pour into mixing bowl with walnuts and stir in flour. Cover and let rise in warm place for 1 hour, or until double in bulk.

5. Punch dough down. Shape into 1-inch balls. Place these 1-inch apart in oiled baking pans. Cover and let rise for 15 minutes. Bake in preheated oven 350° F. for 45 minutes, or until golden.

6. While rolls are still warm, roll each first in melted butter, then the poppy seed mixture.

GARLIC HERB BREAD

Makes 1 loaf

1 cup lukewarm water
1 envelope active dry yeast
2 tablespoons butter
1 egg
1 teaspoon salt

1 tablespoon tarragon or dill weed
1 large clove garlic, peeled
3 cups all-purpose flour

1. Put into container the water and yeast. Let soak for 5 minutes, then cover, and blend on HIGH speed for 20 seconds.

2. Add butter, egg, salt, herb, and garlic. Cover and blend on HIGH speed for 10 seconds.

3. Add 1 cup flour, stir to mix, cover, and blend on HIGH speed for 20 seconds. Cover container and let batter rise for 1 hour. Blend on HIGH speed for 3 minutes longer.

4. Pour batter into mixing bowl and stir in remaining 2 cups flour. Grease an 8¼ x 4½-inch loaf pan.

5. Pick up dough with floured hands and form into a loaf. Put loaf into prepared pan, cover, and let rise for 1 hour, or until dough is nicely rounded over edges of pan.

6. For a golden crust, brush with beaten egg. Bake in preheated 375° F. oven for 35 to 40 minutes.

WHOLE-WHEAT RYE BREAD

Makes 4 small loaves

1¼	cups lukewarm water	1	cup water-ground rye flour
1	envelope active dry yeast	2	cups water-ground
1	cup dry milk solids		whole-wheat flour
1½	teaspoons salt	1	tablespoon soft butter or cook-
1	teaspoon sugar		ing oil

1. Put 1 cup of the water and yeast into container. Let soak for 5 minutes, then cover, and blend on HIGH speed for 20 seconds.

2. Add dry milk solids, salt, sugar, and rye flour. Stir to mix, cover, and blend on HIGH speed for 60 seconds. Pour into a mixing bowl.

3. Add remaining ¼ cup water to container, blend on MEDIUM speed for 10 seconds, and stir into bowl with the batter. Cover and let rise for 30 minutes. Stir down and let rise again for 30 minutes, or until double in bulk.

4. Mix in enough whole-wheat flour to make a soft dough. Turn dough out onto floured surface and knead in enough additional whole-wheat flour to make a firm dough.

5. Shape dough into 4 small loaves and place on oiled baking sheet. Spread surface of loaves with soft butter or oil and let rise for about 1 hour, or until almost double in bulk.

6. Bake in preheated 375° F. oven for 25 to 30 minutes, or until well browned.

CHEESE BREAD

Makes 1 loaf

1   cup lukewarm water
1   envelope active dry yeast
½   pound Cheddar cheese, diced
1   teaspoon salt
1   egg
3   cups all-purpose flour

1. Put into container the water and yeast. Let soak for 5 minutes, then cover, and blend on HIGH speed for 20 seconds.

2. Add cheese, salt, and egg. Cover and blend on HIGH speed for 15 seconds.

3. Pour into a mixing bowl and add flour. Mix until all liquid ingredients are blended into the flour.

4. Cover with a towel and let rise in a warm place for 2 hours.

5. Oil an 8½ x 4¼-inch loaf pan, then punch dough down, pick up with floured hands, and press into prepared pan.

6. Let rise for 1 hour, then bake in a preheated 375° F. oven for 45 to 50 minutes.

Sweet Yeast Breads

ANADAMA BREAD

Makes 1 loaf

1½   cups boiling water   ¼   cup molasses
⅓   cup yellow corn meal   ½   cup cold water
1   teaspoon salt   1   envelope active dry yeast
2   tablespoons butter   3¾   cups all-purpose flour

1. Be sure water is boiling hot. Put water, corn meal, salt, and butter into container. Cover and blend on HIGH speed for 20 seconds.

2. Add molasses and cold water, cover, and blend on HIGH speed for 5 seconds. Add yeast, and blend on HIGH speed for 20 seconds longer.

3. Pour into mixing bowl and add flour. Mix until liquid ingredients

are blended with the flour. This will be a soft dough. Cover and let rise for 1½ hours.

4. Oil a 9 x 5½-inch loaf pan. Stir dough down and empty into prepared pan. Cover and let rise for 1 hour.

5. Brush surface of dough with soft butter, sprinkle with corn meal, and bake in preheated 375° F. oven for 40 to 45 minutes. Remove from pan to cake rack to cool.

SCHNECKEN
(Sweet Buns)

Makes 12 buns

* 1 cup pecans, blender-chopped
  1 cup blanched almonds
  ½ cup granulated sugar
  1 cup lukewarm milk
  1 envelope active dry yeast
  1 cup soft butter

  5 egg yolks
  ¾ teaspoon salt
  About 3 cups all-purpose flour
  1 cup brown sugar
  ¼ pound butter (1 stick)

1. Blender-chop the pecans and empty onto a piece of waxed paper.

2. Put almonds and granulated sugar into container. Cover and blend on HIGH speed for 10 seconds. Empty mixture out onto a second piece of waxed paper. Set aside.

3. Put milk and yeast into container. Let stand 5 minutes, then cover, and blend on HIGH speed for 20 seconds.

4. Add the 1 cup soft butter, egg yolks, and salt. Cover and blend on HIGH speed for 15 seconds.

5. Empty into a mixing bowl and stir in 2½ cups of the flour. Turn dough out onto floured surface and knead in enough additional flour to make a dough that is soft, but not sticky.

6. Roll dough out into a 12-inch square and sprinkle with the almond-sugar mixture. Roll jelly-roll fashion.

7. Melt the stick of butter in a 13 x 9½ x 2-inch baking pan. Remove from heat and sprinkle with the brown sugar and pecans.

8. Cut the roll into ½ inch slices and place cut side down in prepared pan. Cover and let rise for 30 minutes, or until well puffed.

9. Bake in preheated 375° F. oven for 25 to 30 minutes, or until golden. Turn buns out immediately onto cake rack to cool.

PRUNE BREAD

Makes 1 loaf

½	cup lukewarm water	2	tablespoons soft butter
1	package dry yeast	¼	cup sugar
¼	cup milk	1	teaspoon salt
1	cup pitted, cooked prunes	½	cup pecan meats
	Thin rind from 1 lemon	½	cup glacé cherries
2	eggs	3½	cups all-purpose flour

1. Put water and yeast into container. Let stand for 5 minutes. Then cover and blend on HIGH speed for 20 seconds.

2. Add milk, prunes, lemon rind, eggs, butter, sugar, and salt. Cover and blend on HIGH speed for 10 seconds, or until smooth. With motor on, remove cover, add nuts and cherries, and continue blending only until nuts and cherries are chopped.

3. Pour into a mixing bowl and stir in flour. Cover and let rise until double in bulk (about 1½ hours).

4. Shape into loaf and place in greased 9 x 5 x 3-inch loaf pan. Cover and let rise until nicely rounded over edge of pan.

5. Bake in preheated 375° F. oven for 50 minutes. Cool and if desired, top with a glaze made by mixing confectioners' sugar with a little water.

SWEDISH SAFFRON BRAID

Makes 1 loaf

3	tablespoons sugar	¼	pound soft butter or
⅓	cup blanched almonds		margarine (1 stick)
½	cup lukewarm milk	¼	teaspoon salt
1	envelope dry yeast	¾	cup milk
½	teaspoon saffron	½	cup seedless raisins
2	eggs	3½	cups all-purpose flour
½	cup sugar		

1. Put into container 3 tablespoons sugar and almonds. Cover and blend on HIGH speed for 2 to 3 seconds, or until nuts are chopped. Empty onto piece of waxed paper.

2. Put into container the water, yeast, and saffron. Let stand for 5 minutes, then cover, and blend on HIGH speed for 20 seconds. Add one egg,

sugar, butter or margarine, salt, and milk. Cover and blend on HIGH speed for 15 seconds, or until smooth.

3. Empty into a mixing bowl and stir in raisins and flour. Cover and let rise in warm place for 1 hour, or until double in bulk.

4. Punch dough down and knead briefly on lightly floured board. Shape into a 14-inch-long sausage shape.

5. Place on greased baking sheet. Cut to within one inch from one end into 3 long strips and braid. Pinch loose ends together. Cover and let rise for 15 minutes.

6. Beat remaining egg lightly and brush over loaf. Sprinkle with mixture of sugar and chopped almonds.

7. Bake in preheated 350° F. oven for 45 minutes, or until top is golden. Cool on cake rack.

QUICK COFFEE CAKE

Makes one 9-inch square

1 package hot-roll mix	2 tablespoons flour
1 cup warm water	½ cup brown sugar
½ teaspoon cinnamon	¼ teaspoon cinnamon
½ teaspoon nutmeg	½ cup chopped nuts
2 tablespoons sugar	4 tablespoons melted butter
1 egg	(½ stick)
1 cup seedless raisins	

1. Put into container yeast from package of hot-roll mix, warm water, cinnamon, nutmeg, sugar, egg, and seedless raisins. Cover and blend at HIGH speed for about 15 seconds, or until thoroughly blended.

2. Empty flour from package of mix into mixing bowl, add blended mixture, and stir to make a stiff dough.

3. Grease top of dough and cover with waxed paper. Let rise in warm place until dough is light and double in bulk, about 45 minutes to 1 hour.

4. Spread dough evenly in greased baking pan about 9 inches square and 2 inches deep. Combine the 2 tablespoons flour, brown sugar, cinnamon, nuts, and butter to make crumbly mixture and sprinkle lightly over top of dough.

5. Let rise until light in warm place until nearly double in bulk. Bake in moderately hot oven, 375° F., until lightly browned, about 30 minutes.

CAKES, FROSTINGS
& COOKIES

Cakes, Frostings & Cookies

YOUR ELECTRIC blender was not designed for whipping batters for cakes. Generally speaking an electric mixer or a hand beater is superior for cake making, and just a wooden spoon and a strong arm are hard to beat in the cookies department.

However, there are certain types of cakes, such as nut and crumb tortes and other old-fashioned rich, moist cakes and cookies that your blender can produce easily and quickly. It can also perform many short cuts for you in the making of the lighter-textured cakes so popular today.

The blender grates chocolate, nuts, and fruit rinds; chops candied fruits, dates, and raisins; purées fruit for fillings; creams soft butter and sugar; and blends chocolate to a sauce. Your blender can also play an important role in the making of fillings, frosting, and crumbly-type toppings for cakes and cookies. But, perhaps, best of all, it saves many minutes of tedious sieving of cheese to produce some of the best cheesecakes that you have ever put in your mouth. We begin with these.

Cheese Cakes

QUICK CHEESE CAKE

Serves 6

* 10 zwieback, blender-crumbed	½ tablespoon lemon juice
4 tablespoons soft butter (½ stick)	¼ cup boiling water
	2 egg yolks
1 tablespoon sugar	¼ cup sugar
½ teaspoon cinnamon	One 8-ounce package soft cream
1 tablespoon plain gelatin	cheese, quartered
Thin yellow peel from ½ lemon	½ cup heavy cream
	2 egg whites
2 tablespoons cold water	

1. Blender-crumb 5 zwieback at a time and empty into bowl. Mix into crumbs the butter, 1 tablespoon sugar, and cinnamon.

296

2. Line bottom of a 4-cup loaf pan with waxed paper and butter sides heavily. Press crumbs onto sides and bottom of pan.

3. Put into container the gelatin, lemon peel, cold water, and lemon juice. Let gelatin soak for 1 minute, then add the boiling water, cover, and blend on HIGH speed for 30 seconds.

4. Remove cover, and with blades spinning, add egg yolks, the ¼ cup sugar, and the cream cheese, and blend until mixture is smooth.

5. Gradually pour in the heavy cream and blend for 2 seconds longer.

6. In a mixing bowl, beat egg whites until stiff but not dry. Pour blended cheese mixture over egg whites and fold together lightly.

7. Spoon mixture into prepared loaf pan and chill for several hours before serving.

SOUR-CREAM CHEESE CAKE

Serves 6 to 8

	Graham cracker crust	⅓	cup sugar
	(page 232)	¼	teaspoon salt
1	cup sour cream	¼	cup flour
3	egg yolks	2	cups cottage cheese (16 ounces)
1	tablespoon lemon juice	3	egg whites
	Strip of yellow lemon rind	¼	cup sugar

1. Line a 9-inch spring form pan or round cake pan, 3 inches deep, with crust crumbs and set aside.

2. Put sour cream, egg yolks, lemon juice and rind, the ⅓ cup sugar, salt, flour, and cottage cheese into container. Cover and blend on HIGH speed for 30 seconds, stopping to stir down if necessary.

3. In a mixing bowl, beat egg whites until stiff, but not dry. Gradually beat in the ¼ cup sugar. Pour cheese mixture over egg whites and fold together gently but thoroughly.

4. Spoon cheese mixture into crumb-lined pan and bake in preheated 325° F. oven for 1¼ hours or until center of cake is firm.

5. Remove from oven and cool completely before removing from pan.

STRAWBERRY CHEESE CAKE

Serves 6 to 8

* 1½ cup blender-crumbed graham   2 teaspoons vanilla
      crackers   1½ cups sour cream
  6 tablespoons melted butter   Two 8-ounce packages soft cream
      (¾ stick)   cheese, quartered
      Dash of salt   1 pint fresh strawberries
  2 eggs   ½ cup red currant jelly
  ½ cup sugar

1. In a bowl, combine crumbs, 4 tablespoons of the melted butter, and salt. Press on bottom and sides of an 8-inch spring form pan.

2. Put eggs, sugar, vanilla, and sour cream into container. Cover and blend on HIGH speed for 15 seconds. Remove cover and with blades spinning, gradually add the cheese. Finally, add remaining 2 tablespoons melted butter.

3. Pour cheese mixture into prepared pan and bake in preheated 350° F. oven for 20 to 30 minutes, or until set. Cool and remove sides of pan.

4. Top cheese cake with whole or halved strawberries.

5. Melt jelly over low heat in a small saucepan, stirring until smooth. Spoon jelly over strawberries and chill until ready to serve.

Cakes & Tortes

JIFFY SPONGE CAKE

Makes one 9-inch layer

  5 egg whites   3 tablespoons cold water
  ¼ teaspoon salt   1 tablespoon lemon juice
  ¼ teaspoon cream of tartar   5 egg yolks
  1 cup sugar   1 cup sifted cake flour

1. In a large mixing bowl, beat egg whites, salt, and cream of tartar until they stand in smooth peaks. Gradually beat in ½ cup of the sugar.

2. Put remaining sugar into container. Add cold water, lemon juice, egg yolks, and cake flour. Cover and blend on HIGH speed for 1½ minutes.

3. Pour egg yolk mixture over egg whites and fold together until there are no streaks.

4. Pour batter into an ungreased 9-inch tube pan. Bake in preheated 350° F. oven until cake springs back into shape after being pressed lightly with finger, about 45 minutes.

5. Invert cake and pan on cake rack to cool thoroughly before removing cake from pan.

ORANGE CHIFFON CAKE

Makes one 9-inch cake

½	cup egg whites	¼	cup sugar
	(4 egg whites)	1½	teaspoons baking powder
¼	teaspoon cream of tartar	½	teaspoon salt
½	cup sugar	1⅛	cups sifted cake flour
¼	cup cooking oil		A few walnut halves
2	egg yolks		Orange Frosting (page 307)
1	strip orange rind		
	Juice of 1 orange plus water		
	to make ⅜ cup		

1. In a large mixing bowl, beat egg whites until stiff and glossy. Gradually beat in the ½ cup sugar.

2. Put remaining ingredients into container. Cover and blend on HIGH speed for about 1 minute, or until smooth.

3. Pour blended mixture over beaten whites and fold together gently until there are no streaks.

4. Spoon into ungreased tube pan 9 × 3½-inches and bake in a preheated 325° F. oven for 50 to 55 minutes, until cake surface springs back after being pressed lightly with finger.

5. Invert on cake rack and remove from pan when thoroughly cool.

6. Frost with Orange Frosting and garnish with walnut halves.

OLD-FASHIONED CHOCOLATE CAKE

Makes one 9-inch layer.   Here is a delicious moist chocolate cake.

2	eggs	½	cup cocoa
½	cup sugar	2	teaspoons baking powder
¼	cup milk	¼	teaspoon salt
¼	pound soft butter (1 stick)		Chocolate Butter Cream
1½	cups presifted all-purpose		(page 306)
	flour		

1. Put eggs, sugar, and milk into container. Cover and blend on HIGH speed for 10 seconds.

2. Add butter and blend on HIGH speed for 5 seconds, or until smooth.

3. In a mixing bowl, combine flour, cocoa, baking powder, and salt. Add blender mixture and mix well.

4. Spoon batter into oiled 9-inch layer-cake pan and bake in a preheated 325° F. oven for 40 minutes, or until cake tests done.

5. Cool in pan for 5 to 10 minutes, then turn out on cake rack to cool.

6. When cool, split crosswise and fill and frost with Chocolate Butter Cream.

NOTE: ½ cup blender-chopped walnuts or pecans may be added to batter, if desired.

TWO-EGG CAKE WITH MACAROON TOPPING

Makes one 8 × 12-inch cake

2¼	cups sifted cake flour	2	eggs
3	teaspoons baking powder	1½	cups sugar
½	teaspoon salt	2	egg whites
¼	pound soft butter or mar-	1	cup confectioners' sugar
	garine (1 stick)	1	teaspoon vanilla
1	cup milk	One	3½-ounce can shredded
1	teaspoon vanilla		coconut

1. In a mixing bowl, combine cake flour, baking powder, and salt.

2. Put butter or margarine, milk, 1 teaspoon vanilla, eggs, and sugar into container. Cover and blend on HIGH speed for about 1 minute or until mixture is smooth. Pour over dry ingredients and stir lightly until just combined.

3. Spoon batter into oiled 8 × 12-inch baking pan, lined with wax paper, and bake in a preheated 350° F. oven for 40 minutes, or until cake tests done.

4. Meanwhile put egg whites, confectioners' sugar, and 1 teaspoon vanilla into container. Cover and blend on HIGH speed for 8 seconds. Add coconut and continue to blend for 15 seconds.

5. Spread the coconut mixture on top of the hot cake and place under broiler heat for 3 to 5 minutes, or until lightly browned.

CHOCOLATE PICNIC CAKE WITH MARSHMALLOW TOPPING

Makes one 8 × 12-inch cake

* ½ cup blender-chopped walnuts
½ cup brown sugar
1¾ cups sifted cake flour
1 teaspoon baking powder
½ teaspoon soda
½ teaspoon salt
2 squares bitter chocolate, diced

½ cup hot water or strong coffee
½ cup milk
1 teaspoon vanilla
2 eggs
1½ cups sugar
Marshmallows

1. Blender-chop walnuts, combine with brown sugar, and set aside.

2. In a mixing bowl, combine flour, baking powder, soda, and salt.

3. Into container put chocolate and hot water. Cover and blend on HIGH speed for 20 seconds.

4. Add milk, vanilla, eggs, and sugar. Cover and blend on HIGH speed for 30 seconds longer.

5. Pour blended mixture over dry ingredients and stir lightly until smooth.

6. Spoon batter into greased and waxed-paper-lined 8 × 12-inch baking pan. Arrange marshmallows over batter, keeping them 1 inch from sides of pan. Sprinkle the marshmallows with the brown sugar-walnut mixture.

7. Bake the cake in a preheated 350° F. oven for 40 minutes, or until cake tests done.

8. Cool and serve from pan.

COFFEE NUT TORTE

Makes three 8-inch layers

6	egg yolks	⅛	teaspoon salt
¼	cup strong coffee	6	egg whites
1	cup sugar		Coffee Cream Filling
¾	cup walnut meats		(page 308)
⅓	cup flour		Mocha Frosting (page 307)

1. Put egg yolks, coffee, sugar, walnuts, flour, and salt into container. Cover and blend on HIGH speed for 15 seconds, or until smooth, stopping to stir down if necessary.

2. In a large mixing bowl, beat egg whites until stiff, but not dry. Scrape blended ingredients into egg whites and fold together gently but evenly.

3. Spread batter in 3 oiled and waxed-paper-lined 8-inch layer pans. Bake in preheated 375° F. oven for 30 minutes.

4. Remove from oven and loosen edge of cake from pans with spatula to allow them to sink evenly. Cool, then turn out of pans and carefully peel off paper from bottom of each layer.

5. Make Coffee Cream Filling and spread between cake layers. Frost with Mocha Frosting.

ALMOND TORTE

Serves 12

6	egg yolks	⅛	teaspoon salt
¾	cup sugar	½	teaspoon almond extract
1½	cups blanched almonds	One	12-ounce jar apricot preserves
6	egg whites		Sour-Cream Chocolate Frost-
¼	teaspoon cream of tartar		ing (page 306)

1. Put egg yolks and sugar into container. Cover and blend on HIGH speed for 10 seconds.

2. Remove cover and, with blades spinning, gradually add the almonds, and continue blending until nuts are finely chopped, stopping to stir down if necessary.

3. In a large mixing bowl, beat egg whites, cream of tartar, salt, and almond extract until stiff but not dry. Fold egg yolk mixture into egg whites.

4. Spread batter in 2 greased and waxed-paper-lined 9-inch layer pans. Bake in preheated 300° F. oven for 1 hour.

5. Remove cakes from oven and loosen from sides of pans to allow them to sink evenly. When cool remove from pans, cut each layer in half crosswise to make 4 layers, then put the layers together again with apricot preserves spread between.

6. Frost top and sides of cake with Sour-Cream Chocolate Frosting and chill for several hours before serving.

HAZELNUT TORTE

Serves 12

* 1½	cups blanched hazelnuts, blender-grated	⅛	teaspoon salt
		½	teaspoon almond extract
6	eggs, separated	One	12-ounce jar cherry preserves
¾	cup sugar		Chocolate Frosting (page 307)
¼	teaspoon cream of tartar		

1. Blender-grate nuts and empty onto piece of waxed paper.

2. Into container put egg yolks and sugar. Cover and blend on HIGH speed for 10 seconds, or until smooth and lemon colored.

3. Beat egg whites with cream of tartar, salt, and almond extract until stiff but not dry. Fold blended egg yolk mixture and nuts into beaten egg whites.

4. Spread batter into 2 oiled and waxed-paper-lined 9-inch layer cake pans. Bake in preheated 300° F. oven for 1 hour.

5. Run spatula around edges of cakes to allow for even sinking. When cool remove from pans.

6. Cut each layer in half crosswise to form 4 layers. Spread cherry preserves between layers. Frost sides and top of cake with chocolate frosting. Chill several hours before serving.

SWEDISH APPLECAKE

Serves 6

* 2 cups blender-grated zwieback crumbs
¼ cup water
½ cup brown sugar
2 strips lemon rind
  Dash of salt
⅛ teaspoon cinnamon

  Dash of cloves
2 large apples, peeled, cored, and quartered
1 tablespoon soft butter or margarine
  Vanilla Custard Sauce (page 253)

1. Crumb zwieback and set aside.

2. Into container put water, sugar, lemon rind, salt, cinnamon, and cloves. Cover and blend on HIGH speed for 15 seconds, or until smooth and rind is finely chopped.

3. With blades spinning, remove cover and gradually add apple quarters and butter or margarine. Continue blending to a smooth purée.

4. Spread 1 cup crumbs in bottom of well-greased 8-inch layer pan. Spread apple purée over crumbs and top with remaining crumbs.

5. Bake in preheated 375° F. oven for 35 minutes. Cool.

6. Unmold and chill until serving time. Serve with Vanilla Custard Sauce.

SICILIAN CUP CAKES

Makes 18

⅔ cup blanched almonds
½ cup confectioners' sugar
1 teaspoon vanilla
¼ cup orange juice
3 egg whites
9 blanched almonds for decoration

1. Put almonds into container. Cover and blend on HIGH speed for 10 seconds.

2. Add sugar, vanilla, orange juice, and 1 egg white. Cover and blend on HIGH speed for 40 seconds, or until smooth, stopping to stir down if necessary.

3. In a mixing bowl, beat remaining 2 egg whites until stiff but not dry. Scrape blended mixture into egg whites and fold together lightly but thoroughly.

4. Spoon into 18 small paper cups and top each with half a blanched almond.

5. Bake in preheated 250° F. oven for 25 minutes. Cool before serving.

CANDIED FRUIT CAKE

Makes 8 × 4-inch loaf

* One 7¼-ounce package vanilla wafers, blender-crumbed
* 1 cup walnuts, blender-chopped
2 cups mixed fruit (seedless raisins, candied orange and lemon peel, candied pine-apple and glacé cherries)
½ cup pecan halves or blanched almonds

⅔ cup hot evaporated milk
2 teaspoons vanilla
1 tablespoon brandy or rum
¼ pound marshamallows
Candied fruit and nuts for decoration

1. Blender-crumb 10 vanilla wafers at a time. Empty into a mixing bowl and repeat until all are crumbed.

2. Blender-chop the walnuts and empty into the bowl with the crumbs.

3. Stir the mixed fruit and pecan halves or almonds into the crumbs.

4. Into container put evaporated milk, vanilla, brandy or rum, and marshmallows. Cover and blend on HIGH speed for 10 seconds, or until mixture is smooth. Empty into bowl with crumbs and fruit and mix well.

5. Pack mixture into foil-lined loaf pan, decorate top with candied fruit and nuts, cover with foil and refrigerate for 48 hours before serving.

Frostings & Fillings

CHOCOLATE BUTTER CREAM

Makes about 2 cups

6   ounces semi-sweet chocolate pieces
⅓   cup boiling water or strong coffee
3   egg yolks
1   teaspoon vanilla
¼   pound soft butter (1 stick)

1.   Empty chocolate pieces into container. Add water or coffee, cover, and blend on HIGH speed for 20 seconds.

2.   Remove cover and with blades spinning, add remaining ingredients. Continue to blend until mixture is smooth, stopping to stir down if necessary.

NOTE: For a larger quantity use 12 ounces chocolate pieces, ½ cup boiling water, 6 egg yolks, 2 teaspoons vanilla, and ⅜ pound (1½ sticks) soft butter.

MOCHA BUTTER CREAM

Add 1 teaspoon instant coffee to the chocolate and the water or coffee in the container.

RUM BUTTER CREAM

Reduce hot liquid to ¼ cup. Omit vanilla, and add 2 tablespoons Jamaica rum.

SOUR-CREAM CHOCOLATE FROSTING

Makes 1½ cups

6   ounces semi-sweet chocolate pieces
¼   cup boiling water
½   cup sour cream

1. Empty chocolate pieces into container. Add water, cover, and blend on HIGH speed for 20 seconds.

2. Add sour cream. Cover and blend on HIGH for 5 seconds, or until smooth.

CREAMY FROSTINGS

Makes 1⅔ cups

5	tablespoons light cream
1	teaspoon vanilla extract
¼	pound soft butter (1 stick)
2½–3	cups confectioners' sugar

1. Put cream, vanilla, butter, and 2 cups of the sugar into container. Cover and blend on HIGH speed for 10 seconds.

2. Add ½ cup sugar, cover, and blend on HIGH for 10 seconds longer.

3. If necessary, add remaining ½ cup sugar and continue to blend, stopping to stir down once or twice.

CHOCOLATE OR MOCHA FROSTING

Substitute ¼ cup cocoa for ¼ cup of the confectioners' sugar. Add also 1 teaspoon instant coffee for Mocha Frosting.

ORANGE FROSTING

Omit vanilla and substitute concentrated orange juice for the cream.

LEMON FROSTING

Omit vanilla and substitute lemon juice for the cream.

COFFEE CREAM FILLING

Makes about 2 cups

2 eggs
1 cup hot milk
1 cup heavy cream
⅓ cup sugar
3 tablespoons cornstarch
1 tablespoon instant coffee powder

1. Put all ingredients into container, cover, and blend on HIGH speed for 5 seconds, or until smooth.

2. Pour into a small saucepan and cook over low heat, stirring constantly, until smooth and thickened. Cool, stirring occasionally.

Cookies

ALMOND COOKIES

Makes 24

	Almond Paste (below)	¾	cup sugar
1	egg	2	cups presifted flour
2	teaspoons almond extract	¼	teaspoon salt
⅜	pound soft butter (about 1½ sticks)	24	blanched almonds for decoration

1. Make Almond Paste and leave in container. Add egg, almond extract, butter, and sugar, cover, and blend on HIGH speed for 1½ minutes, stopping to stir down well after 30 seconds.

2. In a mixing bowl, combine flour and salt. Add blended mixture and mix until smooth. Chill for 1 hour.

3. Form dough into 1½-inch balls and arrange on ungreased baking sheet. Flatten each ball to about ⅓ inch thick. Place a blanched almond in center of each and bake in a preheated 325° F. oven for 25 minutes, or until lightly browned.

ALMOND PASTE

Makes 1 cup

¼ cup water
¼ cup sugar
¼ cup confectioners' sugar
½ teaspoon lemon juice
¾ cup blanched almonds (4 ounces)

Put all ingredients into container. Cover and blend on HIGH speed for about 3 minutes, or until mixture is blended to a paste consistency. Stop motor occasionally to stir mixture down in container.

PRUNE PINWHEELS

Makes 2 dozen

½ cup pitted, cooked prunes
2 strips yellow lemon rind
½ teaspoon cinnamon
⅛ teaspoon nutmeg
½ cup sugar
1 tablespoon lemon juice
½ cup walnut meats
Pastry for a 1-crust pie

1. Put prunes, lemon rind, cinnamon, nutmeg, sugar, and lemon juice into container. Cover and blend on HIGH speed for 15 seconds.

2. Remove cover and, with blades spinning, add walnut meats. Turn off motor as soon as last walnut has been drawn down into the blades.

3. Roll out pastry into a 12-inch square. Spread prune filling over pastry and roll up jelly-roll fashion. Cut into ½-inch slices and place on greased baking sheet.

4. Bake in preheated 375° F. oven for 20 minutes, or until edges of pastry are golden.

APRICOT PINWHEELS

Substitute cooked apricots for the prunes.

CHOCOLATE TRUFFLES
(Truffettes Dauphinoise)

Makes about 2 dozen

6   ounces semi-sweet chocolate pieces
¼   cup hot cream
4   tablespoons soft butter (½ stick)
2   egg yolks
3   tablespoons cocoa
¼   teaspoon cinnamon

1. Empty chocolate pieces into container. Add hot cream. Cover and blend on HIGH speed for 15 seconds, or until smooth.

2. Remove cover and, with blades spinning, add butter and egg yolks. Continue blending until smooth, stopping to stir down if necessary.

3. Chill mixture until firm, then shape into 1-inch balls.

4. Combine cocoa and cinnamon on piece of waxed paper. Roll the balls in the cocoa-cinnamon mixture until well coated on all sides.

5. Store in the refrigerator.

BROWN-SUGAR FUDGE COOKIES

Makes 3 dozen

¼   pound butter or margarine
     (1 stick)
½   cup milk
Two 1-ounce squares unsweetened
     chocolate, diced

1   egg
1   cup firmly-packed brown
     sugar
2   cups presifted flour
2   teaspoons baking powder

1. In a small saucepan, heat together butter or margarine and milk until butter is melted. Empty into container and add chocolate. Cover and blend on HIGH speed for 10 seconds, or until smooth.

2. Remove cover and, with blades spinning, add egg and brown sugar. Continue blending until smooth.

3. In a mixing bowl, combine flour and baking powder. Stir in chocolate mixture.

4. Drop batter by teaspoonfuls onto greased baking sheets and bake in preheated 375° F. oven for 15 minutes. Cool on wire racks.

HUNGARIAN DEVIL'S PILLS

Makes 2½ dozen rich cookies

* 1 cup toasted blanched almonds, blender-grated
* ½ cup semi-sweet chocolate pieces, blender-grated
  1 cup sugar

2 tablespoons orange juice
   Thin orange rind from 1 large orange
½ cup mixed candied fruits

1. Grate almonds and empty into a mixing bowl.

2. Grate chocolate pieces and empty onto piece of waxed paper.

3. In a small saucepan, heat sugar and orange juice until sugar is melted and syrup is hot. Pour syrup into container. Add orange rind. Cover and blend on HIGH for 15 seconds, or until rind is finely chopped.

4. Remove lid and, with blades spinning, add the candied fruits. Blend only until fruit is chopped.

5. Empty blended mixture into mixing bowl and mix well with the ground nuts. Shape into 1-inch balls, roll in grated chocolate, and chill before serving.

OATMEAL COOKIES

Makes 6 dozen

½ cups presifted flour
2 teaspoons baking powder
½ teaspoon salt
½ teaspoon cinnamon
* ½ cup walnut meats, blender-chopped
2 cups old-fashioned rolled oats

½ cup milk
2 eggs
¼ pound soft butter or margarine (1 stick)
1 teaspoon vanilla
1 cup sugar
1 cup seedless raisins

1. In a mixing bowl, combine flour, baking powder, salt, and cinnamon.

2. Blender-chop walnuts and add to ingredients in mixing bowl.

3. Put 1 cup oats into container. Cover and blend on HIGH speed for 15 seconds. Add to flour-nut mixture. Repeat with remaining cup of oats.

4. Put remaining ingredients into container. Cover and blend on HIGH speed for 2 minutes. Add to flour-oat mixture and mix until all dry ingredients are moistened. Chill for 5 minutes.

5. Spoon batter by teaspoonfuls onto greased baking sheet. Flatten each mound slightly.

6. Bake in a preheated 375° F. oven for about 12 minutes, or until lightly browned.

BEVERAGES FOR PLEASURE & FOR SPECIAL DIETS

Beverages for Pleasure & for Special Diets

ORIGINALLY, the electric blender was bought and used primarily for making alcoholic beverages such as frozen daiquiris, whiskey sours, and a variety of frappéed drinks. But over the years, this function of the blender has become trivial, compared with its more important culinary uses—jobs it performs more efficiently than any other electric appliance. The blender has become essential in homes where special diets are needed and in the diet kitchens of every hospital in the country.

In the case of digestive disorders, where only the minimum of cellulose can be tolerated, the blender purées raw or cooked fruits or vegetables, breaking down cellulose into such minute particles that important nutrients can be included in the diet in the form of a smooth, thin purée, soup, or beverage. The blender has fed and nourished thousands of people with broken jaws, liquefying prescribed food combinations so that a complete balanced diet could be fed via a tube or straw. It quickly blends smooth, nourishing eggnogs and frothy malteds to strengthen those recuperating from a serious illness, and it comes to the rescue of children and senior citizens suffering from vitamin, protein, or other nutrient deficiencies.

So I am not going to waste space on alcoholic beverages in this book. The basic technique of making a frozen daiquiri is given in the Mini-Course, on page 33. In this section, we begin with refreshing fruit frappés and proceed to nourishing malteds, frosteds, nogs, and various milk beverages —high-protein, high-vitamin-and-mineral drinks that have maximum flavor combined with modern-day practicality.

Frappés

COFFEE TROPICAL

Makes 2 servings. Here is a fascinating, refreshing frappéed coffee drink. For those who are not watching waistlines, add ¼ cup heavy cream.

Half fill blender container with ice cubes. Add ¾ cup double-strength, cold black coffee and 1 tablespoon sugar. Cover and blend on HIGH speed until thick and creamy. Pour into tall slim glasses and serve at once.

FRUIT CREAM FRAPPÉS

For each drink:

1   cup diced pineapple, papaya, or mango
2   tablespoons sugar
½   cup evaporated milk
½   cup cracked ice cubes

1. Into the container put the fruit, sugar, and milk and blend on HIGH speed.

2. Add the ice and blend for 10 seconds longer.

3. Pour into glass or goblet.

CREAM OF COCONUT FRAPPÉ

Makes 2 drinks

½   cup diced fresh coconut
1   cup water
1   tablespoon sugar

1. Put coconut, water, and sugar into container. Cover and blend on HIGH speed for 30 seconds.

2. Strain blended mixture into a bowl, pressing coconut with back of a spoon to extract the creamy coconut milk.

3. Fill wine goblets with cracked ice and pour the coconut liquid over the ice.

Fruit Drinks

FRESH FRUIT SODAS

For each drink:

　 Juice of 1 lime, lemon, or orange
1   thin strip fruit peel
2–3   tablespoons sugar
　 Sparkling water

1. Put the fruit juice, fruit peel, and sugar into container. Cover and blend on HIGH speed for 1 minute.

2. Pour into glasses filled with cracked ice and fill glass with soda. Serve with a straw.

PINEAPPLE TWIST

Makes 2 tall drinks

2   lemons
1   cup pineapple juice
2   tablespoons maraschino cherry juice
1   tablespoon sugar
     Ice cubes
     Maraschino cherries

1. Peel each lemon in one continuous spiral. Hang a spiral in each tall glass or pilsner glass, with just enough over the edge of glass to keep peel in place.

2. Squeeze lemons and strain juice into container. Add pineapple juice, maraschino cherry juice, and sugar. Add ice cubes to fill container ¾ full. Cover and blend on HIGH speed until thick and creamy.

3. Pour into prepared glasses and top each drink with a cherry.

AFTER-SKI CRANBERRY WARM-UP

Makes 2 warming drinks

1   cup fresh or frozen cranberries
1   cup water
½   cup sugar
¼   teaspoon cinnamon
1   tablespoon lemon juice
¼   cup sherry
     Nutmeg

1. Put all ingredients except nutmeg into container. Cover and blend on HIGH speed for 10 seconds.

2. Empty into saucepan and heat to simmering.

3. Strain into serving cups and sprinkle each serving with a little nutmeg.

Frosteds & Shakes

FROSTED CHOCOLATE MALTED

Makes 1 large drink

2 tablespoons chocolate syrup
1 tablespoon malted milk
1 teaspoon sugar
1 large scoop chocolate ice cream
½ cup milk

Put all ingredients into container. Cover and blend on HIGH speed until thick and smooth.

STRAWBERRY FROSTED

Makes 2 drinks

1 cup milk
1 10-ounce package strawberries, partially defrosted
2 scoops vanilla ice cream

Put all ingredients into container. Cover and blend on HIGH speed for 10 seconds. Pour into tall glasses.

MOCHA FROSTED

Makes 3 large drinks

1½ cups milk
2 large scoops vanilla ice cream
2 teaspoons cocoa powder
1 teaspoon instant coffee powder
2 tablespoons sugar

Put all ingredients into container. Cover and blend on HIGH speed for 10 seconds.

COFFEE FROSTED

Makes 2 drinks

2 cups cold water
1½ tablespoons instant coffee powder
1 pint vanilla ice cream

Put all ingredients into container. Cover and blend on HIGH speed until thick and fluffy.

BANANA FROSTED

Makes 1 large drink

1 cup milk
1 large scoop vanilla, strawberry, or chocolate ice cream
1 small, ripe banana

1. Put milk and ice cream into container. Cover and turn motor on HIGH speed.

2. Remove cover and, with blades spinning, slice in banana.

3. Pour immediately into tall glass and enjoy.

FRUIT MILK SHAKE

Makes 2 drinks

1 cup fresh or canned fruit such as peeled and sliced melon, peaches, pineapple, apricots, plums, apple, berries
½ cup milk
1 tablespoon lemon juice
1–2 tablespoons sugar to taste
2 large scoops vanilla ice cream or orange sherbet

1. Put fruit, milk, lemon juice, and sugar into container. Cover and blend on HIGH speed for 10 seconds.

2. Remove cover and, with blades spinning, add ice cream or sherbet, and blend until thick and smooth.

3. Pour into tall glasses.

Nogs

BANANA NOG

Makes 1 drink

1   cup skim milk
1   medium banana, peeled and cut in chunks
1   teaspoon vanilla extract
⅛   teaspoon nutmeg

Combine all ingredients in container. Cover and blend on HIGH speed for about 1 minute, or until smooth.

APRICOT NOG

Makes 2 drinks

½   cup apricot nectar
½   cup cream
2   teaspoons sugar
1   egg
1   cup ice cubes

Put all ingredients into container. Cover and blend on HIGH speed for 10 seconds, or until frothy.

SHERRY NOG FOR SIX

Makes almost 1 quart

6   eggs
1   cup hot milk
¼   cup sugar
½   cup sherry

1   cup heavy cream
    Nutmeg

1. Put eggs, milk, and sugar into container. Cover and blend on HIGH speed for 5 seconds.

2. Reduce blending speed to LOW. With motor on, remove cover and pour in sherry and cream.

3. Serve in nog cups sprinkling each serving with a little nutmeg.

WHEAT GERM EGGNOG

Makes about 1 quart

2   cups cold milk
1   cup heavy cream
One   3-ounce package egg custard mix
¼   cup wheat germ
1   teaspoon vanilla extract
Nutmeg

1. Put all ingredients into container. Cover and turn blender on LOW speed. As soon as blades reach full speed, switch to HIGH and blend for 20 seconds.

2. Chill for 1 to 2 hours before serving.

3. Stir well, pour into glasses or cups, and sprinkle each serving with nutmeg.

COFFEE NOG

Makes 3 drinks

½   cup strong cold coffee
2   tablespoons sugar
2   cups milk
½   cup heavy cream
4   ice cubes
Nutmeg

1. Put all ingredients except nutmeg into container. Cover and blend on HIGH speed for15 seconds.

2. Pour into punch glasses and sprinkle with freshly ground nutmeg.

Health Beverages

GREEN-EYED TIGER

Makes 32 ounces.   The first health beverage, according to *The Composition of Foods* (U.S. Department of Agriculture), contains more protein and natural vitamins and minerals than any prepared weight control drink In addition to this, it tastes quite delicious.

½	bunch watercress, leaves and stems	½	cup brewer's yeast
1	cup non-fat dry milk solids	1	egg yolk
2	cups orange juice	1	teaspoon corn oil
		1	cup water

1. Put all ingredients except water into container. Cover and turn motor on LOW. As soon as blades reach full speed, switch to HIGH and blend for 30 seconds.

2. Remove cover and, with blades spinning, add water.

3. Chill or serve over ice cubes. Store, covered, in refrigerator. Drink 8 ounces four times daily. Total calories: 940

ADELLE DAVIS'S PEP-UP

Makes 1½ quarts. An electric blender is a necessity for making this fortified, milk health drink or pep-up, recommended by Adelle Davis in her excellent book entitled *Let's Get Well.*

2	egg yolks or whole eggs	4	cups whole or skim milk
1	tablespoon lecithin	½	cup yeast fortified with calcium
1	tablespoon mixed vegetable oils	½	cup non-fat powdered milk
1½	teaspoons calcium lactate or 4 teaspoons calcium gluconate	¼	cup soy flour or powder
		½	cup wheat germ (optional)
½	teaspoon magnesium oxide	1	teaspoon pure vanilla extract
¼	cup yogurt or 1 tablespoon acidophilus culture	½	cup frozen undiluted orange juice
1	teaspoon granular kelp (optional)		

1. Put egg yolks or eggs into container and add lecithin, vegetable oils, calcium lactate or calcium gluconate, magnesium oxide, yogurt, and kelp. Cover and blend on HIGH speed for 20 seconds.

2. With blades spinning, remove cover and gradually add 2 cups of the milk and the remaining ingredients.

3. Pour into container and stir in the remaining 2 cups milk. Cover and refrigerate. Stir each time before using.

PINEAPPLE WATERCRESS COCKTAIL

Makes 6 drinks. Here is another health drink, extremely high in Vitamins A and C, plus calcium, phosphorous, and iron.

        2   cups pineapple juice
        2   cups watercress leaves
    ½   cup lemon juice
        2   teaspoons honey
        1   cup cracked ice cubes

Blend on HIGH speed for 20 seconds. 40 calories per drink.

PRUNE SMOOTHEE

Makes 2 drinks.   This one contains 10 grams of protein, in addition to appreciable quantities of Vitamin A, calcium, and phosphorous.

        1   cup milk
        4   cooked, pitted prunes
    ½   cup prune juice
        1   teaspoon honey

Blend on HIGH speed for 20 seconds. 120 calories per drink.

NO TIME TO DINE DRINK

Makes 1 large drink.   Forty grams protein, and high in all important vitamins and minerals.

    ¼   cup non-fat dry milk solids
    ½   cup orange juice
        2   tablespoons brewer's yeast
        1   cup plain yogurt
        1   whole egg
        1   tablespoon plain gelatin

Put all ingredients into container and blend on HIGH speed for 10 seconds. About 600 calories.

MEAL IN A HALF A MINUTE

Makes 1 tall drink. Here is one for people in a hurry who can't take time to eat. It will sustain you until your next meal.

¾ cup orange juice
1 egg yolk
1 tablespoon honey wheat germ

Blend on HIGH for 20 seconds. About 150 calories.

SLEEP WELL NIGHTCAP

Makes 1 drink. Eighteen grams protein. High in calcium and phosphorous.

½ cup fat-free milk
3 tablespoons non-fat dry milk solids
2 tablespoons cottage cheese
2 slices fresh pineapple, or melon, or half a fresh peach or apricot

Put all ingredients into container and blend on HIGH speed until smooth and frothy. About 200 calories.

BEAUTY BEVERAGE

Makes 2 drinks. Twenty-five grams protein plus Vitamins A and C, calcium, and phosphorous.

1 cup orange juice
½ cup grape or apple juice
2 tablespoons brewers' yeast
1 cup yogurt
1 whole egg
1 tablespoon plain gelatin

Put all ingredients into container and blend on HIGH speed until smooth and frothy. About 165 calories per drink.

INSTANT PEP-UP

Makes 1 drink.   Twenty grams protein. High in Vitamins B complex and C, calcium, and phosphorous.

1   cup fruit-flavored yogurt
1   tablespoon molasses
1   tablespoon brewer's yeast
¼   cup non-fat milk solids
¼   cup orange juice
6   ice cubes

Put all ingredients into container. Blend on HIGH speed for 15 seconds. About 290 calories.

APRICOT YOGURT REVIVER

Makes 2⅔ cups

1½   cups cold orange juice
One   8-ounce carton apricot yogurt
3   tablespoons wheat germ
2   tablespoons brown sugar

Put all ingredients into container. Cover and blend on HIGH speed for 30 seconds. Chill before serving.

VITAMIN NOG

Makes 1 drink.   Twenty grams protein, plus Vitamins B complex and C.

1   egg
1   tablespoon brewer's yeast
½   cup non-fat dry milk solids
¾   cup apple, cranberry, orange, or pineapple juice

Put all ingredients into container. Cover and blend on HIGH speed for 20 seconds. About 440 calories.

PRESERVES

Preserves

IT WOULD BE very easy to devote an entire book to the virtues of the electric blender in the field of preserving. It's such a great time-saver! It can save hours of tedious preparation and make preserving lots of fun. Don't limit your blender's use or your own imagination just to the recipes in this chapter. You can adapt almost any of your favorite recipes for piccalillis, chutneys, catsups, chili sauces, marmalades, jams, and so on to blender use. Use it to liquid-chop vegetables, especially onions, cabbage, carrots, cucumbers, and green peppers, instead of the grinder or food chopper normally specified in preserving recipes. I call it the "liquid-chopping" method here, as opposed to the "water-chopping" method, for in many of the recipes vinegar or the juice extracted from soft fruit is used as the liquid medium in place of water. In other recipes, the water used for chopping is either added to the ingredients in the recipe, or is utilized to refresh and crisp vegetables that would otherwise become wilted in the vinegar sauce.

Your blender is an aid in extracting juice from fruit for jellies, for puréeing soft fruits and vegetables, for jams and butters, and for chopping citrus fruit and rind for marmalades. It can, of course, prepare only a small quantity (a quart) at a time. But small batches of jams and marmalades are far superior to those made in large quantities. As for pickles, you can double or triple any of the recipes, blending several batches and combining them in the preserving kettle to cook all at one time.

There is quite a revival today in the making of homemade preserves, so put your blender to work and you'll find yourself creating all kinds of specialties of your own with unusual flavors and different textures that money can't buy.

Jams, Jellies & Butters

APRICOT JAM

Makes about 5 pints

1 pound dried apricots
1 orange, peeled, seeded, and sectioned
One 1-pound can crushed pineapple with juice
6 cups sugar

1. Put apricot and orange into container. Add water to cover the fruit by 1 inch. Cover and blend on HIGH speed for 30 seconds, or until fruit is finely cut.

2. Empty into saucepan and let stand overnight.

3. Next day, add pineapple and sugar. Bring to a boil and cook over low heat for 1 hour, stirring frequently.

4. Pour into hot clean jars and seal.

HEAVENLY JAM

Makes about 5 pints

3   pounds ripe peaches, peeled, pitted, and quartered
One   4-ounce jar maraschino cherries
2   unpeeled oranges, coarsely cut and seeded
6   cups sugar

1. Blend half the peaches at a time on HIGH speed until reduced to a purée, stopping to stir down if necessary. Empty into preserving kettle.

2. Put maraschino cherries and juice and oranges into container. Cover and blend on HIGH speed for 30 seconds, or until fruit is finely chopped. Empty into preserving kettle with the peaches.

3. Add sugar, cover, and let stand overnight.

4. Next day, bring to a boil and cook over medium heat for 1 hour, stirring occasionally.

5. Pour into hot clean jars and seal.

RAISIN JAM

Makes four 8-ounce glasses

¾   cup coarsely diced, unpeeled, seeded lemon
2   cups water
3   cups seedless raisins
2   cups sugar
1   cup pineapple juice

1. Put lemon in container and add water. Cover and blend on HIGH speed until fruit is finely cut, about 30 seconds.

2. Add raisins and continue blending for 1 minute longer.

3. Pour blended mixture into saucepan. Add sugar and pineapple juice. Bring to a boil. Cook until thickened to jam consistency, about 220° F., stirring frequently.

4. Pour into sterilized glasses and seal with melted paraffin.

PARSLEY JELLY

Makes five 6-ounce jars. An unusual recipe for an excellent jelly to serve with meats.

Leaves from 1 large bunch parsley or 4 cups firmly packed parsley clusters	2 tablespoons lemon juice
	1 package fruit pectin
	4½ cups sugar
3 cups boiling water	Green food coloring

1. Put half the parsley and half the boiling water into container. Cover and blend on HIGH speed for 30 seconds. Empty into a sieve lined with a piece of cheesecloth or kitchen toweling and set over a large pitcher or bowl. Repeat with remaining parsley and boiling water.

2. Let the parsley liquid drip through the sieve, then form cloth and parsley into a ball and squeeze out any remaining moisture. You should have 3 cups of parsley "stock."

3. Pour the stock into a saucepan and add lemon juice and pectin. Bring to a full rolling boil over high heat. Add the sugar and let come again to a rolling boil. Boil hard for 1 minute. Add green food coloring to taste.

4. Remove from stove and skim surface well of any froth or foam.

5. Strain into jelly glasses.

MINT JELLY FOR LAMB

Make as above using fresh mint leaves in place of the parsley.

HERB JELLIES

Make as above using fresh herbs in place of the parsley—tarragon, dill, oregano, sage are all delicious.

APPLE JELLY

Makes about 2 pints

4 pounds firm, tart apples
2 cups water
   Sugar

1. Wash, core, and coarsely slice the apples.

2. Put apples and water in a large pot. Bring to a boil and cook over low heat for 15 minutes, or until soft.

3. Remove from heat and blend half the apples and juice at a time on HIGH speed for 20 seconds, or until well puréed.

4. Empty into collander lined with clean toweling and set over a container. Repeat with remaining apples and juice.

5. Let juice drip into container below. Then measure juice and return to pot. Add ¾ cup sugar for every 1 cup juice.

6. Bring slowly to a boil, then cook rapidly to the jell stage (220° F.).

7. Remove from heat, skim surface, pour into hot clean jars and seal.

GRAPE JELLY

Follow recipe above substituting slightly underripe Concord or wild grapes for the apples.

RASPBERRY JELLY

Makes four 6-ounce glasses

1   pound fresh raspberries
1½ cups water
3   cups sugar

4   tablespoons lemon juice
6   tablespoons liquid pectin

1. Put raspberries and water into saucepan. Bring to a boil, cover, and simmer for 10 minutes.

2. Empty half the raspberries and liquid into container. Cover and turn blender on HIGH speed. Remove lid and with blades spinning, pour in remaining raspberries and liquid. Blend until smooth.

3. Strain through a sieve lined with a piece of kitchen toweling. You should have 2 cups raspberry juice.

4. Put juice into a large saucepan with sugar and lemon juice. Bring to a full rolling boil, stirring occasionally. Boil for 1 minute.

5. Add pectin and bring again to the boil. Boil for 1 minute.

6. Remove from heat, skim surface well with a metal spoon, and pour into clean glasses. Seal.

APRICOT BUTTER

Makes six 6-ounce glasses

1	pound dried apricots	1	teaspoon cinnamon
2	cups water	½	teaspoon cloves
1	cup sugar	2	cups orange juice

1. Put apricots and water in container. Cover container and blend on HIGH speed until apricots are finely chopped, about 1 minute.

2. Pour blended mixture into a saucepan. Add sugar, spices, and orange juice. Bring to a boil and cook over low heat until of jam consistency, about 30 to 40 minutes. Pour into sterilized jars and seal with melted paraffin.

APPLE BUTTER

Makes 1 pint

½	cup water or apple juice	¼	teaspoon cloves
1	teaspoon cinnamon	⅛	teaspoon salt
¾	cup sugar	1	pound green cooking apples, peeled, cored, and cut in eighths
1	½-inch slice of lemon		
¼	teaspoon allspice		
½	teaspoon nutmeg		

1. Into container put all the ingredients. Cover and blend on HIGH speed for 15 seconds.

2. Pour into a saucepan and cook over very low heat for 45 minutes, stirring occasionally.

3. Pour at once into hot jars and seal.

Marmalades

ORANGE MARMALADE

Makes four 6-ounce glasses

1½   cups coarsely cut, unpeeled, seeded orange
¾   cup coarsely cut, unpeeled, seeded lemon
3   cups water
3   cups sugar

1. Put orange and lemon in container. Add 2 cups of the water. Cover and blend on HIGH speed until fruit is finely cut, about 30 seconds.

2. Empty blended mixture into a saucepan and add remaining water. Cover and bring to a boil. Boil for 10 minutes.

3. Add sugar and bring again to a boil. Cook, uncovered, until a few drops will jell when dropped on a cold saucer, about 221° F. Pour into clean glasses and seal.

LIME MARMALADE

Follow recipe above using 1¼ cups each of coarsely cut, unpeeled, seeded lemons and limes in place of oranges and lemons.

THREE-FRUIT MARMALADE

Makes ten 6-ounce jars

1	medium grapefruit	Water
2	oranges	3½ pounds sugar
3	lemons	

1. Remove the thin yellow rind from grapefruit and set aside. Discard the bitter white pith from around the grapefruit. Coarsely cut the grapefruit, unpeeled orange, and lemons, discarding any seeds.

2. Put half the prepared fruit and grapefruit rind into container. Cover to within 1 inch from top of container with cold water. Cover and blend on HIGH speed for 5 seconds, or until all fruit is chopped. Empty into large saucepan. Repeat with remaining fruit.

3. Add an additional 2 cups water to fruit in saucepan and bring to a boil. Simmer for 1½ hours, stirring occasionally.

4. Add sugar and boil rapidly for 5 minutes, or until setting point is reached (221° F.)

5. Remove from heat and let stand for 5 minutes to allow fruit to settle; then skim surface, stir once, and pour into jars. Seal immediately.

GREEN GRAPE MARMALADE

Makes four 6-ounce glasses

1½   cups coarsely diced, unpeeled, seeded orange
¾   cup coarsely diced, unpeeled, seeded lemon
1½   cups water
3   cups sugar
3   cups halved green seedless grapes

1. Put orange and lemon in container and add water. Blend on HIGH speed until fruit is finely cut, about 1 minute.

2. Pour blended mixture into a saucepan. Cover and bring to boil. Cook for 10 minutes.

3. Add sugar and grapes. Bring to a boil again and cook, uncovered, until a few drops will jell when dropped on a cold saucer, about 221° F.

4. Pour into sterilized glasses and seal with melted paraffin.

BLUEBERRY MARMALADE

Makes 4 eight-ounce glasses

¾   cup coarsely diced, unpeeled, seeded orange
¾   cup coarsely diced, unpeeled, seeded lemon
1   cup water
3   cups sugar
3   cups fresh blueberries

1. Put orange and lemon in container and add water. Cover container and blend on HIGH speed until fruit is finely cut, about 30 seconds.

2. Pour blended mixture into saucepan. Cover and bring to boil. Cook 10 minutes. Add sugar and blueberries. Bring to boil and cook, un-

covered, until a few drops will jell when dropped on a cold saucer, 221° F.

3. Pour into sterilized glasses and seal with paraffin.

STRAWBERRY MARMALADE

Makes six 6-ounce glasses

Follow recipe for Blueberry Marmalade, substituting halved, fresh strawberries for the blueberries.

CHERRY MARMALADE

Makes six 5-ounce glasses

1½ cups coarsely diced, unpeeled, seeded orange
¾ cup coarsely diced, unpeeled, seeded lemon
1½ cups water
3 cups sugar
4 cups pitted sour red cherries (2 pounds)

1. Put orange and lemon in container and add water. Cover and blend on HIGH speed until fruit is finely cut, about 30 seconds.

2. Pour blended mixture into saucepan. Cover and bring to boil. Cook 10 minutes.

3. Add sugar and cherries. Bring to boil again and cook, uncovered, until a few drops will jell when dropped on a cold saucer, 221° F.

4. Pour into sterilized glasses and seal with melted paraffin.

ORANGE-PINEAPPLE MARMALADE

Makes five 8-ounce glasses

Follow recipe above substituting a 1-pound, 4 ounce can crushed pineapple for the sour cherries.

CRANBERRY-RAISIN MARMALADE

Makes eight 8-ounce glasses

Follow recipe above substituting 4 cups (1 pound) raw cranberries, fresh or defrosted, for the sour cherries and add 1½ cups seedless raisins.

Chutneys

APPLE CHUTNEY

Makes 3 pints

2 medium onions, quartered	2 teaspoons dry mustard
1 medium green pepper, seeded and cut in strips	1 tablespoon ground ginger
	1 teaspoon ground allspice
6 medium apples, peeled, cored, and quartered	1 teaspoon celery seeds
	2 teaspoons salt
1 large clove garlic	½ teaspoon hot red pepper flakes
3 cups cider vinegar	1 cup seedless white raisins
3 cups brown sugar	

1. Into container put half the onions, green pepper, apples, and the garlic clove. Add half the vinegar. Cover and blend on HIGH speed for 3 to 4 seconds, or until vegetables are coarsely chopped. Empty into a large saucepan and repeat using remaining onion, green pepper, apples, and vinegar.

2. Add remaining ingredients except raisins to saucepan, bring to a boil, and simmer for 30 minutes.

3. Add raisins and simmer for 30 minutes longer, stirring occasionally, until reduced to about half.

4. Turn into pint jars and seal at once.

PEACH CHUTNEY

Makes 2½ pints

2 pounds firm peaches, halved and pitted	1½ cups brown sugar
	1 tablespoon mustard seeds
1 medium onion, quartered	2 teaspoons chili powder
¼ cup crystallized ginger	2 teaspoons salt
2 cups cider vinegar	¼ teaspoon hot pepper flakes
1 clove garlic	1 cup seedless raisins

1. Put half the peaches, onion, ginger, and the garlic into container. Add half the vinegar. Cover and blend on HIGH speed for 2 to 3 seconds, or

until peaches and onions are chopped. Empty into large saucepan. Repeat with remaining peaches, onion, ginger, and vinegar.

2. Add remaining ingredients to saucepan and bring to a boil. Simmer for 1 hour, stirring occasionally.

3. Pack at once into hot jars and seal.

Pickles & Relishes

EVERY FALL I make large batches of "grandmother's mustard pickles." I've never found any commercially made that can compare with them. My blender saves me many hours of chopping and many tears in making the mustard sauce in which I cook small pickling onion, cauliflower flowerets, and small gherkin pickles or strips or slices of cucumber. String beans and other vegetables may be mustard-pickled in the same way.

MUSTARD PICKLES

Makes 3 quarts

6	medium cucumbers	¾	cup salt
3	large onions	4	cups sugar
3	red peppers	4	cups cider vinegar
1	head cauliflower	¾	cup flour
2	quarts mixed prepared veg-	¼	cup dry mustard
	etables (tiny pickling onion,	1½	tablespoons turmeric
	gherkins or cucumber slices,	1	tablespoon celery salt
	thickly sliced carrots,		
	coarsely cut celery or small		
	string beans)		

1. Coarsely cut the cucumbers. Peel and coarsely cut the onions. Seed red peppers and cut in strips.

2. Fill container with prepared vegetables and add water to come just about 1 inch from top of container. Cover and blend on HIGH speed for 2 to 3 seconds, or until last piece of vegetable at top of container takes a nose dive down into the blades. Drain and empty vegetables into a large bowl. Repeat until all cucumbers, onions, and peppers are chopped.

3. Trim cauliflower and break into flowerettes. Put in a bowl. Put the other prepared, mixed vegetables into a bowl, giving you 2 bowls of chunky vegetables and 1 bowl of chopped vegetables.

4. Sprinkle each bowl of vegetables with 4 tablespoons salt. Cover the chunky vegetables with water and let all vegetables stand overnight.

5. Next day, drain chopped vegetables in a colander. Drain chunky vegetables and dry on a towel.

6. Put all vegetables into preserving kettle and stir in sugar and 3 cups of the vinegar. Bring mixture to a boil.

7. Combine flour, mustard, turmeric, celery salt, and remaining vinegar to a smooth paste. Stir paste into the vegetables and continue to cook, stirring, until sauce is slightly thickened.

8. Turn into clean jars and seal at once.

TOMATO PICKLE RELISH

Makes about 1 quart

2 pounds ripe tomatoes, quartered	1 cup brown sugar
	1 tablespoon salt
3 cups cider vinegar	½ teaspoon pepper
2 medium onions, quartered	1 teaspoon dry mustard
1 green pepper, seeded and cut cut in strips	1 teaspoon sweet basil
1 cucumber, cut in chunks	½ teaspoon cloves

1. Into container put 1 cup tomatoes and ½ cup vinegar. Cover and turn motor on HIGH. Remove cover and, with blades spinning, gradually add remaining tomatoes, and continue to blend until tomatoes are chopped. Turn into a large saucepan.

2. Fill container with half the onions, green pepper, and cucumber and add 1¼ cups vinegar. Cover and blend on HIGH speed for 3 to 4 seconds, or until vegetables are chopped. Empty into saucepan with tomatoes. Repeat with remaining vegetables and vinegar.

3. Stir into saucepan remaining ingredients. Bring to a boil and boil for 35 minutes, stirring occasionally, until mixture is reduced to about half.

4. Ladle into prepared jars and seal at once.

BARBECUE RELISH FOR STEAKS OR HAM

Makes about 3 cups

⅓ cup wine vinegar
1 tablespoon Worcestershire
   sauce
3 medium tomatoes, peeled and
   quartered
⅓ cup brown sugar

½ cup parsley clusters
1½ teaspoons salt
¼ teaspoon Tabasco sauce
2 medium onions, quartered
2 dill pickles, quartered

1. Put wine vinegar, Worcestershire sauce, tomatoes, brown sugar, parsley, Tabasco, and salt into container. Cover and blend on HIGH speed for 10 seconds.

2. Remove cover and, with blades spinning, add onions and pickles. Continue to blend for 10 seconds, or until vegetables are chopped.

3. Turn into saucepan, bring to a boil, and simmer for 30 minutes, stirring occasionally.

BEET RELISH

Makes about 4 pints

2 pounds beets, cooked, peeled,
   and quartered
½ head cabbage, coarsely cut
1 large onion, quartered
1 sweet red pepper, seeded and
   cut in strips

A 2-inch piece fresh horseradish
   root, coarsely sliced
3 cups vinegar
1½ cups sugar
1 tablespoon salt

1. Put ⅓ of the vegetables into container with 1 cup vinegar. Cover and blend on HIGH speed for 3 seconds, or until vegetables are coarsely chopped. Empty into a saucepan. Repeat until all vegetables have been chopped and all vinegar has been used as the chopping liquid.

2. Stir in sugar and salt, bring to a boil, and boil for 10 minutes.

3. Pack into hot jars and seal at once.

CORN RELISH

Makes 2 pints

1	large onion, quartered	1	teaspoon celery seed
1	green pepper, seeded and cut in strips	2	teaspoons salt
1	cup coarsely cut cabbage	1	teaspoon turmeric
1½	cups cider vinegar	1	teaspoon cumin seed
1	tablespoon prepared mustard	3	cups cut corn
1	teaspoon mustard seed	⅔	cup sugar

1. Into container put the onion, green pepper, cabbage, vinegar, and seasonings. Cover and blend on HIGH speed for 10 seconds, or until vegetables are finely chopped.

2. Turn into a saucepan with corn and sugar. Bring to a boil and simmer for 30 minutes, stirring occasionally.

3. Pour at once into hot jars and seal.

BREAD-AND-BUTTER PICKLE RELISH

Makes 1½ pints

2   medium cucumbers, coarsely cut
1   large onion, peeled and coarsely cut
3   teaspoons salt
¼   cup vinegar
¼   cup sugar
¼   teaspoon pepper

1. Put half the cucumbers and onion into container. Cover and blend on HIGH speed for 2 to 3 seconds only, or until vegetables are coarsely chopped. Drain and empty into a bowl. Repeat with remaining vegetables.

2. Add half a dozen ice cubes to the chopped vegetables and the salt and store in refrigerator overnight.

3. Next day, drain and empty vegetables into a saucepan. Add remaining ingredients. Bring to a boil and boil for 2 minutes.

4. Turn into prepared jars and seal at once.

MUSTARD RELISH

Makes 1½ pints

½ cup cider vinegar	⅓ cup sugar
2 medium tomatoes, quartered	2 teaspoons prepared mustard
1 large onion, quartered	½ teaspoon dry mustard
1 large green pepper, seeded	½ teaspoon turmeric
and cut in strips	3 tablespoons flour
2 stalks celery, coarsely cut	4 tablespoons water
1 tablespoon salt	

1. Into the container put the vinegar and tomatoes. Cover and blend on HIGH speed for 5 seconds.

2. Add onion, green pepper, celery, salt, sugar, mustards, and turmeric. Cover and blend on HIGH speed for 2 to 3 seconds, or until vegetables are coarsely chopped.

3. Turn into a saucepan and bring to a boil. Simmer for 10 minutes.

4. Mix flour with the water and stir into the relish. Simmer for 10 minutes longer, stirring occasionally.

5. Turn at once into hot jars and seal.

PICKLE RELISH

Makes about 1 quart

2 pounds ripe tomatoes,	1 cup brown sugar
quartered	1 tablespoon salt
3 cups cider vinegar	½ teaspoon black pepper
2 medium onions, quartered	1 teaspoon dry mustard
1 medium green pepper, seeded,	1 teaspoon sweet basil
and cut into strips	½ teaspoon cloves
1 cucumber, cut into chunks	

1. Put 1 cup of the tomatoes and ½ cup of the vinegar into container. Cover and turn on HIGH. Remove cover and, with blades spinning, gradually add remaining tomatoes. Blend until all tomatoes are chopped. Turn into a large saucepan.

2. Put half the remaining vinegar into container with half the onions, green pepper, and cucumber. Cover and blend on HIGH speed for 3 to 4 seconds, or until vegetables are chopped. Empty into a saucepan and repeat with remaining vinegar and vegetables.

3. Add remaining ingredients to saucepan, bring to a boil, and simmer for 35 minutes, stirring occasionally, until pickle is reduced to about half.

4. Turn into prepared jars and seal at once.

TOMATO-CORN RELISH

Makes 1 quart

1	cup cider vinegar	1	teaspoon salt
2	medium tomatoes, peeled and quartered	½	tablespoon mustard seed
		½	tablespoon celery seed
1	medium onion, quartered	1	teaspoon turmeric
1	cucumber, coarsely cut	½	cup sugar
¼	teaspoon hot pepper flakes	1½	cups corn kernels

1. Into container put ½ cup vinegar and tomatoes. Cover and blend on HIGH speed for 5 seconds.

2. Add onion, cucumber, pepper flakes, salt, mustard seed, celery seed, and turmeric. Cover and blend on HIGH speed for 5 seconds, or until vegetables are finely chopped.

3. Turn into a saucepan with remaining vinegar, sugar, and corn. Bring to a boil and simmer for 45 minutes, stirring occasionally. Pack at once into hot jars and seal.

UNCOOKED CRANBERRY CURAÇAO RELISH

Makes about 2 cups

1½ cups coarsely diced, unpeeled, seeded orange
¼ cup Curaçao or Grand Marnier
¾ cup sugar
2 cups raw cranberries, fresh or defrosted

1. Put orange and Curaço or Grand Marnier into container. Cover and blend on HIGH speed for 10 seconds.

2. Remove cover and, with blades spinning, gradually add sugar and cranberries. Stop motor as soon as the last cranberry is pulled down into the blades.

3. Store in refrigerator until ready to serve.

Chili Sauces & Catsup

CHILI SAUCE

Makes 2 pints

1 cup cider vinegar	½ cup sugar
2 quarts ripe, quartered tomatoes	1½ tablespoons salt
	½ tablespoon mustard seed
1 very large onion, coarsely cut	½ tablespoon celery seed
2 sweet red peppers, seeded and cut in strips	1½ tablespoons mixed pickling spices
1 hot red pepper	

1. Put ⅓ cup vinegar in container. Fill container with one-third of the tomatoes, onion, and peppers. Cover and blend on HIGH speed until vegetables are chopped. Empty into preserving kettle. Repeat twice more using ⅓ cup vinegar and ⅓ of the remaining vegetables each time.

2. Add sugar and salt, bring to a boil, and boil for 45 minutes.

3. Add spices, tied in a small bag, and continue to boil until sauce is thick, stirring frequently.

4. Discard spice bag and seal in clean hot jars.

RED-HOT PEPPER SAUCE

Makes 3 cups of your own Tabasco when hot peppers are in season.

12	long hot peppers
6	ripe tomatoes
2	cups vinegar

½   cup sugar
½   tablespoon salt
1   tablespoon mixed pickling spices

1. Seed and coarsely cut the peppers. Core and quarter the tomatoes.

2. Put vegetables into a saucepan with half the vinegar, bring to a boil, and boil for 30 minutes, or until vegetables are very soft.

3. Empty vegetables and liquid into container. Cover and blend on HIGH speed for 10 seconds. Return to saucepan. Add sugar, salt, and the spices, tied in a small cloth bag, and boil until sauce is thick.

4. Add remaining vinegar and continue to boil for about 15 minutes, or until sauce is the desired consistency.

5. Discard spice bag and seal boiling hot in hot clean jars or bottles.

TOMATO CATSUP

Makes 1½ pints. For a larger quantity, multiply ingredients by 2 or 4. Blend the vegetables and vinegar in 2 or 4 batches. Add required seasonings and sugar, also multiplied, and continue as directed.

1 cup cider vinegar	½ teaspoon dry mustard
1½ pounds ripe tomatoes, quartered	⅛ teaspoon cayenne pepper
	⅛ teaspoon allspice
1 small red pepper, seeded and cut in strips	⅛ teaspoon cloves
	⅛ teaspoon cinnamon
1 large onion, quartered	½ cup sugar
1 tablespoon salt	

1. Put ⅓ cup of the vinegar and the tomatoes into container. Cover and blend on HIGH speed for 10 seconds.

2. Add green pepper and onion. Cover and blend on HIGH speed for 10 seconds longer, or until smooth. Turn into saucepan.

3. Add remaining ingredients, bring to a boil and simmer for 1 hour, stirring occasionally, or until catsup is reduced to half.

4. Pack into hot jars and seal.

Index